RIGHT CHOICES

www.xulonpress.com

THANK YOU!

I dedicate this book to my family. Thank you everyone, for your love and support. I especially thank my wife for her useful critique. I also want to thank my church family, the members of the Full Gospel Church in Southwest City, Missouri, and my Wal-Mart family, the associates of the Grove, Jay, and Miami, Oklahoma Wal-Mart stores.

I spent an hour in prayer each day before I began work on this book project. I always prayed that God's Spirit would flow through me as I wrote the words that would become this book. Therefore, I don't consider myself to be the author. I'm just the person who wrote the words down. Thank you Lord for allowing these experiences to pass through my life on their way to each reader.

CONTENTS:

25. Ask Jesus to Forgive Your Sins
26. Accept Jesus As Your Savior
27. Receive God's Power
28. Tell People About Jesus
29. Give Your Possessions to God
30. Give Your Children to God
31. Take Your Children to Church with You
32. Bless Others Anonymously
33. Give God Opportunities to Bless You
34. Live Every Day for God

CHOOSE TO BE WISE
35. Keep Your Priorities in the Right Order
36. Live Within Your Means
37. Spend Money Wisely
38. Seek Simple Solutions to Simple Problems
39. Utilize Your Available Resources
40. Get the Facts Before Giving the Advice
41. Keep Your Composure During Stressful Situations
42. Tell the Truth, Even if it Hurts
43. Analyze Your Actions
44. Take Responsibility for Your Actions

CHOOSE TO SUCCEED
45. Set Achievable Goals and Pursue Them Aggressively
46. Work Hard and be Dependable at Your Level of Responsibility
47. Take Charge When Responsibility is Given to You
48. Stand Up to Confrontation
49. Respond With Action!
50. Learn From Your Mistakes
51. Learn From Failure and Try Again

52. Develop a Purpose for Your Life

Conclusion: Ecclesiastes 12: 13, 14

INTRODUCTION

You are not a victim of your circumstances. You will always have an opportunity to choose. This is a book about choices. Each chapter's title is a right choice. You will find some form of the word - choice - in every story, every set of bullet points, and every set of questions. The book's fifty-two chapters allow the reader to study and meditate on one choice topic per week, and complete the study in one year's time.

Several symbolic representations were incorporated into the planning of this book. The book cover features the words RIGHT CHOICES in an acrostic pattern representing the cross upon which Jesus was crucified. The cross is standing on a rock base symbolizing a firm foundation of obedience (Matthew 7:24). The red background represents the blood that Jesus shed to pay for our sins (Romans 5:9). The fruit tree represents the tree of the knowledge of good and evil. Partaking of its fruit caused man's sentence of death (Genesis 2:17). The oak tree represents the tree of life (Genesis 3:22). The trees are located on opposite sides of the cross to symbolize that there is only one way to pass from death unto life, and that is through the cross (Ephesians 2:16). Numerically, chapter twenty-six is the central chapter of the book. The title of chapter twenty-six is ACCEPT JESUS AS YOUR SAVIOR. The central location of the salvation chapter symbolizes the premise that all other choices must be based on the fundamental right choice of receiving salvation by accepting the sacrifice of Jesus (Acts 4:12).

All primary scripture was taken from a THOMPSON CHAIN - REFERENCE BIBLE, FOURTH IMPROVED EDITION, KING JAMES VERSION. The Hebrew and Greek definitions used in the scripture analysis were defined by STRONG'S EXHAUSTIVE CONCORDANCE OF THE BIBLE. Also contained within the scripture analysis are references from UNGER'S BIBLE DICTIONARY, Webster's New Collegiate Dictionary, the ZONDERVAN NIV STUDY BIBLE, New International Version.

The *preface* states the five fundamental beliefs which form the basis of the book.

Right is always right, wrong is always wrong, regardless of the circumstance.
Right is always right, wrong is always wrong, no matter what other people do.
Right choices produce right results.
Wrong choices produce wrong results.
Always strive to make right choices.

The stories were written over a period of two years. During that time the father passed away, the youngest daughter married, and the author retired from Wal-Mart.
The chapters do not follow the sequential order of events as they occurred. Instead, each chapter is listed in an order that develops a naturally flowing process for making choices.
Some liberality has been taken to include implied choices for each story's *bullet points*. The chapters which contain God or Jesus in the title, have additional scripture instead of bullet points.
The *scripture analysis* is intended to enhance the reader's understanding of the King James version of scripture. The analyzed portions of scripture are placed directly beneath the corresponding King James version of scripture so the reader can compare both renderings. Pronouns were changed at the author's discretion to either the subject's proper names or to other expanded identifications. Old English words were changed to their modern English equivalence. Additional words deemed necessary to properly convey the intended meanings were enclosed within brackets. Definitions within word groups (be, become, became / you, your, yourself, etc.) were interchanged at the author's discretion without reference. The following fifty words were interchanged or otherwise defined at the author's discretion, without the use of referenced definitions: after, also, an, and, are, as, at, be, before, but, by, came, did, even, for, forth, from, have, how, I, if, in, is, it, may, me, my, o, of, on, shall, should, that, the, their, them, this, those, through, to, unto, upon, was, were, when, will, with, what, which, *and* yet.

EXAMPLE OF SCRIPTURE ANALYSIS:

Psalms 119: 11

Thy
- *(Thy* is changed from Old English to the modern translation of *your*. Lord, *(God)* is inserted to designate who is being spoken to. Brackets are placed around Lord, *(God)* to designate that it is entered additionally.)
  - [Lord (God)] your
Word
- From the Hebrew word *imrah*, Strongs #565: commandment.
  - (Hebrew definition is used but changed to plural form)
  - Commandments
Have I hid
- From the Hebrew word *tsaphan*, Strong's #6845: hoard.
- (Hebrew definition is used but changed to past tense. The words *have* and *I* are placed in the order of *I have* to create a more natural flow of modern English.)
  - I have hoarded
In mine
- *(Mine* is changed to *my* without reference because it is in the same word group.)
  - In my
Heart,
- From the Hebrew word *leb*, Strong's #3820: the feelings, the will and even the intellect.
  - (Appropriate portions of the Hebrew definition is used.)
  - Feelings, will and intellect,
That I
- *(So* is inserted additionally to create a more natural flow of modern English. Brackets are placed around *so* to designate that it is entered additionally.)
  - [So] that I
Might not sin
- Unger's Bible Dictionary states: "The underlying idea of sin is that of law and of a lawgiver. The lawgiver is God. Hence sin

is everything in the disposition and purpose and conduct of God's moral creatures that is contrary to the expressed will of God... The sinfulness of sin lies in the fact that it is against God, even when the wrong we do is to others or ourselves."

- (*Sin* is defined by portions of commentary from Unger's Bible Dictionary. The commentary is informational only, so the scripture analysis is repeated with identical wording from the King James Version.)

- Might not <u>sin</u>

Against <u>thee</u>.

- (*Thee* is changed from Old English to the modern translation of you. *Thee* is not identified as *Lord (God)*, because that identification was already made within this statement.)

- Against <u>you</u>.

By following the bottom line from each portion of analyzed scripture, you will read the analyzed scripture in the following manner:

> Lord (God) your commandments
> I have hoarded
> in my feelings, will and intellect,
> so that I might not sin against you.

Chapters one through fifty one contain six questions in the *choice examination.* Man was created on the sixth day (Genesis 1:26, 31). The burden of making choices lies with man. Chapter fifty two contains seven questions. The creation of the heavens and the earth were finished on the seventh day (Genesis 2: 1, 2). Chapter fifty two is the final chapter of the book, and is intended to represent the final stage of the choice process. The book's seventh and final question asks - "Why do you need to make RIGHT CHOICES?"

The answer is found by analyzing the choices in God's Holy Word, the Bible. The author prays that all readers would be liberated by the concept of striving to make RIGHT CHOICES.

And ye shall know the truth, and the truth shall make you free. John 8: 32

MAKE RIGHT CHOICES

Right is always right
Wrong is always wrong
Regardless of the circumstance

Right is always right
Wrong is always wrong
No matter what other people do

Right choices produce
Right results

Wrong choices produce
Wrong results

Always strive to make
Right choices

DO WHAT'S RIGHT EVEN IF IT BREAKS A RULE

≈1≈

And, behold, there was a woman which had a spirit of infirmity eighteen years, and was bowed together, and could in no wise lift up herself. And when Jesus saw her, he called her to him, and said unto her, Woman, thou art loosed from thine infirmity. And he laid his hands on her: and immediately she was made straight, and glorified God.

And the ruler of the synagogue answered with indignation, because that Jesus had healed on the sabbath day, and said unto the people, There are six days in which men ought to work: in them therefore come and be healed, and not on the sabbath day.

The Lord then answered him, and said Thou hypocrite, doth not each one of you on the sabbath loose his ox or his ass from the stall, and lead him away to watering? And ought not this woman, being a daughter of Abraham, whom Satan hath bound, lo, these eighteen years, be loosed from this bond on the sabbath day?

And when he had said these things, all his adversaries were ashamed: and all the people rejoiced for all the glorious things that were done by him.

Luke 13: 11 - 17

"Don't worry about the rules, *just do what's right.*" That was my advice to a new and insecure service desk clerk. The computer was telling her that a customer had received several refunds for the same item. Through conversation with the customer the clerk had learned that a single situation had caused her to exchange the item several times before she had realized the actual cause of her problem. The woman wasn't a dishonest customer. She wasn't trying to take advantage of Wal-Mart's liberal refund policy. She just needed to get her item exchanged, and the computer had identified her transaction as a repeated situation. The clerk actually wanted to take care of the customer's need. She just needed reassurance that it was all right to break a rule.

How often is a wrong choice made because someone chose to follow a rule, instead of choosing to do what was right for the situation?

When my daughter, Amy, started dating her boyfriend, Matthew, they asked me about their curfew. They wanted to know what time I was going to require Matt to have Amy home from their dates. I refused to give them a curfew. I took quite a lot of time explaining to them that I wanted them to concentrate on being responsible, rather than concentrating on not breaking a rule. I explained to them that not only should their behavior be responsible, their behavior should also appear responsible. People should not even suspect impropriety in their behavior. Therefore, nights of excessive lateness should be avoided. I had no interest in requiring Matt to have Amy home at five minutes before midnight, instead of five minutes after midnight. I was interested in requiring both of them to think about doing what's right. They understood the concept and have behaved appropriately.

Rules are necessary. For the most part, rules are good. But it's impossible to make enough rules to apply to every situation. The end result should always be the right result, regardless of the rules. Sometimes, more than rules, we just need a good philosophy to follow. That philosophy is - *just do what's right*.

Don't ever let a good rule cause you to make a bad choice. Just do what's right, even if it breaks a rule.

BULLET POINTS

Do what's right,
Even if it breaks a rule.
Right always takes priority
Over rules.

Do what's right,
Even if it breaks a rule.
Do it because it's right,
Not because it's a rule.

Wrong is never right,
No matter what the rules say.

People follow rules because
They have to.
People do what's right because
They want to.

Don't ever let a good rule
Cause you
To make a bad decision.

Choose to
Do what's right,
Even if it breaks a rule.

SCRIPTURE ANALYSIS

Luke 13: 11 - 17

11. And, behold, there was a woman <u>which</u> had
- And, behold, there was a woman <u>who</u> had

11. A <u>spirit</u>
- A <u>spiritually [inflicted disease]</u>

11. <u>Of</u>
- <u>Which [had caused her]</u>

11. <u>Infirmity</u> eighteen years, and
- From the Greek word *astheneia*, Strong's #769: <u>feebleness</u>.
- <u>[To be] feeble [for the last]</u> eighteen years, and

11. <u>Was</u> bowed together,
- <u>[Her body] was</u> bowed together,

11. <u>And</u> could in no wise
- <u>So [that she]</u> could in no wise

11. <u>Lift</u> up herself.
- From the Greek word *anakupto*, Strong's #352: <u>unbend</u>.
- <u>Unbend</u> herself [<u>back</u>] up.

12. And when Jesus saw <u>her</u>,
- And when Jesus saw <u>the feeble woman</u>,

12. He called <u>her</u>
- He called [<u>for</u>] <u>the feeble woman</u>

12. <u>To</u> him,
- <u>To [come to]</u> him,

12. And <u>said</u>
- And [<u>Jesus</u>] said

12. Unto <u>her</u>,
- Unto <u>the feeble woman</u>,

12. Woman, <u>thou art</u>
- Woman, <u>you are</u>

12. <u>Loosed</u>
- From the Greek word *apoluo*, Strong's #630: <u>release</u>.

- Released
12. From thine infirmity.
- From your [condition of] feebleness.
13. And he laid his hands
- And Jesus laid his hands
13. On her:
- On the [feeble] woman:
13. And immediately she
- And immediately the [feeble] woman's
13. Was made straight,
- [Posture] was made straight,
13. And glorified God.
- And [she] glorified God.
14. And the ruler of the synagogue
- The Unger's Bible Dictionary states: "The ruler of the synagogue had the care of external order in public worship, and the supervision of the concerns of the synagogue in general. Among his functions is specially mentioned that of appointing who should read the Scriptures and the prayer, and summoning fit persons to preach; to see that nothing improper took place in the synagogue, and to take charge of the synagogue building. For the acts proper to public worship - the reading of the Scriptures, preaching and prayer - no special officials were appointed. These acts were, on the contrary, in the time of Christ still freely performed in turn by members of the congregation."
- And the ruler of the synagogue [who had the care of external order to see that nothing improper took place]
14. Answered with indignation,
- From the Greek word *apokrinomai*, Strong's #611: to begin to speak.
- Began to speak [to the people who saw Jesus heal the feeble woman] with indignation,
14. Because that Jesus
- Because [of the fact] that Jesus
14. Had healed
- Had healed [the feeble woman]
14. On the sabbath day,
- The Unger's Bible Dictionary states: "According to

Mosaic law the Sabbath was observed: 1. By cessation from labor (Exod. 20:10). The idea of work is not more precisely defined in the law, except that the kindling of fire for cooking is expressly forbidden (35:3), and the gathering of wood is treated as a transgression (Num. 15:32, sq.); whence it is evident that work, in its widest sense, was to cease."

   - On the <u>Sabbath</u> day,

14. And <u>said</u>

   - And [<u>the ruler of the synagogue</u>] said

14. Unto the <u>people</u>,

   - Unto the <u>people</u> [<u>who saw Jesus heal the feeble woman</u>],

14. There are six <u>days</u> in which men

   - There are six <u>days</u> [<u>in each week</u>] in which men

14. Ought <u>to</u> work:

   - Ought <u>to</u> [<u>do their</u>] work:

14. In <u>them</u>

   - In [<u>those</u>] six days [<u>of the week</u>]

14. Therefore <u>come and</u> be healed,

   - Therefore [<u>you may</u>] come to be healed,

14. <u>And not</u> on the sabbath day.

   - But [<u>do</u>] not [<u>come to be healed</u>] on the Sabbath day.

15. <u>The Lord</u> then

   - Then <u>Jesus</u>

15. Answered <u>him</u>,

   - Answered <u>the ruler of the synagogue</u>,

15. And said, <u>Thou</u> hypocrite,

   - And said, <u>You</u> hypocrite,

15. <u>Doth</u> not each one of you

   - <u>Do</u> not each one of you

15. On the <u>sabbath</u>

   - On the <u>Sabbath</u> [<u>day</u>]

15. Loose <u>his</u>

   - Loose <u>your</u>

15. Ox or <u>his</u>

   - Ox or <u>your</u>

15. <u>Ass</u> from the stall,

   - From the Greek word *onos*, Strong's #3688: <u>donkey</u>.

⌐ <u>Donkey</u> from the stall,

15. And lead <u>him</u> away

- And lead [<u>your</u>] ox or donkey away

15. <u>To</u> watering?

- <u>For</u> watering?

16. And ought not this woman, being a <u>daughter</u> of Abraham,

- From the Greek word *thugater*, Strong's #2364: <u>a female child or descendant</u>.

- And ought not his woman, being a <u>descendant</u> of Abraham,

16. Whom Satan <u>hath</u> bound,

- Whom Satan <u>has [kept]</u> bound,

16. Lo, <u>these</u> eighteen years,

- Lo, [<u>for</u>] <u>these</u> [<u>last</u>] eighteen years,

16. Be loosed from this <u>bond</u> on the sabbath day?

- From the Greek word *desmon*, Strong's #1199: <u>disability</u>.

- Be loosed from this <u>disability</u> on the Sabbath day?

17. And <u>when he</u> had said these things,

- And <u>after Jesus</u> had said these things,

17. All <u>his</u> adversaries

- All [<u>of</u>] <u>Jesus'</u> adversaries

17. Were <u>ashamed</u>:

- Were <u>ashamed [of themselves]</u>:

17. And all the <u>people</u>

- And all the <u>people [who witnessed the healing and heard Jesus' words]</u>

17. Rejoiced for all the glorious things that were done by <u>him</u>.

- Rejoiced for all the glorious things that were done by <u>Jesus</u>.

CHOICE EXAMINATION

1. Why was the service desk clerk told to break a rule in order to take care of a customer?

2. Why were Amy and Matthew not given a specific curfew when they started dating?

3. In the scripture, why did Jesus heal the feeble woman on the Sabbath day?

4. Why was the ruler of the synagogue upset about Jesus healing the woman?

5. Why were Jesus' adversaries ashamed of themselves?

6. What choices do you need to make in order to *do what's right, even if it breaks a rule*?

CHOOSE TO TAKE CARE OF YOUR HEALTH

KEEP YOURSELF NEW

≈ 2 ≈

Hast thou not known? hast thou not heard, that the everlasting God, the LORD, the Creator of the ends of the earth, fainteth not, neither is weary? there is no searching of his understanding. He giveth power to the faint; and to them that have no might he increaseth strength. Even the youths shall faint and be weary, and the young men shall utterly fall: But they that wait upon the LORD shall renew their strength; they shall mount up with wings as eagles; they shall run, and not be weary; and they shall walk, and not faint.

Isaiah 40: 28 - 31

His eyes were opened wide, his hands were in the air, and he had an incredulous expression on his face. "What! My *new* tractor! You can't sell my *new* tractor!" That was my dad speaking. I had just asked him if he would allow me to trade in his International Harvester H-Farmall tractor when we bought our new (used), much larger tractor, an Allis Chalmers 190XT. The year was 1992. His Farmall was built in 1952.

There's no telling how many thousands of hours we've spent circling the fields on that old Farmall. My brothers and I practically grew up in the seat of that old tractor. Every summer was spent working in the fields and building fences, and the old Farmall was always in the middle of the work.

Old Farmall, that's what I thought it was; but my dad didn't. He still thought it was his new tractor forty years after he bought it. You see, to him, it wasn't forty years *old*; it was forty years *new*.

Indeed, a good part of the tractor was new. We drove it so much that the tread on the tires wore off smooth, so we bought it a set of new tires. The steering shaft got so loose that it was becoming unsafe to operate, so we replaced it with a new steering shaft. The engine started using oil so my brother, Gary, gave it a new engine overhaul. The tractor's paint lost its luster, so we gave it a new paint job. We even put new factory decals on the sides of the hood! The end result of the tractor's ongoing renovation was always this; the old Farmall looked and operated just as well as it did on the day it left the factory. In every sense of the word, the old Farmall really was new, except for its age.

My dad's tractor wasn't old to him because he didn't let it get old. He kept it new.

Why do people quit growing spiritually? Why do people quit exercising? Why do people quit controlling their diets? Why do people quit learning? Why do people quit anticipating good things for the future? Why do people quit having fun? Why do people quit?? --- Is it because they're old? Is it because they're, maybe, forty years old?

That didn't seem to apply to my dad's H-Farmall. My dad chose to keep his tractor new. He kept it forty years *new*.

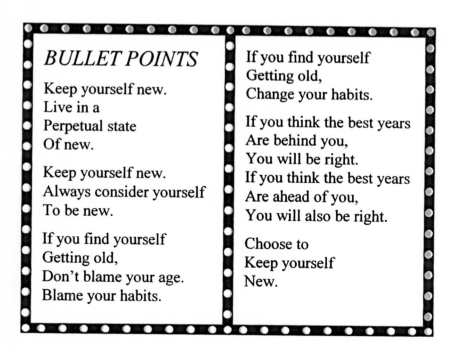

BULLET POINTS

Keep yourself new.
Live in a
Perpetual state
Of new.

Keep yourself new.
Always consider yourself
To be new.

If you find yourself
Getting old,
Don't blame your age.
Blame your habits.

If you find yourself
Getting old,
Change your habits.

If you think the best years
Are behind you,
You will be right.
If you think the best years
Are ahead of you,
You will also be right.

Choose to
Keep yourself
New.

SCRIPTURE ANALYSIS

Isaiah 40: 28 - 31

28. Hast thou not known?
  - Have you not known?
28. Hast thou not heard,
  - Have you not heard,
28. That the everlasting God,
  - From the Hebrew word *owlam*, Strong's #5769: eternal.
  - That the eternal God,
28. The LORD,
  - The Lord, [who is]
28. The Creator of the ends of the earth,
  - From the Hebrew word *qatsah*, Strong's #7098: uttermost part.
  - The Creator of the uttermost parts of the earth,
28. Fainteth not,
  - From the Hebrew word *yaaph*, Strong's #3286: to tire.
  - [Does] not [get] tired,
28. Neither
  - [And] neither
28. Is
  - Does [God become]
28. Weary?
  - From the Hebrew word *yaga*, Strong's #3021: to be exhausted.
  - Exhausted?
28. There is no searching
  - There is no [way of] searching [out to improve]
28. Of his
  - Upon God's
28. Understanding.
  - From the Hebrew word *tabuwn*, Strong's #8394: wisdom.
  - Wisdom.
29. He giveth
  - God gives

29. Power
- From the Hebrew word *koach*, Strong's #3581: <u>vigor, capacity and power</u>.
- <u>Vigor, capacity and power</u>

29. To the faint;
- From the Hebrew word *yaeph*, Strong's #3287: <u>fatigued or exhausted</u>.
- To the [people who are] fatigued or exhausted;

29. And to them that
- And to [the] people who

29. Have no might
- From the Hebrew word *own*, Strong's #202: <u>ability, power, strength or substance</u>.
- Have no <u>ability, power, strength or substance</u>

29. He increaseth
- <u>God increases</u>

29. Strength.
- From the Hebrew word *otsmah*, Strongs #6109: <u>powerfulness, numerousness, abundance, strength</u>.
- [Their] powerfulness, numerousness, abundance [or] strength [as needed].

30. Even the youths shall faint
- Also from the Hebrew word *yaaph*, Strong's #3286: <u>to tire</u>. The same word was translated as *fainteth* in verse #28.
- Even the youths shall [naturally get] tired

30. And be weary, and the young men shall
- And <u>become exhausted</u>, and the young men shall

31. Utterly fall:
- The NIV says " <u>Stumble and fall;</u>"

31. But they that wait
- From the Hebrew word *qavah*, Strong's #6960: <u>bind together, expect, [and] tarry</u>.
- But they that <u>bind together, expecting [and] tarrying</u>

31. Upon the LORD,
- <u>For</u> the Lord,

31. Shall renew their strength;
- Also from the Hebrew word *koach*, Strong's #3581: <u>vigor, capacity, and power</u>. The same word was translated as *power* in

verse #29.

    - Shall renew their <u>vigor, capacity, and power</u>;

31. <u>They</u>

    - <u>The people [who bind together, expecting and tarrying for the Lord]</u>

31. <u>Shall</u>

    - <u>Shall [feel like they are]</u>

31. <u>Mount</u>

    - From the Hebrew word *alah*, Strong's #5927: <u>ascend up</u>.

    - <u>Ascending</u>

31. <u>Up</u> with wings

    - <u>Upwards</u> with wings

31. <u>As</u> eagles;

    - <u>As [if they were]</u> eagles;

31. They shall run, and not <u>be weary</u>;

    - They shall run and not <u>become exhausted</u>;

31. And they shall walk, and not <u>faint</u>.

- And they shall walk, and not <u>[get] tired</u>.

CHOICE EXAMINATION

1. Why did the dad think his forty year old tractor was new?

2. Why did the dad keep his forty year old tractor in new condition?

3. Why do people quit keeping themselves in new condition?

4. In the scripture, what must people, who are fatigued or exhausted, do to renew their vigor, capacity or power?

5. Why do people neglect binding together, expecting and tarrying for the Lord?

6. What choices do you need to make in order to *keep yourself new?*

PROTECT YOUR BRAIN FROM HARMFUL SUBSTANCES

≈ 3 ≈

NOW the serpent was more subtil than any beast of the field which the LORD God had made. And he said unto the woman, Yea, hath God said, Ye shall not eat of every tree of the garden?

And the woman said unto the serpent, We may eat of the fruit of the trees of the garden: But of the fruit of the tree which is in the midst of the garden, God hath said, Ye shall not eat of it, neither shall ye touch it, lest ye die.

And the serpent said unto the woman, Ye shall not surely die: For God doth know that in the day ye eat thereof, then your eyes shall be opened, and ye shall be as gods, knowing good and evil.

And when the woman saw that the tree was good for food, and that it was pleasant to the eyes, and a tree to be desired to make one wise, she took of the fruit thereof, and did eat, and gave also unto her husband with her; and he did eat. And the eyes of them both were opened, and they knew that they were naked; and they sewed fig leaves together, and made themselves aprons. And they heard the voice of the LORD God walking in the garden in the cool of the day: And Adam and his wife hid themselves from the presence of the LORD God amongst the trees of the garden.

And the LORD God said unto the woman, What is this that thou hast done?

And the woman said, The serpent beguiled me, and I did eat.

And unto Adam he said, Because thou hast hearkened unto the voice of thy wife, and hast eaten of the tree, of which I commanded thee, saying, Thou shalt not eat of it: cursed is the ground for thy sake; in sorrow shalt thou eat of it all the days of thy life; Thorns also and thistles shall it bring forth to thee; and thou shalt eat the herb of the field; In the sweat of thy face shalt thou eat bread, till thou return unto the ground; for out

of it wast thou taken: for dust thou art, and unto dust shalt thou return.

Genesis 3: 1 - 8, 13, 17 - 19

She was a responsible young lady. Her work ethic was exemplary. Never had she missed a day of scheduled work, but I thought she should have stayed home on this day.

"Brandy, we know that your mother passed away last night. We don't expect you to be here today. You need to be at home with your family. We will give you bereavement pay for the time you miss. Don't worry about your responsibilities here. Wal-Mart will be fine. We want to take care of you."

She seemed determined to stay at work; yet eager to talk about her situation. I spent the next thirty minutes just listening to her. She told me that her mother was a long-term drug addict. As a teenager, Brandy had played the role of parent to her mother. More than once she had saved her mother's life by calling the ambulance to their house when her mother had overdosed on drugs. She routinely had to pick her mother up from the floor to put her in bed at nights. When Brandy was in high school, she worked at various jobs to help buy groceries for the rest of the family. Sometimes Brandy's income was used to help pay the utility bills too. It was an incredible story. I had to ask her some questions.

"How did you avoid getting hooked on drugs, too? How did you survive your teenage years with all this pressure? Why did you choose to be so responsible?"

"I know this might sound amazing to you," she said. "But when I saw the suffering our family endured because of my mother's drug addiction, I chose to make my life better. I didn't want my family to suffer the way we did, so I chose to stay away from drugs."

She left the office and went back to work. I still thought she should have gone home, but I knew I couldn't persuade her. I knew she had a determined attitude and now I knew why. It had something to do with a choice she had made when she was a teenager.

BULLET POINTS

Protect your brain
From harmful substances.
Avoid getting hooked on
Drugs.

Protect your brain
From harmful substances.
Choose to be responsible.

Drug induced highs are
Temporary.
Brain loss is forever.

Concentrate
On what you can
Educate.

Take care of your brain so
It can take care of you.

Choose to
Protect your brain
From harmful substances.

SCRIPTURE ANALYSIS

Genesis 3: 1 - 8, 13, 17 - 19

1. NOW the <u>serpent</u>
    - From the Hebrew word *nachash*, Strong's #5175: <u>a snake</u>
    - Now the <u>snake</u>
1. Was more <u>subtil</u>
    - From the Hebrew word *aruwm*, Strong's #6175: <u>cunning</u>
<u>(usually in a bad sense)</u>.
    - Was more <u>cunning</u>
1. Than any <u>beast</u> of the field which the LORD God had made.
    - From the Hebrew word *chay*, Strong's #2416: <u>living</u>
<u>creature</u>.
    - Than any [other] <u>living creature</u> of the field which the
Lord God had made.
1. And <u>he</u> said
    - And <u>the snake</u> said
1. Unto <u>the woman,</u>
    - Unto <u>Eve (see 3:20),</u>
1. <u>Yea, hath</u>
    - <u>Yes, has</u>
1. God <u>said,</u>
    - God [really] <u>said [that],</u>
1. <u>Ye</u> shall not eat
    - <u>You</u> shall not eat
1. <u>Of</u> every tree
    - <u>From</u> every tree
1. <u>Of</u>
    - <u>In</u>
1. The <u>garden?</u>
    - The <u>garden [in Eden (see 2: 8)]</u>?
2. And <u>the woman</u>
    - And <u>Eve</u>
2. Said unto the <u>serpent,</u>
    - Said unto the <u>snake,</u>
2. <u>We</u>

- <u>Adam and I (see 2: 16, 19)</u>
2. May eat <u>of</u> the fruit
    - May eat <u>[some] of</u> the fruit
2. <u>Of</u> the trees
    - <u>[From almost all]</u> of the trees
2. <u>Of</u>
    - <u>In</u>
2. The <u>garden</u>:
    - The <u>garden [in Eden]</u>:
3. <u>But</u> of the fruit
    - <u>But [we are not allowed to eat any]</u> of the fruit
3. <u>Of</u> the tree
    - <u>From</u> the tree
3. Which is in the midst of the <u>garden</u>
    - Which is in the midst of the <u>garden [in Eden]</u>,
3. God <u>hath</u> said,
    - God <u>has</u> said,
3. <u>Ye</u> shall not eat
    - <u>You</u> shall not eat
3. <u>Of it</u>,
    - <u>[The fruit] from the tree [in the midst of the garden in</u>
<u>Eden]</u>
3. Neither shall <u>ye</u>
    - Neither shall <u>you</u>
3. Touch <u>it</u>,
    - Touch <u>the fruit [from the tree in the midst of the garden in</u>
<u>Eden]</u>,
3. <u>Lest</u>
    - Defined by Webster's Dictionary as: <u>for fear that - used</u>
<u>after an expression denoting fear or apprehension</u>.
    - <u>For fear that</u>
3. <u>Ye die</u>.
    - <u>You [will]</u> die.
4. And the <u>serpent</u> said
    - And the <u>snake</u> said
4. Unto <u>the woman</u>,
    - Unto <u>Eve</u>,

4. Ye shall not surely
> - Surely you shall not

4. Die:
> - [Actually] die:

5. For God doth know
> - For [what] God does know

5. That in
> - [Is] that on

5. The day ye
> - The day [that] you

5. Eat thereof,
> - Defined by Webster's Dictionary as: of that or it.
> - Eat [some] of that [fruit],

5. Then your eyes shall be
> - Then your eyes shall become

5. Opened,
> - From the Hebrew word *paqach*, Strong's #6491: to be observant.
> - Observant,

5. And ye
> - And you [and Adam]

5. Shall be
> - Shall become

5. As gods,
> - [The same] as gods,

5. Knowing good and evil.
> - Knowing [the difference between] good and evil.

6. And when the woman
> - And when Eve

6. Saw that the tree
> - Saw that the tree [in the midst of the garden in Eden]

6. Was good for
> - Was good for [producing]

6. Food,
> - From the Hebrew word *maakal*, Strong's #3978: fruit.
> - Fruit,

6. And that it was
> - And that the fruit had [a]

6. Pleasant to the eyes,
    - Pleasant [appearance] to the eyes,
6. And
    - And [since the snake had said it was]
6. A tree to be desired to
    - A tree to be desired because [it could]
6. Make one wise,
    - Make someone [become] wise,
6. She
    - Eve
6. Took of the fruit
    - Took [some] of the fruit
6. Thereof,
    - [From] it,
6. And did eat,
    - And [Eve] did eat [some of the fruit],
6. And gave also
    - And [Eve] gave [some of the fruit] also
6. Unto her husband with her;
    - Unto Adam, [who was] with her;
6. And he
    - And Adam
6. Did eat.
    - Did eat [some of the fruit, also].
7. And the eyes of them both
    - And the eyes of both, Adam and Eve
7. Were opened,
    - Became observant,
7. And they knew that they were naked;
    - And [then] Adam and Eve knew that they were naked;
7. And they sewed fig leaves together,
    - And Adam and Eve sewed fig leaves together,
7. And made themselves aprons.
    - And made themselves aprons [to cover their nakedness].
8. And they heard
    - And Adam and Eve heard
8. The voice of the LORD God walking in

- The voice of the Lord God [as he was] walking through

8. The garden

- The garden [in Eden]

8. In the cool of the day:

- From the Hebrew word *ruwach*, Strong's #7307: wind [and] cool.

- In the cool, windy [portion] of the day:

8. And Adam and his wife hid themselves

- And Adam and Eve hid themselves

8. From the presence of the LORD God amongst the trees of the garden.

- From the presence of the Lord God amongst the trees of the garden [in Eden].

13. And the LORD God said unto the woman,

- And the Lord God said unto Eve,

13. What is this that thou hast done?

- What is this that you have done?

13. And the woman said,

- And Eve said [to the Lord God],

13. The serpent

- The snake

13. Beguiled me,

- From the Hebrew word *nasha*, Strong's #5377: (morally) to seduce.

- Morally seduced me,

13. And I did eat.

- And I did eat [some of the fruit from the tree in the midst of the garden in Eden].

17. And unto Adam he said,

- And unto Adam God said,

17. Because thou hast

- Because you have

17. Hearkened

- From the Hebrew word *shama*, Strong's #8085: to hear intelligently.

- Heard intelligently

17. Unto

- [And responded] to
17. The voice of <u>thy wife,</u>
    - The voice of <u>Eve,</u>
17. And <u>hast eaten of</u> the tree,
    - And <u>have eaten [fruit] from</u> the tree,
17. Of which I commanded <u>thee,</u> saying,
    - Of which I commanded <u>you,</u> saying,
17. <u>Thou shalt</u> not
    - <u>You shall</u> not
17. <u>Eat</u>
    - <u>Eat [fruit]</u>
17. <u>Of it:</u>
    - <u>From the tree [in the midst of the garden in Eden]</u>:
17. Cursed is the ground for <u>thy</u> sake;
    - Cursed is the ground for <u>your</u> sake;
17. In <u>sorrow</u>
    - From the Hebrew word *itstsabown*, Strong's #6093: <u>worrisome labor</u>.
    - In <u>worrisome labor</u>
17. <u>Shalt thou</u>
    - <u>You shall</u>
17. Eat <u>of it</u> all the days
    - Eat <u>[what's produced] from the ground [for]</u> all the days
17. Of <u>thy</u> life;
    - Of <u>your</u> life;
18. Thorns also and thistles shall <u>it</u> bring forth
    - Thorns also and thistles shall <u>the ground</u> bring forth
18. To <u>thee;</u>
    - To <u>[hinder] your [efforts]</u>;
18. And <u>thou shalt</u> eat
    - And <u>you shall</u> eat
18. The <u>herb</u>
    - From the Hebrew word *eseb*, Strong's #6212: <u>to glisten (or be green); grass (or any tender shoot)</u>
    - The <u>green or glistening tender shoots</u>
18. <u>Of</u> the field;
    - <u>[That grow] in</u> the field;

19. In the
- [And] through the [labor that causes the beads of]

19. Sweat of thy face
- Sweat [to form] on your face

19. Shalt thou
- You shall [obtain]

19. Eat bread,
- From the Hebrew word *lechem,* Strong's #3899: food.
- Food [to] eat,

19. Till thou return
- Until [the time when] you return

19. Unto the ground;
- Unto the ground [in death];

19. For
- For [from]

19. Out of it wast thou taken:
- Out of the ground was [where] you [were] taken:

19. For dust thou art,
- For dust [is what] you are [made from],

19. And unto dust shalt thou return.
- And unto dust shall your [dead body] return.

CHOICE EXAMINATION

1. Why was Brandy determined to stay at work on the day after her mother died?

2. What things did Brandy do while she was still a teenager, that helped her avoid getting hooked on drugs?

3. Why did Brandy choose to be so responsible?

4. In the scripture, how did the snake persuade Eve to eat some of the fruit from the tree in the midst of the garden in Eden?

5. Why did Adam also take some of the fruit from the tree in the midst of the garden in Eden?

6. What choices do you need to make in order to *protect your brain from harmful substances*?

THINK ABOUT WHAT YOU SHOULD THINK ABOUT

≈ 4 ≈

Finally, brethren, whatsoever things are true, whatsoever things are honest, whatsoever things are just, whatsoever things are pure, whatsoever things are lovely, whatsoever things are of good report; if there be any virtue, and if there be any praise, think on these things.

Philippians 4: 8

When I stepped out onto the sidewalk it caught my attention immediately! The volume was turned up really loud! The song was nothing more than a constant stream of expletives with defiant, crude, vulgar, disrespectful language directed toward the exploitation of women.

"What's going on here?" I asked the young man.

"I'm just listening to my music!" he growled.

I barked out an angry response. "Well, you can't disrupt our customer service with loud music like that! Turn it off right now!" I walked away with a vow to return in a few minutes to insure his compliance.

When I came back to the sidewalk I found the music turned off and the young man standing by his car. I felt that I owed him an explanation for my request. "First of all," I said, "this is a place of business and we have to show our customers a certain degree of professionalism. So really loud music can't be allowed. Secondly, the message I heard in that song was extremely vulgar and it spoke disrespectfully about women. Are you sure that *you* want to be listening to words like that?"

" I never listen to the words," he stated. " I just listen to the beat in the music."

I understood what he was saying. I doubt that he chose that particular song because he intended to participate in its vulgar message. He probably bought that type of music because it was popular, he wanted to feel accepted with his friends, and the music did have a good drum beat. Regardless of his intentions though, I felt that the words in the song would fill his mind with defiant, cruel messages that would attempt to influence his behavior.

I walked away. I didn't feel capable to lecture him on the subject. I was afraid I might say something I'd regret. The words in that song were still fresh in *my* mind.

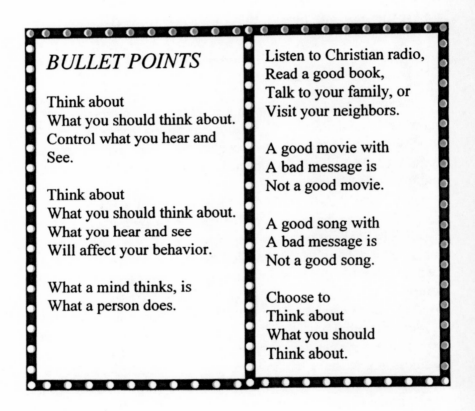

BULLET POINTS

Think about
What you should think about.
Control what you hear and
See.

Think about
What you should think about.
What you hear and see
Will affect your behavior.

What a mind thinks, is
What a person does.

Listen to Christian radio,
Read a good book,
Talk to your family, or
Visit your neighbors.

A good movie with
A bad message is
Not a good movie.

A good song with
A bad message is
Not a good song.

Choose to
Think about
What you should
Think about.

SCRIPTURE ANALYSIS

Phillipians 4: 8

8. Finally, brethren,
    - Finally, [my spiritual] brothers,
8. Whatsoever things
    - Whatever things
8. Are true,
    - From the Greek word *apelegmos*, Strong's #557:
refutation.
    - Are [not] refutable
8. Whatsoever things
    - Whatever things
8. Are honest,
    - From the Greek word *semnos*, Strong's #4586: honorable
    - Are honorable,
8. Whatsoever things
    - Whatever things
8. Are just,
    - From the Greek word *dikaios*, Strong's #1342: equitable,
innocent, holy, righteous.
    - Are equitable, innocent, holy, and righteous,
8. Whatsoever things
    - Whatever things
8. Are pure,
    - From the Greek word *hagnos*, Strong's #53: innocent,
modest, perfect, chaste, clean, pure,
    - Are innocent, modest, perfect, chaste, clean and pure,
8. Whatsoever things
    - Whatever things
8. Are lovely,
    - From the Greek word *prosphiles*, Strong's #4375: friendly
towards, acceptable, lovely.
    - Are friendly, acceptable, and lovely,
8. Whatsoever things

- Whatever things

8. Are of good

- Are good because [they]

8. Report;

- From the Greek word *euphemos*, Strong's #2163: well spoken of, reputable

- [Are] well spoken of [and] reputable;

8. If there be any virtue,

- From the Greek word *arete*, Strong's #703: valor, excellence, praise

- If there be any valor, excellence, [or if it's worthy of] praise,

8. And if there be any praise,

- From the Greek word *epainos*, Strong's #1868: A commendable thing.

- And if there be any commendable [attributes],

8. Think

- From the Greek word *logizomai*, Strong's #3049: to take an inventory.

- Take an inventory [in your mind]

8. On these things.

- Of these things.

CHOICE EXAMINATION

1. Why was the young man listening to vulgar music?

2. What type of messages was the young man allowing into his mind?

3. Why did the store manager not try to lecture the young man at that time?

4. In the scripture, what commendable attributes are we told to think about?

5. Why should we take an inventory of commendable attributes in our minds?

6. What choices do you need to make in order to *think about what you should think about*?

REST ONE DAY EACH WEEK
≈5≈

Remember the sabbath day, to keep it holy. Six days shalt thou labour, and do all thy work: But the seventh day is the sabbath of the LORD thy God: in it thou shalt not do any work, thou, nor thy son, nor thy daughter, thy manservant, nor thy maidservant, nor thy cattle, nor thy stranger that is within thy gates: For in six days the LORD made heaven and earth, the sea, and all that in them is, and rested the seventh day: wherefore the LORD blessed the sabbath day and hallowed it.

Exodus 20: 8 - 11

I felt my head drifting toward the tractor's steering wheel as I was passing out. I reached out with my left hand, and without using the clutch, forced the gearshift into neutral. The tractor coasted to a full stop. My body went limp. I slumped over the left side of the tractor, rolled across the left wheel, turned a complete somersault and landed on the ground next to the tractor. When my dad found me, I was still lying on the ground with my head resting against the tractor's tire. The tractor's engine was revved up at full throttle and the hay mower was still operating.

When I was a teenager we baled our hay into small square bales. We had an old hay truck and a bale loader. Much of the hay we baled for our own livestock was stored in the hay lofts of our two barns. It was dirty, dusty, hard work which was done during the hottest part of the summer. It took a crew of three to four people to haul in the hay. I usually wasn't the biggest or strongest member of the crew, but I did take pride in my stamina. "I may not be the strongest," I thought, "but I can last the longest."

The work ethic I developed as a young person on the farm carried over into my work habits on the job. My hard work as an hourly associate at Wal-Mart was noticed and was a factor in getting me promoted to assistant manager. During my first year as an assistant manager I earned the nickname of "Midnight Manning." The associates gave me that name because I had a habit of staying late to get more work accomplished.

"Galen, I want to know what's wrong with you. You're grumpy, you're argumentative, and you're not paying attention to your associates." I was a store manager at the time. My district manager had me cornered in a back office. He wanted a truthful answer.

"Sir, I've been working my full schedule here at the store. I've worked hard and the store's in good condition. My attitude has probably been affected by the farm work that I'm doing at home. After getting off work here, I've been jumping on a tractor and pulling a plow around the field until about midnight each night. I'm tired, but I'm not neglecting my job."

"No," he said, "you are neglecting your job. You're overworking yourself, and it's affecting your behavior toward people. You need to take better care of yourself so you will take better care of your associates."

I listened to his advice - partially. I apologized to the appropriate people and I improved my behavior, but I chose to keep working too many hours. It was a few months later when I passed out while driving the tractor.

"Your EKG looks good," the doctor said, "and your blood sugar looks good. I see nothing medically wrong with you. Are you perhaps, dealing with some kind of stress which could be affecting your body this way?"

Oh boy! I knew I was in trouble now! (Barbie was with me.) Barbie turned to the doctor and gave him the lowdown on my excessive work habits. If I wasn't going to listen to what my district manager was telling me, and if I wasn't going to listen to what my *body* was telling me, then I would have to be monitored by my wife. And now she had all the ammunition she needed to straighten me up!!

I learned my lesson. I continued to work hard when it was time to work, but I also chose to sleep eight hours a night and rest one day each week.

My health and my attitude both improved.

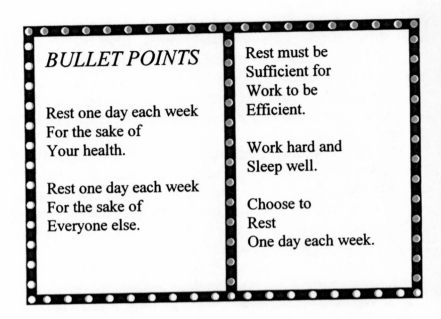

BULLET POINTS

Rest one day each week
For the sake of
Your health.

Rest one day each week
For the sake of
Everyone else.

Rest must be
Sufficient for
Work to be
Efficient.

Work hard and
Sleep well.

Choose to
Rest
One day each week.

SCRIPTURE ANALYSIS

Exodus 20: 8 - 11

8. Remember the <u>sabbath</u> day,
　　　- From the Hebrew word *shabbath*, Strong's #7676: <u>intermission</u>.
　　　- The Unger's Bible Dictionary states: "According to Mosaic law the Sabbath was observed … by cessation from labor…The object of this cessation and coming together in holy convocation was to give man an opportunity to engage in such mental and spiritual exercises as would tend to the quickening of soul and spirit and the strengthening of spiritual life. In this higher sense it is evident that our Lord meant that 'the Sabbath was made for man' (Mark 2:27)."
　　　- Remember the day [of] intermission [from labor],
8. To keep <u>it</u>
　　　- To keep <u>the day of intermission [from labor]</u>

8. <u>Holy</u>.

> \- From the Hebrew word *qadash*, Strong's #6942: <u>to be clean (ceremonially or morally)</u>.
> \- <u>Ceremonially and morally clean</u>.

9. <u>Six days shalt thou</u>

> \- <u>[For] six days [of the week] you shall</u>

9. Labour, and do all <u>thy</u> work:

> \- Labor and do all <u>your</u> work:

10. But the seventh day is the <u>sabbath</u>

> \- But the seventh day is the <u>day of intermission [from labor]</u>

10. <u>Of</u> the LORD

> \- <u>[Given to you] by</u> the Lord

10. <u>Thy</u> God:

> \- <u>Your</u> God:

10. <u>In it thou shalt</u> not do any work,

> \- <u>On the day of intermission [from labor] you shall</u> not do any work,

10. <u>Thou,</u>

> <u>[Neither] you,</u>

10. Nor <u>thy</u> son,

> \- Nor <u>your</u> son,

10. Nor <u>thy</u> daughter,

> \- Nor <u>your</u> daughter,

10. <u>Thy</u>

> \- <u>Your</u>

10. <u>Manservant,</u>

> \- From the Hebrew word *ebed*, Strong's #5650: <u>a servant</u>.
> \- <u>[Male] servant,</u>

10. Nor <u>thy</u>

> \- Nor <u>your</u>

10. <u>Maidservant,</u>

> \- From the Hebrew word *amah*, Strong's #519: <u>a maid-servant or female slave</u>.
> \- <u>Female servant,</u>

10. Nor <u>thy</u> cattle,

> \- Nor <u>your</u> cattle,

10. Nor <u>thy</u>

> \- Nor <u>the</u>

10. Stranger
    - From the Hebrew word *ger*, Strong's #1616: <u>guest</u>.
    - <u>Guest</u>

10. That is
    - <u>Who</u> is

10. Within thy
    - <u>[Staying] within your</u>

10. Gates:
    - From the Hebrew word *shaar*, Strong's #8179: <u>door</u>.
    - <u>Doors:</u>

11. For in six days the LORD made <u>heaven</u>
    - From the Hebrew word *shamayim*, Strong's #8064: <u>the sky</u>
    - For in six days the Lord made <u>the sky</u>

11. And <u>earth,</u>
    - From the Hebrew word *erets*, Strong's #776: <u>land</u>.
    - And <u>[the] land,</u>

11. The sea,
    - <u>[As well as] the</u> sea,

11. And all that in <u>them</u> is,
    - And all that is in <u>the sky, land, and sea,</u>

11. And <u>rested</u> the seventh day:
    - And <u>[then God] rested [from creating on]</u> the seventh day:

11. <u>Wherefore</u>
    - From the Hebrew word *al*, Strong's #5921: <u>after</u>. And from the Hebrew word *ken*, Strong's #3651: <u>therefore</u>.
    - <u>Therefore, after [setting this precedent]</u>

11. The LORD blessed the <u>sabbath</u> day,
    - The Lord blessed the day <u>of intermission [from labor],</u>

11. And <u>hallowed it.</u>
    - From the Hebrew word *qadash*, Strong's #6942: <u>to be clean (ceremonially or morally)</u>. The same word was translated as *holy* in verse # 8.
    - And <u>[made] the day of intermission [from labor] ceremonially and morally clean.</u>

CHOICE EXAMINATION

1. Why did Galen pass out while driving the tractor?

2. How did Galen's pride affect his work habits?

3. Why did the district manager tell Galen he needed to take better care of himself?

4. In the scripture, what spiritual benefit did God intend for mankind to receive by involving in the day of intermission?

5. Who should participate in the day of intermission?

6. What choices do you need to make in order to *rest one day each week*?

CHOOSE TO TAKE CARE OF YOUR FAMILY

KEEP YOUR VIRGINITY UNTIL YOU'RE MARRIED

≈ 6 ≈

AND it came to pass after this, that Absalom the son of David had a fair sister, whose name was Tamar; and Amnon the son of David loved her. And Amnon was so vexed, that he fell sick for his sister Tamar; for she was a virgin; and Amnon thought it hard for him to do anything to her. So Amnon lay down, and made himself sick: and when the king was come to see him, Amnon said unto the king, I pray thee, let Tamar my sister come, and make me a couple of cakes in my sight, that I may eat at her hand.

Then David sent home to Tamar, saying , Go now to thy brother Amnon's house, and dress him meat.

So Tamar went to her brother Amnon's house; and he was laid down. And she took flour and kneaded it, and made cakes in his sight, and did bake the cakes. And she took a pan and poured them out before him; but he refused to eat. And Amnon said, Have out all men from me. And they went out every man from him. And Amnon said unto Tamar, Bring the meat into the chamber, that I may eat of thine hand. And Tamar took the cakes which she had made, and brought them into the chamber to Amnon her brother. And when she had brought them unto him to eat, he took hold of her, and said unto her, Come lie with me, my sister.

And she answered him, Nay, my brother, do not force me; for no such thing ought to be done in Israel: do not thou this folly. Howbeit, he would not hearken unto her voice: but, being stronger than she, forced her, and lay with her.

Then Amnon hated her exceedingly; so that the hatred wherewith he hated her was greater than the love wherewith he had loved her. And Amnon said unto her, Arise, be gone.

II Samuel 13:1, 2, 6 - 12, 14, 15

The young man purchased some condoms.

I'm accustomed to parents bringing young children to me when they find out their son or daughter has stolen an item from the store. They usually want me to give their child a good lecture on the subject of personal integrity. I'm supposed to tell the child that stealing is wrong. I'm supposed to tell the child how his or her misplaced actions can hurt other people. I'm supposed to let the child know how much trouble he or she can get into if he or she continues to steal. I've had parents tell me to speak harshly to their child so the lecture will have a lasting impact. I take this responsibility very seriously.

One day, however, when I was asked to speak to a teenager about his sex life, I realized that a normal good lecture delivered in a harsh manner would not be effective. This conversation would have to be delivered in a very personal and delicate way if it was going to have any chance of making an impact on his life. I took him into a back office and told him the most personal information I had ever shared with another person.

"My wife and I were both virgins when we got married and we've never regretted that fact. I realize that you're a teenager now and this may not seem important to you today, but know this - nobody regrets on their wedding night that they had kept their virginity until they got married. Indeed, there is a special trust that develops between a husband and a wife that comes from knowing they had saved themselves for each other, and neither party has a need to worry about their spouse's faithfulness in marriage. It's natural for a young person to be curious and a young person's hormones run strong, but the choice you're about to make will be exciting for one night only. Yet, the consequences of your action will last for a lifetime."

BULLET POINTS

Keep your virginity until you're married.
You will never regret that decision.

Keep your virginity until your married.
Nobody regrets, on their wedding night,
That they had kept their virginity
Until they got married.

There is a special trust that
Develops between
A husband and a wife that
Comes from knowing they had
Saved themselves
For each other.

Loosing your virginity is exciting for
One night only, yet
The consequences of that action will last
For a lifetime.

Choose to
Keep you virginity
Until you're married.

SCRIPTURE ANALYSIS

II Samuel 13: 1, 2, 6 - 12, 14, 15

1. AND it came to pass after <u>this</u>,
- And it came to pass after <u>this - [David's conquering of the city of Rabbah (see 12: 29)]</u>,
1. That Absalom the son of <u>David</u>
- That Absalom, the son of <u>[king] David [who]</u>

1. Had a fair

- From the Hebrew word *yapheh*, Strong's #3303: <u>beautiful</u>.

- Had a <u>beautiful</u>

1. <u>Sister, whose name was Tamar;</u>

- <u>[Half] sister (See II Samuel 3: 2, 3 and II Samuel 13: 1),</u> whose name was Tamar;

1. <u>And</u> Amnon

- <u>That</u> Amnon

1. The son of <u>David</u>

- The son of [king] David

1. <u>Loved her.</u>

- [Fell in] love [with] Tamar.

2. And Amnon was so <u>vexed</u>,

- From The Hebrew word *yatsar*, Strong's #3334: <u>be in distress</u>.

- And Amnon was so <u>distressed</u>,

2. That <u>he</u>

- That <u>Amnon</u>

2. Fell <u>sick</u>

- Fell [emotionally] sick

2. For his <u>sister</u> Tamar;

- For his [half] sister Tamar;

2. For <u>she</u> was a virgin;

- For <u>Tamar</u> was a virgin;

2. And Amnon thought it <u>hard</u> for him

- And Amnon thought it [would be] hard for him

2. <u>To</u> do anything to her.

- To [get permission to] do anything to her.

6. So Amnon lay down, and made himself <u>sick</u>:

- So Amnon lay down, and made himself [to look as though he was phsically] sick:

6. And when the <u>king was</u> come

- And when the <u>king [David, Amnon's father,] had</u> come

6. To see <u>him</u>,

- To see <u>Amnon</u>,

6. Amnon said unto the <u>king</u>,

- Amnon said unto the <u>king [David, his father]</u>,

6. I pray
- The NIV says: "I would like"

6. Thee,
- [For] you [to],

6. Let Tamar my sister come,
- Let Tamar my [half] sister come [to my house],

6. And make me a couple of cakes in
- And make me a couple of cakes within

6. My sight,
- [The vision of] my eyesight,

6. That I may eat
- [So] that I may eat

6. At her hand.
- [Directly] from her hand.

7. Then David
- Then [king] David [Amnon and Tamar's father,]

7. Sent home to Tamar,
- Sent [a message] home to Tamar,

7. Saying, Go now to thy brother Amnon's house,
- Saying, Go now to your brother Amnon's house,

7. And dress him
- From the Hebrew word *asah*, Strong's #6213: prepare.
- And prepare him

7. Meat.
- From the Hebrew word *biryah*, Strong's #1279: food.
- [Some] food.

8. So Tamar went to her brother Amnon's house;
- So Tamar went to her [half] brother Amnon's house;

8. And he
- Where he

8. Was laid down.
- Was lying down [pretending to be sick].

8. And she
- And Tamar

8. Took flour, and kneaded
- Took [some] flour, and kneaded

8. It,

49

- The flour,

8. And made cakes in his sight,
- And made cakes within [the vision of] Amnon's eyesight,

8. And did bake the cakes.
- And then [Tamar] baked the cakes.

9. And she took
- And Tamar took

9. A pan, and poured them out
- A pan and poured the cakes out

9. Before him;
- Before Amnon;

9. But he
- But Amnon

9. Refused to eat. And Amnon said,
- Refused to eat [the cakes]. And Amnon said,

9. Have out all men from me
- Have all [the] men [moved] out [of the room, away] from
me.

9. And they went out every man
- And they went out [from the room,] every man

9. From him.
- [Away] from Amnon.

10. And Amnon said unto Tamar, Bring the meat
- And Amnon said unto Tamar, Bring the food

10. Into the chamber,
- Into the [bed] chamber,

10. That I may eat
- [So] that I may eat

10. Of thine hand.
- [Directly] from your hand.

10. And Tamar took the cakes that she had made, and brought them
- And Tamar took the cakes that she had made, and brought
the cakes

10. Into the chamber
- Into the [bed] chamber

10. To Amnon her brother.

- To Amnon her [half] brother.

11. And when _she_
- And when <u>Tamar</u>

11. Had brought _them_
- Had brought <u>the cakes</u>

11. Unto _him_ to eat,
- Unto <u>Amnon</u> to eat,

11. _He_
- <u>Amnon</u>

11. Took hold of _her,_
- Took hold of <u>Tamar,</u>

11. And said unto _her,_
- And said unto <u>Tamar,</u>

11. Come _lie_ with me,
- From the Hebrew word _shakab_, Strong's #7901: <u>to lie down for sexual connection.</u>
- Come <u>lie down to [have] sex</u> with me,

11. My _sister._
- My [half] sister.

12. And _she_
- And <u>Tamar</u>

12. Answered _him,_
- Answered [to] <u>Amnon,</u>

12. _Nay,_
- <u>No,</u>

12. My _brother,_
- My [half] brother,

12. Do not force _me;_
- Do not force <u>me [to have sex with you]</u>;

12. For no _such_ thing ought to be done in Israel:
- For no thing <u>such [as this wickedness]</u> ought to be done in Israel:

12. Do not _thou_
- <u>You [must]</u> not do

12. This _folly._
- From the Hebrew word _nbalah_, Strong's #5039: <u>wickedness.</u>

- This <u>wicked [thing]</u>.

14. <u>Howbeit he</u>
- <u>However Amnon</u>

14. Would not <u>hearken</u>
- From the Hebrew word *shama*, Strong's #8085: <u>listen</u>.
- Would not <u>listen</u>

14. Unto <u>her</u> voice:
- Unto <u>Tamar's</u> voice:

14. But, <u>being</u> stronger
- But, [<u>Amnon,</u>] being stronger

14. Than <u>she</u>,
- Than <u>Tamar</u>,

14. Forced <u>her, and</u>
- Forced <u>Tamar [onto the bed with him]</u> and,

14. <u>Lay with</u> her.
- The NIV says: "<u>He raped</u> her"

15. <u>Then</u>
- <u>Then [after Amnon had raped Tamar]</u>

15. Amnon hated <u>her</u> exceedingly;
- Amnon hated <u>Tamar</u> exceedingly;

15. <u>So</u> that
- <u>So [much]</u> that

15. The hatred <u>wherewith</u>
- From the Hebrew word *asher*, Strong's #834: <u>which</u>.
- The hatred [<u>for] which</u>

15. <u>He</u> hated
- <u>Amnon</u> hated

15. <u>Her</u> was greater than the love
- <u>Tamar</u> was greater than the love

15. <u>Wherewith he</u>
- <u>[For] which Amnon</u>

15. Had loved <u>her</u>.
- Had loved <u>Tamar</u>.

15. And Amnon said unto <u>her</u>,
- And Amnon said unto <u>Tamar</u>,

15. <u>Arise, be gone</u>.
- <u>Arise [from here, and] be gone [from me]</u>.

CHOICE EXAMINATION

1. What special trust is developed between virgin married couples?

2. What consequences, which can last for a lifetime, can occur after unmarried couples loose their virginity?

3. In the scripture, why was it inappropriate for Amnon to develop lustful feelings for Tamar?

4. How should Amnon have dealt with his feelings for Tamar?

5. What could Tamar have done if she would have recognized Amnon's intentions when all the men were ordered out of the room?

6. What choices do you need to make in order to *keep your virginity until you're married?*

MARRY ONLY FROM THE OPPOSITE SEX

≈ 7 ≈

For the wrath of God is revealed from heaven against all ungodliness and unrighteousness of men, who hold the truth in unrighteousness; Because that which may be known of God is manifest in them; for God hath shewed it unto them. For the invisible things of him from the creation of the world are clearly seen, being understood by the things that are made, even his eternal power and Godhead; so that they are without excuse: Because that, when they knew God, they glorified him not as God, neither were thankful; but became vain in their imaginations, and their foolish heart was darkened. Professing themselves to be wise, they became fools, And changed the glory of the incorruptible God into an image made like to corruptible man, and to birds, and four footed beasts, and creeping things.

Wherefore God also gave them up to uncleanness through the lusts of their own hearts, to dishonour their own bodies between themselves: Who changed the truth of God into a lie, and worshipped and served the creature more than the Creator, who is blessed forever. Amen. For this cause God gave them up unto vile affections: for even their women did change the natural use into that which is against nature: And likewise also the men, leaving the natural use of the woman, burned in their lust one toward another; men with men working that which is unseemly, and receiving in themselves that recompense of their error which was meet. And even as they did not like to retain God in their knowledge, God gave them over to a reprobate mind, to do those things which are not convenient;

Romans 1: 18 - 28

First it was her, then it was him. Next it was her and him. Then it was him and him.

It's been exciting to see the romances that have developed among the young men and women I've hired over the years. I've had a role in initiating several marriages. Through the normal interactions that occur when people work together, associates often develop friendships which turn into dating relationships. Sometimes those relationships progress into marriage.

I was pleased when I heard he was dating her. I was happy when they got married. I was saddened, a few years later when I learned they had divorced. I was perplexed when he married again. He married another man.

I'm not a scientist, a geneticist, or a psychologist. I don't understand the mysteries of the hormonal changes that take place in people's bodies. I don't understand the predetermined tendencies that work in people's minds persuading them to behave in certain ways. I don't understand the psychology of the emotional baggage that people carry around in response to events that have occurred in their lives. What I do understand is this: Marriage is a choice. He chose to marry her, and he chose to marry him. No one forced him to love and marry her. No one forced him to love and marry him. It was a choice on both accounts.

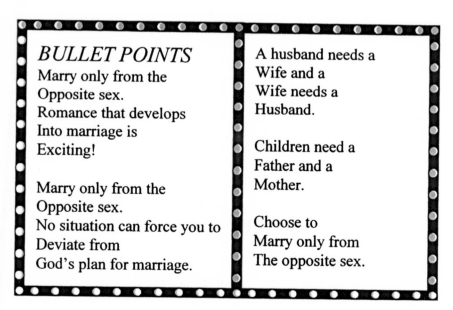

BULLET POINTS
Marry only from the
Opposite sex.
Romance that develops
Into marriage is
Exciting!

Marry only from the
Opposite sex.
No situation can force you to
Deviate from
God's plan for marriage.

A husband needs a
Wife and a
Wife needs a
Husband.

Children need a
Father and a
Mother.

Choose to
Marry only from
The opposite sex.

SCRIPTURE ANALYSIS

Romans 1: 18 - 28
18. For the <u>wrath</u> of God
 - From the Greek word *orge*, Strong's #3709: <u>justifiable abhorrence</u>.
 - For the <u>justifiable abhorrence</u> of God
18. Is revealed from heaven <u>against</u>
 - From the Greek word *epi*, Strong's #1909: <u>because of</u>.
 - Is revealed from heaven <u>because [of]</u>
18. <u>All</u> ungodliness and unrighteousness
 - <u>All [the]</u> ungodliness and unrighteousness
18. <u>Of</u> men,
 - <u>[That is done] by</u> men,
18. Who <u>hold</u>
 - Who <u>hold [back]</u>
18. The <u>truth</u>
 - The <u>truth [of godliness and righteousness]</u>
18. <u>In</u> unrighteousness;
 - <u>By [their]</u> unrighteousness;
19. Because that which may <u>be</u> known
 - Because that which may <u>be [obvious and well]</u> known
19. <u>Of</u> God
 - <u>From</u> God
19. Is manifest in <u>them;</u>
 - Is manifest in <u>people [who do ungodly and unrighteous things]</u>;
19. For God <u>hath shewed it</u>
 - For God <u>has shown [what] ungodliness and unrighteousness [is]</u>
19. Unto <u>them.</u>
 - Unto <u>[the] people who do ungodly and unrighteous things [by the normal processes that take place in things that are made by God]</u>.
20. For the invisible things of <u>him</u>
 - For the invisible things of <u>God [which we take for</u>

granted, and which have been in place]
20. From the creation of the world
- [Ever] since the creation of the world
20. Are clearly seen,
- Are clearly seen [by all of mankind],
20. Being understood by the things
- Being understood by [the normal processes that take place in] the things
20. That are made,
- That are made [by God],
20. Even his eternal power
- Through God's eternal power
20. And Godhead;
- From the Greek word *theiotes*, Strong's #2305: divinity.
- And [through God's] divinity;
20. So that they
- So that people [who do ungodly and unrighteous things]
20. Are without excuse:
- Are without excuse [for their behavior]:
21. Because that,
- Because [of the fact] that,
21. When
- [Even] though
21. They
- The people [who did ungodly and unrighteous things]
21. Knew God,
- Knew [the normal processes that took place in the things that were made by] God,
21. They glorified him not as God,
- They glorified God not as God,
21. Neither were thankful;
- Neither were [they] thankful [to God for the normal processes];
21. But became
- But [they] became
21. Vain
- From the Greek word *mataioo*, Strong's #3154: foolish.

- Foolish

21. In their imaginations,
- From the Greek word *dialogismos*, Strong's #1261: reasoning.
- In their reasoning,

21. And their foolish heart
- From the Greek word *kardia*, Strong's #2588: thoughts or feelings.
- And their foolish thoughts and feelings

21. Was
- Became

21. Darkened.
- From the Greek word *skotizo*, defined by Strong's Concordance as: to obscure.
- Obscured [to God's normal processes].

22. Professing themselves to be wise,
- [By] professing themselves to be wise,

22. They became fools,
- The people [who did ungodly and unrighteous things instead] became fools,

23. And changed the
- Because [they] changed the

23. Glory of the uncorruptible God
- From the Greek word *aphthartos*, Strong's #862: immortal.
- Glory of the immortal God

23. Into an image made like to
- Into an image made like a

23. Corruptible man,
- From the Greek word *phthartos*, Strong's #5349: perishable.
- Perishable man,

23. And to birds,
- And [also like images] of birds,

23. And four footed beasts,
- And [images of] four footed beasts,

23. And creeping things.

- And [images of] creeping things.

24. Wherefore God also
- Therefore God also

24. Gave them up to
- Gave up to people [who did ungodly and unrighteous things]

24. Uncleanness through
- From the Greek word *akatharsia*, Strong's #167: impurity.
- Impure [desires, evidenced] through

24. The
- Their

24. Lusts
- from the Greek word *epithumia*, Strong's #1939: a longing (espec. for what is forbidden) [or a] desire.
- Longing desires for what is forbidden

24. Of
- Through

24. Their own hearts, to dishonour their own bodies between themselves:
- Their own thoughts and feelings, [desiring] to dishonor their own bodies between themselves:

25. Who changed the
- [These are people] who [have] changed the

25. Truth of God into
- Truth of God's [normal processes] into

25. A lie, and worshiped and served
- A lie [to themselves,] and [they have] worshiped and served

25. The creature
- The creatures [which they created]

25. More than
- More than [they have worshipped and served]

25. The Creator,
- Their [own] Creator (God),

25. Who is blessed forever. Amen.
- From the Greek word *amen*, Strong's #281: so be it.

- Who is blessed forever. <u>So be it</u>.

26. For this <u>cause</u>
- From the Greek word *dia*, Strong's #1223: <u>by reason of</u>.
- For this <u>reason</u>

26. God gave <u>them</u> up unto
- God gave up unto <u>people [who did ungodly and unrighteous things]</u>

26. <u>Vile</u>
- From the Greek word *atimia*, Strong's #819: <u>shame</u>.
- <u>Shameful</u>

26. <u>Affections</u>:
- From the Greek word *pathos*, Strong's #3806: <u>a passion</u>.
- <u>Passions</u>:

26. For even <u>their</u> women
- For even <u>the</u> women

26. Did change the natural <u>use</u>
- From the Greek word *chresis*, Strong's #5540: <u>sexual intercourse as an occupation of the body</u>.
- Did change the natural <u>[process of] sexual intercourse</u>

26. Into <u>that</u> which is
- Into <u>[a process of] sexual intercourse</u> which is

26. <u>Against</u> nature:
- From the Greek word *para*, Strong's #3844: <u>contrary to</u>.
- <u>Contrary to</u> nature:

27. And likewise also <u>the</u> men,
- And likewise also <u>[did] the</u> men,

27. <u>Leaving</u> the natural
- From the Greek word *aphiemi*, Strong's #863: <u>forsake</u>.
- <u>Forsaking</u> the natural

27. <u>Use</u>
- <u>[Process of] sexual intercourse</u>

27. <u>Of</u> the woman,
- <u>With</u> the woman,

27. <u>Burned</u> in their lust one toward another;
- <u>[The men] burned</u> in their lust one toward another;

27. Men <u>with</u> men
- Men <u>[having sexual intercourse] with [other]</u> men

27. Working that
    - From the Greek word *katergazomai*, Strong's #2716: perform.
    - Performing that

27. Which is unseemly,
    - From the Greek word *aschemosune*, Strong's #808: an indecency.
    - Which is indecent,

27. And receiving in themselves
    - And receiving for themselves

27. That
    - The

27. Recompense
    - Defined by Webster's Dictionary as: compensation.
    - Compensation

27. Of their error which was
    - For their error which was

27. Meet.
    - The NIV says: "Due".

28. And even as they
    - And even as they [intended, the people who did ungodly and unrighteous things]

28. Did not like
    - From the Greek word *dokimazo*, Strong's #1381: try.
    - Did not try

28. To retain God in their knowledge,
    - To retain [the normal processes of] God in their knowledge,

28. God
    - [So] God

28. Gave them over
    - Gave the people [who did ungodly and unrighteous things] over

28. To a reprobate
    - From the Greek word *adokimos*, Strong's #96: unapproved [or] rejected.
    - To a rejected and unapproved

28. Mind,
  - From the Greek word *nous*, Strong's #3563:
<u>understanding</u>.
   - <u>Understanding [of God's normal processes</u>],
28. To do those things which <u>are</u> not
   - To do those things which <u>do</u> not
28. <u>Convenient;</u>
   - From the Greek word *katheko*, Strong's #2520: <u>fit</u>.
   - <u>Fit [the normal processes intended by God</u>];

CHOICE EXAMINATION

1. Why did he love and marry her?

2. Why did he love and marry him?

3. What was common for both accounts?

4. In the scripture, how is the truth of godliness and righteousness clearly seen by all of mankind?

5. Why did God give people who did ungodly and unrighteous things a rejected and unapproved understanding of God's normal processes?

6. What choices do you need to make in order to *marry only from the opposite sex*?

KEEP YOUR WEDDING VOWS
≈ 8 ≈

And the Pharisees came to him, and asked him, Is it lawful for a man to put away his wife? tempting him.

And he answered and said unto them, What did Moses command you?

And they said, Moses suffered to write a bill of divorcement, and to put her away.

And Jesus answered and said unto them, For the hardness of your heart he wrote you this precept. But from the beginning of the creation God made them male and female. For this cause shall a man leave his father and his mother, and cleave to his wife; and they twain shall be one flesh: so then they are no more twain, but one flesh. What therefore God hath joined together, let not man put asunder.

Mark 10: 2 - 9

We held the celebration at our house. We borrowed sixty folding chairs and four folding tables from the church. We had people everywhere! Some were standing on the porch, some had walked upstairs, most had crowded into the living / dining room area. Everyone had a plate of food on their laps. Our son, Joshua, owned a 1940 Chevrolet sedan. He chauffeured Mother and Dad the short distance from their house to ours. It was a grand entrance. My brother, Gary, opened the ceremony with prayer. Then he took a few minutes to tell a couple of funny stories. My daughters, Charity and Amy, and their cousins, Kayla and Karissa, stood in the open space upstairs and sang a love song. The celebration ended with a video which the kids had made. It showed the progression of my parents' lives with highlights from different areas of the farm. It was their fiftieth wedding anniversary! I've never seen my parents happier, more proud, or more in love with each other. It was a good day to celebrate good memories of a long life together!

It's been seven years since we had that day of celebration. Parkinson's disease and cancer took a heavy toll on my father's health. Caring for my father was a difficult task. Mother spent most of her time in the later years of their marriage attending to her husband. Her devotion to Dad was remarkable! She was relentless in her effort to provide and care for him. No effort was considered too great, if it served to lengthen Dad's life or to aid in his comfort.

Our daughter, Amy, and her fiance, Matthew, are getting married in two weeks. Matt's former youth pastor is going to conduct a portion of the ceremony. He gave them copies of different wedding vows to choose from. They were excited to read them to Barbie and me. A portion of one copy read:

> For better or worse,
> For richer or poorer,
> In sickness or in health,
> Until death do us part.

Perhaps it was the same vows that my mother chose to repeat to my dad when they got married.

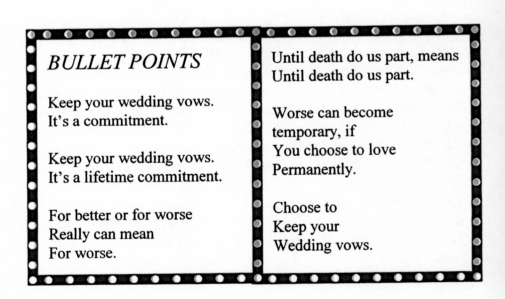

BULLET POINTS

Keep your wedding vows.
It's a commitment.

Keep your wedding vows.
It's a lifetime commitment.

For better or for worse
Really can mean
For worse.

Until death do us part, means
Until death do us part.

Worse can become
temporary, if
You choose to love
Permanently.

Choose to
Keep your
Wedding vows.

SCRIPTURE ANALYSIS

Mark 10: 2 - 9

2. And the <u>Pharisees</u>
- The Unger's Bible Dictionary states: "It was a leading aim of the Redeemer [Jesus] to teach men that true piety [religious duty] consisted not in forms, but in substance; not in outward observances, but in inward spirit; not in small details, but in great rules of life. The whole system of Pharisaic piety led to exactly opposite conclusions. Under its influence 'the weightier matters of the law, judgment, mercy, and faith' were undervalued and neglected; the idea of religion as that which should have its seat in the heart disappeared; the most sacred obligations were evaded; vain and trifling questions took the place of serious inquiry into the great principles of duty; and even the most solemn truths were handled as mere matters of curious speculation or means to entrap an adversary."
- And the <u>Pharisees</u>

2. Came to <u>him</u>,
- Came to <u>Jesus</u>,

2. And asked <u>him</u>,
- And asked <u>Jesus</u>,

2. Is it lawful for a man to <u>put away</u> his wife?
- Both *put* and *away*, come from the Greek word *apoluo*, Strong's #630: <u>divorce</u>.
- Is it lawful for a man to <u>divorce</u> his wife?

2. <u>Tempting</u>
- From the Greek word *peirazo*, Strong's #3985: <u>to test</u>.
- <u>Testing</u>

2. <u>Him</u>.
Jesus.

3. And <u>he</u> answered
- And <u>Jesus</u> answered

3. And said unto <u>them</u>,
- And said unto <u>the Pharisees</u>,

3. What did <u>Moses</u> command you?
- What did [the law which God gave you through] Moses
command you?
4. And <u>they</u> said,
- And the Pharisees said,
4. <u>Moses</u>
- [The law which God gave us through] Moses
4. <u>Suffered</u> to write
- From the Greek word *epitrepo*, Strong's #2010: <u>allow</u>.
- [Made] allowance [for a husband] to write
4. A bill of <u>divorcement</u>,
- A bill of <u>divorcement (see Deuteronomy 24:1</u>),
4. And to <u>put</u>
- And to <u>divorce</u>
4. <u>Her away</u>.
- [His] wife [with a bill of] divorcement.
5. And Jesus answered <u>and said</u> unto them,
- And Jesus answered [the Pharisees] by saying unto them,
5. <u>For</u> the
- Because [of] the
5. <u>Hardness</u> of your
- From the Greek word *sklerokardia*, Strong's #4641:
destitution of spiritual perception.
- <u>Destitution</u> of your
5. <u>Heart</u>
- Also from the Greek word *sklerokardia*, Strong's #4641:
destitution of spiritual perception.
- <u>Spiritual perception</u>
5. <u>He</u> wrote you
- [God, through] Moses wrote you
5. This <u>precept</u>.
- Webster's Dictionary defines *precept* as: <u>a command or
principle intended as a general rule of action</u>.
- This <u>general rule</u>.
6. But from the beginning of the <u>creation</u>
- But from the beginning of the <u>creation [of mankind]</u>
6. God made <u>them</u>

- God made <u>the people [he created to be both]</u>

6. Male and <u>female</u>.

    - Male and <u>female [for the purpose of marrying each other]</u>.

7. For this <u>cause</u>

    - From the Greek word *heneka*, Strong's #1752: <u>by reason of</u>.

    - For this <u>reason</u>

7. <u>Shall</u>

    - <u>Does</u>

7. A man <u>leave</u> his father and mother,

    - A man <u>[have the opportunity to]</u> leave his father and mother,

7. And <u>Cleave</u> to his wife;

    - From the Greek word *proskollao*, Strong's #4347: <u>join self</u>.

    - And <u>join himself</u> to his wife;

8. And they <u>twain</u>

    - From the Greek word *duo*, Strong's #1417: <u>two [or] both</u>.

    - And they <u>both [together, being] two [separate people]</u>

8. Shall <u>be</u>

    - Shall <u>become [only]</u>

8. One <u>flesh</u>:

    - From the Greek word *sarx*, Strong's #4561: <u>a human being</u>.

    - One <u>human being [from God's perspective]</u>:

8. So then they are no more <u>twain</u>,

    - So then they are no more <u>[considered to be]</u> two [human beings],

8. But <u>one flesh</u>.

    - But [instead,] one human being.

9. What therefore God <u>hath</u> joined together,

    - What therefore God <u>has</u> joined together,

9. Let not man <u>put asunder</u>.

    - The NIV says, "Let not man <u>separate</u>."

CHOICE EXAMINATION

1. How did the mother develop remarkable devotion for her husband?

2. What things did the mother do which made her remarkable devotion apparent?

3. How might the mother's remarkable devotion influence Amy and Matthew as they chose their wedding vows?

4. In the scripture, why did the law which was given through Moses, allow for a husband to divorce his wife?

5. What is God's perception of a male and a female who are married to each other?

6. What choices do you need to make in order to *keep your wedding vows*?

HAVE DAILY CONVERSATIONS WITH YOUR FAMILY AROUND THE DINNER TABLE

≈ 9 ≈

Now it came to pass, as they went, that he entered into a certain village: and a certain woman named Martha received him into her house. And she had a sister called Mary, which also sat at Jesus' feet, and heard his word. But Martha was cumbered about much serving, and came to him, and said, Lord, dost thou not care that my sister hath left me to serve alone? Bid her therefore that she help me.

And Jesus answered and said unto her, Martha, Martha, thou art careful and troubled about many things: But one thing is needful: and Mary hath chosen that good part, which shall not be taken away from her.

Luke 10: 38 - 42

"When dinner is on the table, the television is turned off." Barbie set that rule on the first day we arrived home from our brief honeymoon. We chose to make that rule permanent. Dinner is an event around our house. We sit around the table as a family, we eat our meal together, and we have a conversation.

Conversation. All families need to understand this concept. When families gather around the dinner table, conversation occurs - naturally.

"How was school today? How was college today? How was work today? How was cheerleading practice? How was ball practice? How did you do on your spelling test? How did you do on your algebra test? Did you hear about that story in the news today? Who do you think we should vote for? Why? Was Billy mean to you at recess again or was he nice today? Where do you want to go for vacation this year? What color should we paint the house? How big was that fish? How big was that buck? What college classes did the counselor recommend for your career choice? What did that pretty dress at the store look like? What did your friends think? How can I help you with that? Would you be able to help me with this? How do you like this new recipe? What's your thoughts on today's sermon? What do you plan to do tonight? With whom? What time will you be back?"

How many of these questions would have been asked if the whole family had not gathered together at one time around one table with no outside distractions… and had a conversation?

There are appropriate times for wholesome entertainment, and there are appropriated times for unobstructed conversation.

"When dinner is on the table, the television is turned off," and conversation is turned on.

BULLET POINTS

Have daily conversations with your family
Around the dinner table.
Make it an event.

Have daily conversations with your family
Around the dinner table.
It's the reason you eat dinner
Together.

The TV talks, but it never listens.

Children will listen to
The TV and the stereo if
They are the only ones
Talking.

Children will listen to you if
You are the only one
Talking.

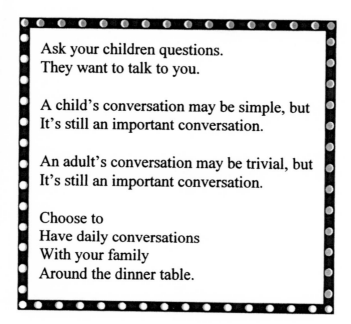

Ask your children questions.
They want to talk to you.

A child's conversation may be simple, but
It's still an important conversation.

An adult's conversation may be trivial, but
It's still an important conversation.

Choose to
Have daily conversations
With your family
Around the dinner table.

SCRIPTURE ANALYSIS

Luke 10: 38 - 42

38. Now it came to pass, as <u>they went,</u>
- Now it came to pass, as <u>Jesus and his disciples went [to Martha and Mary's house],</u>

38. That <u>he</u> entered into a certain village:
- That <u>Jesus</u> entered into a certain village:

38. And a certain woman named Martha received <u>him</u> into her house.
- And a certain woman named Martha received <u>Jesus</u> into her house.

39. And <u>she</u>
- And <u>Martha</u>

39. Had a sister <u>called</u> Mary,
- Had a sister <u>called [by the name of]</u> Mary,

39. Which also sat
  - Who also sat

39. At Jesus' feet,
  - At [an area near] Jesus' feet

39. And
  - So [she could]

39. Heard
  - From the Greek word *akouo*, Strong's #191: understand.
  - [Listen to and] understand

39. His word.
  - Jesus' words.

40. But Martha was cumbered
  - From the Greek word *perispao*, Strong's #4049: to distract.
  - But Martha was distracted

40. About much
  - From the Greek word *peri*, Strong's #4012: by.
  - By [the] much

40. Serving,
  - Serving [that was needed to attend to Jesus and his disciples],

40. And came
  - And [Martha] came

40. To him, and said,
  - To Jesus, and said,

40. Lord, dost thou not care
  - Lord, do you not care

40. That my sister hath left me
  - That Mary has left me

40. To serve alone?
  - To serve [you and your disciples] alone?

40. Bid
  - From the Greek word *epo*, Strong's #2036: tell.
  - Tell

40. Her therefore
  - Mary therefore

40. That she help me.

- That she [needs to] help me.

41. And Jesus answered and said unto her, Martha, Martha, thou art

- And Jesus answered and said unto her, Martha, Martha, you are

41. Careful

- From the Greek word *merimnao*, Strong's #3309: to be anxious about.

- Anxious

41. And troubled about

- From the Greek word *turbazo*, Strong's #5182: disturb.

- And disturbed about

41. Many things:

- [The] many things [that need to be done in order to serve your guests]:

42. But one thing

- But [only] one thing

42. Is needful:

- From the Greek word *chreia*, Strong's #5532: necessary.

- Is necessary:

42. And Mary hath chosen

- And Mary has chosen

42. That good part,

- From the Greek word *agathos*, Strong's #18: benefit.

- That [more] beneficial part,

42. Which shall not be taken away from her.

- Which [I] shall not [ask to] be taken away from her.

CHOICE EXAMINATION

1. Why did Barbie make a rule about turning the television off when dinner is on the table?

2. Why is it important to gather for dinner at the same time and in a single location?

3. Why is conversation with the entire family important?

4. In the scripture, why did Mary sit at an area near Jesus' feet?

5. What was Jesus referring to when he told Martha that Mary had chosen the more beneficial part?

6. What choices do you need to make in order to *have daily conversations with your family around the dinner table*?

BE A PARENT TO YOUR CHILDREN

≈ 10 ≈

Train up a child in the way he should go: and when he is old, he will not depart from it.

Proverbs 22: 6

Each of our children heard this speech a few days before they got married. "Your role is changing," we said. "But our role with you will never change. Even though you're getting married in a few days we will still be your parents. You can always come to us when you need us. We will always have your best interest in mind."

Charity and Jon married first. Joshua and Lauren were next. Amy and Matt were married in June of this year. We are proud of our three children, and we are proud of our sons-in-law and our daughter-in-law. We are so pleased that each of our children chose Christian spouses to marry. They are all involved in their churches. They are all college educated. They are all developing good careers. (That's counting motherhood as Lauren's present career. She's currently raising their twins. She does, however, have a teaching degree.) It's been Barbie's and my pleasure to watch our children grow and develop into responsible adults. I don't think it's happened by accident.

When we got married Barbie was a college student. I was working as a clerk in a convenience store. A few months later I got an hourly job working for Wal-Mart. Two years into our marriage Barbie became pregnant with our first child, Joshua. Even though she was only one college year away from obtaining her teaching degree, we both felt she should delay finishing her education so she could stay at home to raise our children. For the next twelve years, until Amy entered kindergarten, we lived on my single income. We had to be frugal with expenses. We lived in an old house. We drove an old car and pickup. We didn't eat out. We didn't spend money on anything frivolous. Even though two incomes would have afforded us a more comfortable lifestyle, we still chose to live off of my single income so Barbie could stay at home to raise our children.

Barbie is my image of the consummate mother. She's tough when she needs to be tough, and she's tender when she needs to be tender. She knows when she needs to get involved, and she knows when she needs to stay away. Nothing slips past her. She knows when any of our children are upset, confused, or if their feelings are hurt - even if they try to not show it. She's empathetic. If a son, daughter, or one of their spouses feels hurt, Barbie feels hurt too - only worse. Her attentiveness to our children has helped me become a better father than I naturally would have been.

I know there are parents who, because of circumstances beyond their control, cannot afford for the mother to stay at home to raise their children. I know too, there are families who have made arrangements for their children to be raised by grandparents or other loving people who are good influences for the children. I recommend however, if it's possible, that the parents choose a lifestyle that allows for the mother stay at home to raise the children. It will be worth the sacrifice in income for the children's sake, and the bond between the mother and the children will develop into a relationship that will last for a lifetime.

Our children are all adults now, but they still come to Barbie and me for advice. Sometimes we ask *our* parents for advice, too. They always have our best interests in mind. A parent's role never changes.

BULLET POINTS
Be a parent to your children.
The child's role will
Change, but the
Parent's role will never
Change.

Be a parent to your children.
The mother and child bond
Will develop into a
Relationship that will last
For a lifetime.

Living on one income
May affect
Your lifestyle, but
It will be worth the
Sacrifice in income
For the children's sake.

Always have your
Child's best interest
In mind.

Choose to
Be a parent
To your children.

SCRIPTURE ANALYSIS

Proverbs 22: 6

6. Train
 - [If you will] train
6. Up a child
 - A child [while he is growing] up
6. In
 - About
6. The way he should go:
 - *Way is* from the Hebrew word *derek,* Strong's #1870: a course of life or mode of action.
 - The course his life should [take and his] mode of action [to] go [there]:
6. And
 - Then
6. When he is old,
 - When he has [grown] old,

6. He will not __depart__
- From the Hebrew word *cuwr*, Strong's #5493: <u>rebel</u>.
- He will not <u>rebel</u>

6. From <u>it</u>.
- From [his] <u>training</u>.

CHOICE EXAMINATION

1. What did the parents mean when they said, "Our role with you will never change"?

2. Why was it important for the mother to stay at home to raise the children?

3. What helped cause Barbie to develop into Galen's image of a consummate mother?

4. In the scripture, why must parents train their child at the stage of life when he (or she) is growing up?

5. What attributes are needed in order for parents to train a child while he (or she) is growing up?

6. What choices do you need to make in order to *be a parent to your children*?

KEEP YOUR FAMILY CONNECTED
≈ 11 ≈

And Elimelech Naomi's husband died; and she was left, and her two sons. And they took them wives of the women of Moab; the name of the one was Orpah, and the name of the other Ruth: and they dwelled there about ten years. And Mahlon and Chilion died also both of them; and the woman was left of her two sons and her husband. Then she arose with her daughters in law, that she might return from the country of Moab: for she had heard in the country of Moab how that the LORD had visited his people in giving them bread. And they lifted up their voice, and wept again: and Orpah kissed her mother in law; but Ruth clave unto her. And she said, Behold, thy sister in law is gone back unto her people, and unto her gods: return thou after thy sister in law. And Ruth said, Intreat me not to leave thee, or to return from following after thee: for whither thou goest, I will go; and where thou lodgest, I will lodge: thy people shall be my people, and thy God my God: Where thou diest, will I die, and there will I be buried: the LORD do so to me, and more also, if ought but death part thee and me.

Ruth 1: 3 - 6, 14 - 17

It was mass confusion, utter chaos, constant turmoil.... And everyone was having a great time!! I'm describing Christmas at Grandma Barker's, also Easter at Grandma Barker's, as well as Thanksgiving at Grandma Barker's, and someone's birthday at Grandma Barker's, and just about any excuse for a get-together that you could ever come up with, at Grandma Barker's. She never had an agenda. Nothing was ever organized. Basically the children in the family ended up playing together (running, screaming), while the adults sat around the kitchen table and talked. Grandma constantly teased and laughed. You never saw her happier than you did when she had all of her family around her.

I've always admired the way the Barker family stayed connected. It didn't matter if people got married, if they moved far away, or if they were really busy; when it was time for the family to join together at Grandma Barker's house, everyone came. It was a ritual. It was the normal expectation. Keeping the family connected was important, so everyone chose to come.

Grandma was ninety-two years old when she passed away. The Barker family, of course, all gathered together to mourn her passing. There was a sadness in the air, but there was also a measure of joy.... Because everyone was glad to see each other.... Like they always were.... Like Grandma would have wanted it....

It was a fitting tribute.

BULLET POINTS

Keep your family connected,
Even if they get married,
Or move far away,
Or if they're really busy.

Keep your family connected.
The bond of friendship is
Subject to change, but
The bond of family is
Forever.

Families still enjoy each other,
Even after they have
Grown up.

No one has more memories of
You than
Your family.

Nobody knows you
Better than
Your family.

You don't have to
Pretend when you're
With
Your family.

Your family will be your
Best support group.

Families can grow apart.
You must choose to
Keep them connected.

Choose to
Keep your family
Connected.

SCRIPTURE ANALYSIS

Ruth 1: 3 - 6, 14 - 17

3. And Elimelech Naomi's husband died; and <u>she</u>
- And Elimelech, Naomi's husband, died; and <u>Naomi</u>
3. Was <u>left,</u>
- Was <u>left [without a husband]</u>,
3. <u>And</u>
- <u>And [the only family Naomi had left were]</u>
3. Her two <u>sons</u>.
- Her two <u>sons, [Mahlon and Chilion (see verse #2)]</u>.
4. And <u>they</u> took
- And <u>Mahlon and Chilion</u> took
4. <u>Them</u> wives
- <u>Themselves</u> wives
4. <u>Of</u> the women of Moab;
- <u>From</u> the women of Moab;
4. The name of the <u>one</u> was Orpah,
- The name of the <u>one [wife]</u> was Orpah,
4. And the name of the <u>other</u> Ruth:
- And the name of the <u>other [wife was]</u> Ruth:
4. And <u>they dwelled there</u> about ten years.
- And <u>Naomi, Mahlon, Chilion, Orpah, and Ruth dwelled in Moab [for]</u> about ten years.
5. And Mahlon and Chilion died also both of them; and <u>the woman</u>
- And Mahlon and Chilion died also, both of them; and <u>Naomi</u>
5. Was left <u>of</u> her two sons and her husband.
- Was left <u>[alone after the loss]</u> of her two sons and her husband.
6. Then <u>she arose</u>
- Then <u>Naomi arose [to leave Moab]</u>
6. With her <u>daughters in law</u>,

- With her daughters-in-law, [Orpah and Ruth],
6. That she might
    - [So] that she might
6. Return from the country of Moab:
    - Return [to Bethlehem in Judah (see verse #1),] from the country of Moab:
6. For she
    - For Naomi
6. Had heard in the country of Moab how
    - Had heard [it being told] in the country of Moab how
6. That the LORD had visited his people
    - From the Hebrew word *paqad*, Strong's #6485: care for.
    - That the Lord had [expressed his] care for his people
6. In giving
    - By giving
6. Them
    - The people [in Bethlehem in Judah]
6. Bread.
    - From the Hebrew word *lechem*, Strong's #3899: food.
    - Food.
14. And they
    - And Naomi, Ruth, and Orpah
14. Lifted up their voice,
    - Lifted up their voices [together],
14. And wept again: And Orpah kissed her mother in law;
    - And wept again: And Orpah kissed her mother-in-law [Naomi, goodbye];
14. But Ruth clave
    - From the Hebrew word *dabaq*, Strong's #1692: follow close
    - But Ruth followed closely
14. Unto her.
    - Unto Naomi.
15. And she said,
    - And Naomi said,
15. Behold, thy sister in law
    - Behold, your sister-in-law

15. <u>Is</u> gone back

- <u>Has</u> gone back

15. Unto her <u>people</u>,

- Unto her [<u>native</u>] people [<u>the Moabites</u>],

15. And unto her <u>gods</u>:

- And unto her [<u>native, Moabite</u>] gods:

15. Return <u>thou</u>

- <u>You [should also</u>] return

15. After <u>thy</u> sister in law.

- After [<u>the manner of] your</u> sister-in-law.

16. <u>And Ruth said, Intreat me not</u>

- The NIV says: "<u>But Ruth replied, 'Don't urge me'</u>"

16. To leave <u>thee</u>,

- To leave <u>you</u>,

16. Or to return from following after <u>thee</u>:

- Or to return from following after <u>you</u>:

16. For <u>whither thou goest</u>,

- For <u>wherever you go</u>,

16. I will <u>go</u>;

- I will <u>go [with you]</u>;

16. And <u>where thou</u>

- And <u>wherever you</u>

16. <u>Lodgest</u>,

- From the Hebrew word *luwn*, Strong's #3885: <u>to stay permanently</u>.
- [<u>Choose to] stay permanently</u>,

16. I will <u>lodge</u>:

- I will <u>stay [there] permanently [too]</u>:

16. <u>Thy</u> people

- <u>Your [native</u>] people

16. Shall be my <u>people</u>,

- Shall be my [<u>native] people</u>,

16. And <u>thy God</u> my God:

- And <u>your God [shall also be]</u> my God:

17. <u>Where thou diest</u>,

- <u>Wherever you die</u>,

17. <u>Will I die</u>,

- [Is where] I will die [also],

17. And there will I be buried:
- And there [is where] I will be buried:

17. The LORD do so to me,
- The NIV says: "May the Lord deal with me,"

17. And more also,
- The NIV says: "Be it ever so severely,"

17. If ought but death
- From the Hebrew word *dabar*, Strong's #1697: anything.
- If anything but death

17. Part thee and me.
- [Should] part you and me.

CHOICE EXAMINATION

1. Why did Grandma Barker insist that all the family stay connected?

2. Why did Grandma never plan an organized agenda for her family gatherings?

3. Why was there a measure of joy in the air at Grandma Barker's funeral?

4. In the scripture, why did Ruth insist on staying with her mother-in-law, Naomi?

5. Why did Orpah leave?

6. What choices do you need to make in order to *keep your family connected?*

CHOOSE TO TAKE CARE OF PEOPLE

RESPECT LIFE AT EVERY STAGE

≈ 12 ≈

**Then the word of the LORD came unto me, saying,
Before I formed thee in the belly I knew thee; and before thou
camest forth out of the womb I sanctified thee, and I ordained
thee a prophet unto the nations.**

Jeremiah 1: 4, 5

It was a sad funeral. All the relatives and friends of the
family came to give their condolences, share in the grief, and bring
words of comfort and encouragement to the family members who
suffered the loss. The flowers were beautiful. The minister
delivered a wonderful, touching message with scriptures from the
Bible that brought hope and strength to the occasion.

Timmy Hobbs, named after his dad, saw life for only one
day. His lungs were not fully formed, and his body was not yet
ready to sustain itself. Timmy was born pre-mature. His mother,
Barb, was only twenty weeks pregnant at the time of his birth.

I looked up some information about abortions:
Two U.S. Supreme Court decisions, Roe v. Wade and Doe v.
Bolton, make abortion:
- Legal for any woman, regardless of her age
- Legal for any reason during the first six months of
  pregnancy, and
  For virtually any reason thereafter (1)

Abortion Statistics - U. S.
- Approximately 1,370,000 abortions occur in the United
  States annually. (2)
- 165,000 abortions occur each year to unborn babies in
  their second and third trimester.

- 90,000 abortions at 13 - 15 weeks of pregnancy
- 60,000 abortions at 16 - 20 weeks of pregnancy
- 15,000 abortions at 21 or more weeks (3)
- 88% of abortions occur during the first 6 to 12 weeks of pregnancy.
- 60 % of abortions are performed on women who already have one or more children.
- 47% of abortions are performed on women who have already had one or more abortions.

Abortion Statistics - Demographics
- 52% of women getting an abortion are younger than 25 years old and
- 19% are teenagers
- 51% of women who are unmarried when they become pregnant will get an abortion.

Abortion Statistics - Decisions to Have an Abortion (U.S.)
- 25.5% of women deciding to have an abortion want to postpone childbearing.
- 21.3% of women cannot afford a baby.
- 14.1% of women have a relationship issue or their partner does not want a child.
- 12.2% of women are too young (their parents or others object to the pregnancy.)
- 10.8% of women feel a child will disrupt their education or career.
- 7.9% of women want no (more) children.
- 3.3% of women have an abortion due to a risk to fetal health.
- 2.8% of women have an abortion due to a risk to maternal health. (2)

Tim and Barb didn't look up any statistics before they chose to schedule a funeral. They didn't think they needed to. As far as Tim and Barb were concerned, Timmy was not a statistic. Timmy was a person. He was their baby. They scheduled the funeral service so they, their friends, and their family, could share in their expressions of love for Timmy.

They love Timmy very much, and they miss him greatly.

(1) www.family.org/cforum/fosi/bioethics/facts/a0027729.cfm -
33k - Feb 1, 2006
(2) women issues.about,com/cs/
abortionstats/a/aa**abortion**/stats.htm -30k - Feb 1, 2006
(3) www.cakiforniaprolife.org/**abortion**/aborstats.html - 21k,
copyright 2000 California ProLife Council

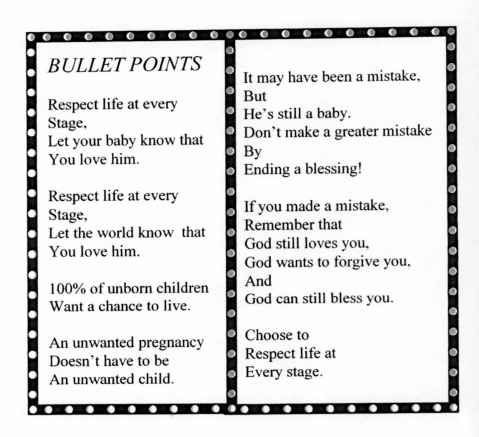

BULLET POINTS

Respect life at every
Stage,
Let your baby know that
You love him.

Respect life at every
Stage,
Let the world know that
You love him.

100% of unborn children
Want a chance to live.

An unwanted pregnancy
Doesn't have to be
An unwanted child.

It may have been a mistake,
But
He's still a baby.
Don't make a greater mistake
By
Ending a blessing!

If you made a mistake,
Remember that
God still loves you,
God wants to forgive you,
And
God can still bless you.

Choose to
Respect life at
Every stage.

SCRIPTURE ANALYSIS

Jeremiah 1: 4, 5

4. Then the word of the LORD came unto <u>me</u> saying,
>   - Then the word of the Lord came unto <u>Jeremiah (see verse #1)</u> saying,

5. Before I formed <u>thee</u>
>   - Before I formed <u>you</u>

5. In <u>the</u>
>   - In <u>your [mother's]</u>

5. <u>Belly</u>
>   - From the Hebrew word *beten*, Strong's #990: <u>the womb.</u>
>   - <u>Womb</u>

5. I knew <u>thee</u>;
>   - I knew <u>you;</u>

5. And before <u>thou camest</u> forth
>   - And before <u>you came</u> forth

5. Out of <u>the</u> womb
>   - Out of <u>your [mother's]</u> womb

5. I <u>sanctified</u>
>   - From the Hebrew word *qadash*, Strong's #6942: <u>to be clean (ceremonially or morally).</u>
>   - I <u>ceremonially and morally cleansed</u>

5. <u>Thee</u>,
>   - <u>You,</u>

5. And I <u>ordained</u>
>   - From the Hebrew word *nathan*, Strong's #5414: <u>appoint.</u>
>   - And I <u>appointed</u>

5. <u>Thee</u> a prophet unto the nations.
>   - <u>You [to be]</u> a prophet unto the nations.

CHOICE EXAMINATION

1. Why did Tim and Barb not look up any statistics before they chose to schedule a funeral?

2. Why did relatives and friends of the family attend the funeral?

3. In the scripture, who took credit for forming Jeremiah?

4. When did God ceremonially and morally cleanse Jeremiah?

5. When did God appoint Jeremiah to be a prophet to the nations?

6 What choices do you need to make in order to *respect life at every stage*?

TREAT EVERYONE WITH RESPECT

≈ 13 ≈

And he spake this parable unto certain which trusted in themselves that they were righteous, and despised others: Two men went up into the temple to pray; the one a Pharisee, the other a publican. The Pharisee stood and prayed thus with himself, God, I thank thee, that I am not as other men are, extortioners, unjust, adulterers, or even as this publican. I fast twice in the week, I give tithes of all that I possess.

And the publican, standing afar off, would not lift up so much as his eyes unto heaven, but smote upon his breast, saying, God be merciful to me a sinner.

I tell you, this man went down to his house justified rather than the other: for everyone that exalteth himself shall be abased; and he that humbleth himself shall be exalted.

Luke 18: 9 - 14

We called him Old Stinky. We didn't know his real name. How could we ever know? We never got close enough to him to actually talk. He was a frequent customer of ours at Wal-Mart.

I suppose the man hadn't taken a bath in several years. The odor was horrific! You could follow the scent up and down each aisle he had walked through for several minutes after he left the building. It made you realize how a dog's keen sense of smell enables him to follow the trail of a rabbit. Pity the poor cashier who waited on Old Stinky! After each visit, the cashier was immediately given a re-sealable plastic sandwich bag to store Old Stinky's money. It protected the rest of the money from the odor of the money which had been in Old Stinky's pocket.

We knew he was stealing from us, but nobody wanted to get close enough to make the apprehension. The day arrived however, when a courageous associate (who could hold his breath for a really long time) agreed to take on the challenge.

Sure enough, Old Stinky had loaded his pockets with a handful of inexpensive items that had not been paid for. I took him to a back office. The office clerk left (out of necessity). I stood outside of the office door (out of necessity) and asked someone to call the police department so an officer could make the arrest.

"He's not riding in *my* car," the officer said to me. He turned to Old Stinky and said, "Do you know where the police station is? It's only a few blocks away. I need you to walk down to the police station. I'll be waiting for you there." The officer was about to leave when I stopped him.

"Wait," I said. "I haven't filled out the forms for Wal-Mart." I turned to Old Stinky and asked, "Can I have you name?"

"It's Marvin* ------."

He had a name! It was a dignified sounding name, and he had a dignified sounding voice!

"What's your address?"

"What's your date of birth?"

"What's your social security number?"

"How tall are you?"

"How much do you weigh?"

To my surprise, he knew the information. *Marvin* knew the information. That means that Marvin had intelligence. Therefore, Marvin had feelings, and Marvin needed respect.

We should never have chosen to call him Old Stinky. It was disrespectful to call him Old Stinky. He wasn't Old Stinky, he was Marvin.

* Name changed

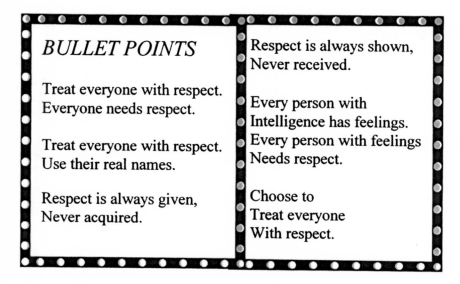

BULLET POINTS

Treat everyone with respect.
Everyone needs respect.

Treat everyone with respect.
Use their real names.

Respect is always given,
Never acquired.

Respect is always shown,
Never received.

Every person with
Intelligence has feelings.
Every person with feelings
Needs respect.

Choose to
Treat everyone
With respect.

SCRIPTURE ANALYSIS

Luke 18: 9 - 14

9. And <u>he spake</u>
    - And <u>Jesus spoke</u>
9. This <u>parable</u>
    - From the Greek word *parabole*, Strong's #3850: <u>a
fictitious narrative of common life conveying a moral</u>.
    - This <u>fictitious story of common life, conveying a moral</u>
9. Unto certain <u>which</u>
    - Unto certain <u>[people] who,</u>
9. <u>Trusted</u>
    - From the Greek word *peitho*, Strong's #3982: <u>to rely by
inward certainty</u>.
    - <u>[With] inward certainty, relied</u>
9. <u>In</u>
    - <u>On</u>
9. <u>Themselves</u>
    - The NIV says: "<u>Their own righteousness</u>"
9. <u>That</u> they were righteous,
    - <u>[Convincing themselves] that</u> they were righteous,

9. And
    While
9. Despised others:
    - Webster's Dictionary defines *despised* as: <u>to look down on with contempt.</u>
    - <u>Looking down on</u> others <u>with contempt.</u>
10. Two men went up into the temple to pray; the <u>one</u>
    - Two men went up into the temple to pray; the <u>one [was]</u>
10. A <u>Pharisee,</u>
    - From the Greek word *Pharisaios*, Strong's #5330: <u>a separatist</u>.
    - Unger's Bible dictionary states: "The characteristic feature of the Pharisees arises from their legal tendency. They had the greatest influence upon the congregations, so that all acts of public worship, prayers, and sacrifices were performed according to their injunctions."
    - A <u>Pharisee,</u>
10. The <u>other</u>
    - The <u>other [was]</u>
10. A <u>publican.</u>
    - From the Greek word telesphoreo, Strong's #5052: <u>to be a bearer to completion.</u>   - Unger's Bible Dictionary states that a publican is "A collector of the Roman revenue. These publicans were encouraged by their superior in vexatious and even fraudulent exactions. They overcharged [and] brought false charges of smuggling in the hope of extorting hush money. The publicans were also regarded as traitors and apostates [religious or political defectors], defiled by their frequent intercourse with the heathen, and willing tools of the oppressor."
    - A <u>publican.</u>
11. The Pharisee stood and prayed <u>thus with</u> himself,
    - The Pharisee stood and prayed [like] <u>this, about</u> himself,
11. God, I thank <u>thee,</u>
    - God, I thank <u>you,</u>
11. That I am not <u>as</u> other men are,
    - That I am not [the same] <u>as</u> other men are,
11. <u>Extortioners,</u>
    - Webster's dictionary defines *extort* as: <u>to obtain from a</u>

person by force or undue or illegal power.

    - [Such as] extortionists [who obtain goods from people by force or undue illegal power],

11. Unjust,

    - From the Greek word *adikos*, Strong's #94: <u>wicked</u>.

    - [Or like people who are] wicked,

11. Adulterers,

    - [Or like people who commit] adultery,

11. Or even <u>as</u> this publican.

    - Or even [people] like this publican.

12. I <u>fast</u>

    - Webster's dictionary defines *fast* as: <u>to abstain from food</u>.

    - I <u>abstain from food</u>

12. Twice in the <u>week</u>,

    - The Unger's Bible dictionary states that "The Pharisees fasted regularly on the second and fifth day of every week…(because Moses was supposed to have ascended the Mount for the second tables of the law on a Thursday and to have returned on a Monday)"

    - Twice in the <u>week [as a recognition of Moses obtaining the tables of the law]</u>,.

12. <u>I</u>

    - [And] <u>I</u>

12. Give <u>tithes</u> of all that I possess.

    - Webster's dictionary defines tithe as: <u>the tenth part of something paid as a voluntary contribution</u>.

    - The Unger's Bible Dictionary states: "[Under the Mosaic law,] the tenth part of all produce, flocks, and cattle was declared to be sacred to Jehovah by way, so to speak, of feu-duty or rent to him who was, strictly speaking, the owner of the land."

    - Give <u>as a voluntary contribution [to God] a tenth part</u> of all that I possess.

13. And the publican, standing afar <u>off</u>,

    - And the publican, standing afar <u>off [from the other people in the temple]</u>,

13. Would not lift up <u>so</u> much as his eyes

    - Would not lift up [even] <u>so</u> much as his eyes

13. Unto <u>heaven</u>,

- From the Greek word *ouranos*, Strong's #3772: <u>sky</u>.
- Unto [the] <u>sky</u>,

13. But <u>smote</u> upon his breast, saying, God be merciful to me
- From the Greek word *tupto*, Strong's #5180: <u>beat</u>.
- But <u>beat</u> upon his breast, saying, God be merciful to me

13. <u>A</u> sinner.
- [For I am] <u>a</u> sinner.

14. I tell you, this <u>man</u>
- I tell you, this <u>publican [is the one who]</u>

14. Went down to his house <u>justified</u>
- From the Greek word *dikaioo*, Strongs #1344: <u>to show or regard as just or innocent</u>.
- Went down to his house <u>regarded as innocent</u>

14. Rather than the <u>other</u>:
-Rather than the <u>Pharisee</u>:

14. For everyone <u>that</u>
- For everyone <u>who</u>

14. <u>Exalteth</u>
- From the Greek word *hupsoo*, Strong's #5312: <u>lift up</u>.
- <u>Lifts up</u>

14. <u>Himself</u>
- <u>Himself [to God]</u>

14. Shall be <u>abased</u>;
- From the Greek word *tapeinoo*, Strong's #5013: <u>humble</u>.
- Shall be <u>humbled</u>;

14. And he that <u>humbleth</u>
- And he that <u>humbles</u>

14. <u>Himself</u>
- <u>Himself [to God]</u>

14. Shall be <u>exalted</u>.
- Shall be <u>lifted up</u>.

CHOICE EXAMINATION

1. Why should Marvin have been shown respect despite his poor hygiene?

2. What do you think was a primary reason that Marvin was a frequent visitor at Wal-Mart?

3. What things could have been done for Marvin which could have helped him gain some self-respect?

4. In the scripture, why did the Pharisee rely on himself with inward certainty?

5. What did the Publican do which made Jesus regard him as innocent?

6. What choices do you need to make in order to *treat everyone with respect*?

IGNORE THE SKIN, LOOK WITHIN

≈ 14 ≈

But the LORD said unto Samuel, Look not on his countenance, or on the height of his stature; because I have refused him: for the LORD seeth not as man seeth; for man looketh on the outward appearance, but the LORD looketh on the heart.

I Samuel 16: 7

It was the largest tree in the county! At least we thought it was. Its trunk measured seventeen feet in circumference. It was situated at the bottom of a valley near the river, but it towered high above the trees on the nearby hills. It was easily the most notable landmark on the entire farm. There was not a blemish to be seen anywhere on its massive trunk. From every vantage point the giant cottonwood appeared to be totally solid. It was nature's monument to life and strength on the Manning farm.

"I want a picture of all my grandchildren holding hands, encircling the big cottonwood," my dad said. Someone from the newspaper borrowed our picture and ran a story about the county's largest tree. We were proud to see our children in the paper and we were proud to show off our massive, giant tree.

Three weeks after our tree found its way to the local newspaper, a strong wind found its way to our giant cottonwood - *and the trunk snapped at ground level.* The wooden rim forming the trunk was no more than three to four inches thick!

Barbie and I have a nephew and a niece of whom we are very proud. They met in Bible college. They're active in their local church. They have good jobs. They recently bought a new house. We always enjoy visiting with them at the family gatherings. Their lives appear to be developing in a normal, healthy fashion despite the fact that his skin is white and her skin is black.

I don't think the contrasting skin colors mattered to my nephew and niece when they chose to get married. The most important issue for them was whether they could find desirable qualities in each other that could produce a long-lasting, loving relationship. They knew that when they struggled through the storms of life that all couples are destined to face, the real strength of their marriage would be tested by what was found on the *inside*, not by what appeared on the *outside*.

Just like cottonwood trees.

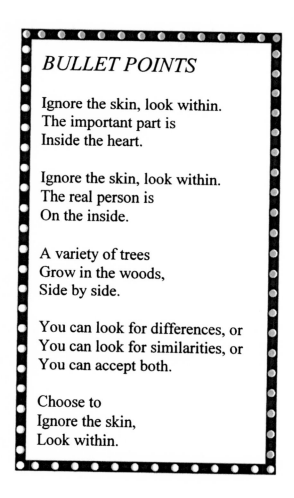

BULLET POINTS

Ignore the skin, look within.
The important part is
Inside the heart.

Ignore the skin, look within.
The real person is
On the inside.

A variety of trees
Grow in the woods,
Side by side.

You can look for differences, or
You can look for similarities, or
You can accept both.

Choose to
Ignore the skin,
Look within.

SCRIPTURE ANALYSIS

I Samuel 16: 7

7. But the LORD said unto <u>Samuel</u>,
> - The Unger's Bible Dictionary states: "Since Saul had been rejected by God, and the government was not to remain in his family, it was necessary, in order to prevent strife and confusion, that his successor should be appointed before the death of the king. Samuel was therefore instructed by the Lord to go to Bethlehem, and anoint David, the youngest son of Jesse, as the chosen one."
> - But the Lord said unto [the prophet] Samuel,

7. Look not on <u>his</u>
> - Look not on <u>Eliab's (see verse #6)</u>

7. <u>Countenance,</u>
> - From the Hebrew word *mareh*, Strong's #4758: <u>an appearance</u>.
> - <u>Appearance,</u>

7. <u>Or</u> on
> - <u>Or [even] on</u>

7. The height of <u>his</u> stature;
> - The height of <u>Eliab's</u> stature;

7. Because I have refused <u>him</u>:
> - Because I have refused [to choose] Eliab [for king (see verse #1)]:

7. For the LORD <u>seeth not</u>
> - For the Lord <u>sees not [in the same way]</u>

7. As <u>man seeth</u>;
> - As [a] <u>man sees</u>;

7. For <u>man looketh on</u>
> - For [a] <u>man looks at</u>

7. The outward <u>appearance,</u>
> - The outward <u>appearance [of a person]</u>,

7. But the LORD <u>looketh on</u>
> - But the Lord <u>looks at</u>

7. The <u>heart</u>.
> - Webster's dictionary defines the heart as: <u>ones innermost</u>

character, feelings, or inclinations.
- The [person's] innermost character, feelings and inclinations.

CHOICE EXAMINATION

1. Why did the niece and nephew choose each other for marriage?

2. What storms of life might the niece and nephew be destined to face?

3. How can the niece and nephew develop real strength in their marriage as they struggle through the storms of life?

4. In the scripture, what influenced Samuel to think that God might have chosen Eliab for king?

5. How can we train ourselves to focus more on the person's innermost character, feelings and inclinations, than on the person's outward appearance?

6. What choices do you need to make in order to *ignore the skin, look within*?

ACCEPT PEOPLE WHO ACT DIFFERENTLY THAN YOU

≈ 15 ≈

And one of the Pharisees desired him that he would eat with him. And he went to the Pharisee's house, and sat down to meat. And, behold, a woman in the city, which was a sinner, when she knew that Jesus sat at meat in the Pharisees house, brought an alabaster box of ointment, And stood at his feet behind him weeping, and began to wash his feet with tears, and did wipe them with the hairs of her head, and kissed his feet, and anointed them with the ointment.

Now when the Pharisee which had bidden him saw it, he spake within himself, saying, This man, if he were a prophet, would have known who and what manner of woman this is that toucheth him: for she is a sinner.

And Jesus answering said unto him, Simon, I have somewhat to say unto thee.

And he saith, Master, say on.

There was a certain creditor which had two debtors: the one owed five hundred pence, and the other fifty. And when they had nothing to pay, he frankly forgave them both. Tell me therefore, which of them will love him most?

Simon answered and said, I suppose that he, to whom he forgave most.

And he said unto him, Thou hast rightly judged. Wherefore I say unto thee, Her sins, which are many, are forgiven; for she loved much: but to whom little is forgiven, the same loveth little.

And he said unto her, Thy sins are forgiven.

Luke 7: 36 - 43, 47, 48

They were excited about coming to church! They wanted to learn more about serving God! Most of them were jumping up and down during the worship service. Some of them were lying on the floor face down endeavoring to make a gesture of honor to God. One of them had orange hair. One of them had a pierced nose. Another had a pierced lip. They were quite a rowdy bunch, shouting "AMEN!" and "HALLELUJAH!" while the pastor preached. And to top it off, they were all sitting *right on the front pews*!

I really like our church. I'm comfortable in it, and I'm growing spiritually. We have a good Sunday school. Our worship time is energetic and meaningful. The preaching is always good. Our Wednesday evening service ministers to over two hundred children and teenagers. That's an amazing number considering the population of our town is only six hundred! On Saturdays some of our church members pull a concession stand downtown to give away free water, coffee, and snacks. We're trying to show the community that we're good neighbors, interested in serving people's needs. Our church's ministries always seems to be inclusive of the entire community. I guess that's what caught their attention.

Brother Frank, a mission oriented evangelist from a nearby town, brought them to our church. He has a special ability to minister to people who are not necessarily ... *conservative.* He understands them well. He used to live a non-conservative kind of lifestyle. After he accepted Jesus as his Savior, he felt a desire to share the message of salvation to people who, like him, did not fit the traditional church crowd stereotype. His ministry consists of frequenting the places where Christians don't normally go. He goes to drug houses, bars, and adult video / book stores, to tell people about Jesus. All of the people he witnesses to are frustrated. They are searching, through drugs, alcohol, sexual gratification, or other means, to find peace of mind, comfort, and security. Frank is able to show them that what they really need to search for is a personal relationship with Jesus.

I guess I'm naturally conservative. I probably won't dye my hair orange. I probably won't pierce my nose or lips. I probably won't jump up and down during the worship service. I probably won't lie on the floor during prayer time at church. I don't feel comfortable doing those things in public. I am glad, however, that people who wish to do those things in public can do them, without condemnation, in our church. I'm proud, too, that people in our church choose to allow people, who have a different background than the rest of us, to express themselves freely. Everyone's accepted at the Full Gospel Church.

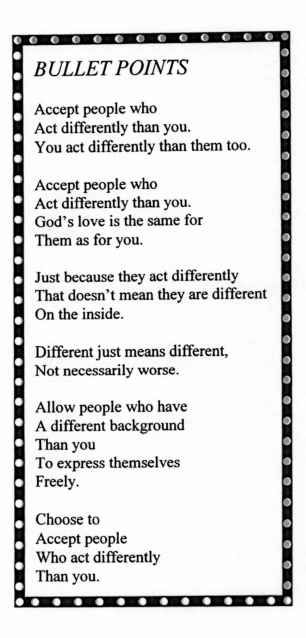

BULLET POINTS

Accept people who
Act differently than you.
You act differently than them too.

Accept people who
Act differently than you.
God's love is the same for
Them as for you.

Just because they act differently
That doesn't mean they are different
On the inside.

Different just means different,
Not necessarily worse.

Allow people who have
A different background
Than you
To express themselves
Freely.

Choose to
Accept people
Who act differently
Than you.

SCRIPTURE ANALYSIS

Luke 7: 36 - 43, 47, 48

36. And one of the <u>Pharisees</u>
- And one of the <u>Pharisees (Simon, see 7:40)</u>

36. <u>Desired</u>
- From the Greek word *erotao*, Strong's #2065: <u>to request</u>.
- [Made a] <u>request</u>

36. <u>Him</u>
- [Of] <u>Jesus [asking]</u>

36. That <u>he</u>
That <u>Jesus</u>

36. Would <u>eat</u> with him.
- Would <u>eat [a meal]</u> with him.

36. And <u>he</u> went
- And <u>Jesus</u> went

36. Into <u>the Pharisee's</u> house,
- Into <u>Simon's</u> house,

36. And sat down to <u>meat</u>.
- From the Greek word *broma*, Strong's #1033: <u>food</u>.
- And sat down to [eat some] <u>food</u>.

37. And, behold, a woman in the city, <u>which</u> was a sinner,
- And, behold, a woman of the city, <u>who</u> was a sinner,

37. When she knew that Jesus sat at <u>meat</u>
- When she knew that Jesus sat at [the table to eat] <u>food</u>

37. In <u>the Pharisee's</u> house,
- In <u>Simon's</u> house,

37. Brought an <u>alabaster</u> box
- From the Greek word *alabastron*, Strong's #211: <u>the name of a stone</u>.
- The Unger's Bible Dictionary states: "This is a variety of carbonate of lime, usually stalagmitic in origin, with a layered structure due to its deposition from water, giving it a banded aspect of slightly varying shades and colors, often very delicate and beautiful."

- Brought an <u>alabaster [stone]</u> box

37. Of <u>ointment</u>,
    - From the Greek word *muron*, Strong's #3464: <u>myrrh [or]</u>
<u>perfumed oil</u>.
    - Of <u>perfumed oil</u>,

38. And <u>stood</u>
    - And <u>[the woman]</u> stood

38. At <u>his</u> feet
    - At <u>Jesus'</u> feet

38. Behind <u>him</u> weeping,
    - Behind <u>Jesus</u> weeping,

38. And <u>began</u>
    - And <u>[the woman]</u> began

38. To wash <u>his</u> feet
    - To wash <u>Jesus'</u> feet

38. With <u>tears</u>,
    - With <u>[her]</u> tears,

38. And <u>did</u>
    - And <u>[the woman]</u> did

38. Wipe <u>them</u> with the hairs of her head,
    - Wipe <u>her tears [onto Jesus' feet]</u> with the hairs of her
head,

38. And <u>kissed</u>
    - And <u>[the woman]</u> kissed

38. <u>His</u> feet,
    - <u>Jesus'</u> feet,

38. And anointed <u>them</u>
    - And anointed <u>Jesus' feet</u>

38. With the <u>ointment</u>.
    - With the <u>perfumed oil</u>.

39. Now when <u>the Pharisee</u>
    - Now when <u>Simon</u>

39. <u>Which</u> had
    - <u>Who</u> had

39. <u>Bidden</u>
    - Webster's Dictionary defines *bid* as: <u>invitation</u>.
    - <u>Invited</u>

39. <u>Him</u>
- <u>Jesus</u>
39. Saw <u>it,</u>
- Saw [the woman] washing, wiping, kissing and anointing [Jesus' feet],
39. He spake
- <u>Simon spoke</u>
39. <u>Within</u> himself, saying,
- From the Greek word *en*, Strong's #1722: <u>to</u>.
- <u>To</u> himself, saying,
39. This <u>man,</u>
- This <u>man (Jesus),</u>
39. If he were <u>a prophet,</u>
- If he were <u>an [authentic] prophet,</u>
39. Would have known who and what manner of woman this is that <u>toucheth</u> him:
- Would have known who and what manner of woman this is that <u>touches</u> him:
39. <u>For she</u> is a sinner.
- <u>Because this woman</u> is a sinner.
40. And Jesus answering said unto <u>him,</u>
- And Jesus answering said unto <u>Simon,</u>
40. Simon, I have <u>somewhat</u>
- Simon, I have <u>something</u>
40. To say unto <u>thee.</u>
- To say unto <u>you</u>.
40. And <u>he saith,</u>
- And <u>Simon said,</u>
40. <u>Master,</u> say on.
- From the Greek word *didaskalos*, Strong's #1320: <u>teacher</u>.
- <u>Teacher,</u> say on.
41. <u>There</u> was a certain creditor
- [<u>And Jesus said</u>] <u>there</u> was a certain creditor
41. <u>Which</u> had two debtors:
- <u>Who</u> had two debtors:
41. The <u>one</u>
- The <u>one [debtor]</u>

41. Owed <u>five hundred pence</u>, and
- Owed <u>$220</u>, and

41. The other <u>fifty</u>.
- The other <u>[owed] $22</u>.

42. And when <u>they</u> had
- And when <u>the two debtors</u> had

42. <u>Nothing</u>
- <u>No [money]</u>

42. To <u>pay</u>,
- To <u>pay [the creditor]</u>,

42. <u>He</u>
- <u>The creditor</u>

42. <u>Frankly</u>
- From the Greek word *charis*, Strong's #5485: <u>graciousness</u>.
- <u>Graciously</u>

42. Forgave <u>them</u> both.
- Forgave both <u>debtors [of their debt]</u>.

42. Tell me therefore, <u>which</u>
- Tell me therefore, <u>which [one]</u>

42. Of <u>them</u>
- Of <u>the debtors</u>

42. Will love <u>him</u> most?
- Will love <u>the creditor [the]</u> most?

43. Simon answered and <u>said</u>,
- Simon answered and <u>said [to Jesus]</u>,

43. I suppose <u>that</u> he,
- I suppose <u>that [would be]</u> he,

43. To whom <u>he</u>
- To whom <u>the creditor</u>

43. Forgave <u>most</u>.
- Forgave <u>[of the] most [debt]</u>.

43. And <u>he</u> said
- And <u>Jesus</u> said

43. Unto <u>him</u>,
- Unto <u>Simon</u>,

43. <u>Thou hast</u>

- You have
43. Rightly judged.
    - From the Greek word *orthos*, Strong's #3723: correctly.
    - Judged correctly.
47. Wherefore I say unto thee,
    - Wherefore I say unto you (Simon),
47. Her sins,
    - [This] woman's sins,
47. Which are many,
    - Which are many [in number],
47. Are forgiven;
    - Are [all] forgiven;
47. For she loved much:
    - For she [indeed] loved much [that is sin]:
47. But to whom
    - But to [the person] whom
47. Little
    - From the Greek word *oligos*, Strong's #3641: little [or] few.
    - Few [sins]
47. Is forgiven,
    - Are forgiven,
47. The same
    - The same [person]
47. Loveth little.
    - Loves [God comparatively] little [in return].
48. And he said
    - And Jesus said
48. Unto her,
    - Unto the woman,
48. Thy sins are forgiven.
    - Your sins are forgiven.

CHOICE EXAMINATION

1. Why were the non-traditional church crowd people so excited about being in church?

2. Why does Brother Frank frequent places where Christians don't normally go?

3. In the scripture, why did the woman wash Jesus' feet with her tears?

4. Why did Jesus allow the woman to wash his feet with her tears?

5. Why did Simon think that Jesus was not an authentic prophet?

6. What choices do you need to make in order to *accept people who act differently than you.*

LOVE PEOPLE LIKE THEY ARE MEMBERS OF YOUR FAMILY

≈ 16 ≈

While he yet talked to the people, behold, his mother and his brethren stood without, desiring to speak with him. Then one said unto him, Behold, thy mother and thy brethren stand without, desiring to speak with thee.

But he answered and said unto him that told him, Who is my mother? and who are my brethren? And he stretched forth his hand toward his disciples, and said, Behold my mother and my brethren! For whosoever shall do the will of my Father which is in heaven, the same is my brother, and sister, and mother.

Matthew 12: 46-50

"You *love* us!" he exclaimed. I was struck by how awesome of a statement this was coming from a fifth grader, a boy, in the middle of a class session, in front of the other students, and directed toward his teacher. She was a first year teacher. She is my daughter, Charity.

The young man's assessment was correct. Charity loves people like they are members of her family. "OK, we have a new rule today," she said on her second day in the classroom. "Before you leave each day you have to either give me a hug or shake my hand, whichever you prefer." Some shook, most hugged. More importantly, each student's last memory of each day was of a special moment with the teacher.

"I think they all want to feel special!" Charity told Barbie and me. "So I always mention something good they did during the day when I give them their hug. (Sometimes I have to think hard and fast, but I always come up with something!") she chuckled.

Charity has a knack for making people feel good about themselves. I've accused her of being the world's friendliest person. You can't walk down the street with Charity without stopping several times for her to share friendly greetings with all the people she knows. "Hey, Joe!" she shouts to someone across the street. "We missed you at the church youth meeting last week. Be sure to come next week!" Two more steps down the sidewalk and she stops again. "Casey, what a lovely dress! Where on earth did you find that?" Two more steps and you're entering the grocery store. "Hey, there's Jose's mom. I'm going to go smile at her!" (Jose's mom doesn't speak English, but she understands smiling really well.) We purchase our groceries. A young man grabs our two sacks to carry them to the car. "Hey Justin, you're really building up muscles carrying out those groceries like that. Are you going to play football again this year?" On the way home Charity is thinking out loud. "I think I'll call Jessica and invite her over to dinner next week. I'll bet she'd like some company."

Someone once told me that there must be something dark and foreboding in Charity's life that she is hiding from all of us. No one, I was told, can be that happy all the time. I totally disagree. Charity is an open book. What you see is what you get. Charity is happy to see people because - *Charity loves people*! She loves people like they're members of her family.

Love covers a lot of territory. Sometimes fifth graders misbehave. Sometimes Charity has to scold or punish some of her students. One young girl decided to act up in class. Charity took her out of the classroom and gave her a lecture on her behavior. The next day she acted up again. Charity gave her another lecture and sent her to the principal's office. At the end of the day, the young girl was sent back to the classroom. When the bell rang, she went to the front of the room, as normal, to get a hug from her teacher. Just as Charity was starting to mention something special about the student, the young girl stopped her. "Mrs. Keith," she said, "I've been thinking. I really shouldn't behave badly in your class. I've decided that starting tomorrow I will be nice again, forever."

"Well, that's a wonderful idea! I'll be looking forward to tomorrow!"

To the young girl, good or bad behavior was simply a choice to be made. She chose that day to exhibit good behavior because she, and all the other students, knew their teacher loved them. She loved them like they were members of her family.

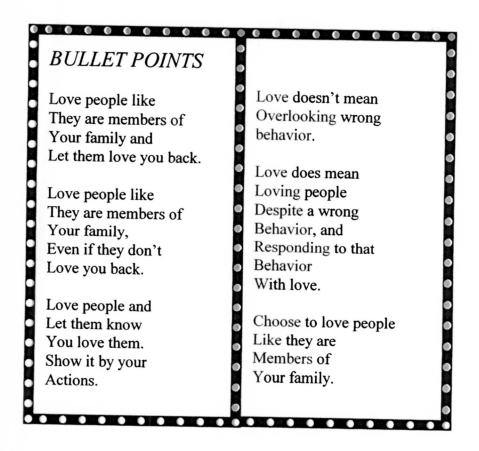

BULLET POINTS

Love people like
They are members of
Your family and
Let them love you back.

Love people like
They are members of
Your family,
Even if they don't
Love you back.

Love people and
Let them know
You love them.
Show it by your
Actions.

Love doesn't mean
Overlooking wrong
behavior.

Love does mean
Loving people
Despite a wrong
Behavior, and
Responding to that
Behavior
With love.

Choose to love people
Like they are
Members of
Your family.

SCRIPTURE ANALYSIS

Matthew 12: 46 - 50

46. While he
- While Jesus

46. Yet talked to
- Was [still] talking to

46. The people,
- The [great multitude (see 12: 15) of] people

46. Behold, <u>his</u> mother
    - Behold, [someone saw] Jesus' mother

46. And his <u>brethren</u>
    - And his <u>brothers</u>

46. <u>Stood</u>
    - <u>Standing</u>

46. <u>Without</u>, desiring to speak with him.
    - From the Greek word *exo*, Strong's #1854: <u>outside</u>.
    - <u>Outside</u>, desiring to speak with him.

47. Then <u>one</u> said
    - Then <u>someone</u> said

47. Unto <u>him</u>,
    Unto <u>Jesus</u>,

47. Behold, <u>thy</u> mother
    - Behold, <u>your</u> mother

47. And <u>thy brethren</u>
    - And <u>your brothers</u>

47. <u>Stand without</u>,
    - <u>[Are] standing outside</u>,

47. Desiring to speak with <u>thee</u>.
    - Desiring to speak with <u>you</u>.

48. But <u>he</u> answered
    - But <u>Jesus</u> answered

48. And said unto <u>him</u>
    - And said unto <u>the person</u>

48. <u>That</u>
    - <u>Who</u>

48. Told <u>him</u>,
    - Told <u>him [the message]</u>,

48. Who is my mother? and who are my <u>brethren</u>?
    - Who is my mother? And who are my <u>brothers</u>?

49. And <u>he</u>
    - And <u>Jesus</u>

49. Stretched <u>forth</u> his hand toward his disciples, and said,
    - Stretched <u>out</u> his hand toward his disciples, and said,

49. <u>Behold</u> my mother
    - The NIV says: "<u>Here are</u> my mother"

49. And my <u>brethren</u>!
> - And my <u>brothers</u>!

50. For whosoever shall do the will of my Father <u>which</u> is in heaven,
> - For whosoever shall do the will of my Father <u>who</u> is in heaven,

50. <u>The same</u> is
> - <u>That same [person]</u> is

50. <u>My</u> brother, and sister, and mother.
> - <u>[Equivalent to] my</u> brother, and sister, and mother.

CHOICE EXAMINATION

1. Why was the fifth grade boy unhesitant to make the statement, "You love us!" in front of the other members of his class?

2. How can people tell that Charity loves them?

3. Why was the fifth grade girl unhesitant to go to the front of the classroom for a hug from her teacher after she misbehaved?

4. In the scripture, what did Jesus mean when he said, "Here are my mother and my brothers?"

5. What actions cause Jesus to think of people as equivalent to his brother, sister and mother?

6. What choices do you need to make in order to *love people like they are members of your family*?

CONTINUE TO CARE ABOUT PEOPLE

≈ 17 ≈

And as they departed from Jericho, a great multitude followed him. And, behold, two blind men sitting by the way side, when they heard that Jesus passed by, cried out, saying, Have mercy on us O Lord, thou son of David. And the multitude rebuked them, because they should hold their peace: but they cried the more, saying, Have mercy on us, O Lord, thou son of David.

And Jesus stood still, and called them, and said, What will ye that I shall do unto you?

They say unto him, Lord, that our eyes may be opened.

So Jesus had compassion on them, and touched their eyes: and immediately their eyes received sight, and they followed him.

Matthew 20: 29 - 34

He was a young man. He was sitting in my office, and he was crying. I had just finished explaining why I couldn't hire him. He had been without a job for four months. His wife had recently lost her job. They had a one year old child at home. They didn't have any money and they didn't have much food.

I opened up my billfold. It had twenty-four dollars in it. I handed him the twenty. "This isn't a loan. You just take this. Professionally, I can't help you today. But on a personal level, I'll do what I can to help you."

I grabbed a notebook and made him a list of businesses which I thought might be able to hire him. I visited with him about his personal situation. I tried to offer suggestions that could improve his situation. I asked if I could pray for him. He said yes. I shut the door to the office. I laid a hand on his shoulder and prayed for him to find a job, to find encouragement, and to find faith that Christ would meet all of his needs. We shook hands and he left. An hour later, store-related business brought me to the

Lowe's store, next door. The young man was there, sitting at a desk, filling out an application for employment.

It was a tough week. The day before the encounter with the young man I had to tell a woman, who was struggling with her job as an office clerk, that I was reassigning her to a position with less responsibility. A few hours later I had to tell a man, a cashier, with whom I had devoted a lot of time for instruction and counseling over a period of several months, that I was terminating his employment.

Merchandising is the easiest part of managing a Wal-Mart store. Almost anyone can learn the merchandise side of the business. The more difficult aspect of managing a store is dealing with all the people issues. Sometimes, the day's activities can keep you so busy that you can almost forget what your job is all about. It's all about *people*. It's interacting with and building relationships with people, whether it's your boss, your co-workers, your employees, or your customers. It's all about people.

Some situations can break your heart, and they should break your heart.

There is a process, however, that enables some people to engage an automatic defense mechanism in their minds. This defense mechanism helps supervisors, administrators, and people in authority to cope with the emotional stress that is caused by constantly dealing with people in need. It can engage all by itself without the implementer even realizing it. It works like this: Choose to stop thinking of people... as people.

What if the young man who applied for a job was just a job applicant? What if the woman who was reassigned to a position with less responsibility was just an office clerk? What if the man whose employment was terminated was just a cashier, and none of these people were thought of as people? They were only a job applicant, an office clerk, and a cashier.

Of course, people are not job applicants, office clerks, and cashiers. They are people. They all have families. They all have personal obligations. They all have personal needs. They all have feelings. They all are people.

Continue to care about people. Do what you can to help people. Your job, no matter what your job, is all about people.

BULLET POINTS

Continue to care about people.
Your job, no matter what your job is,
Is all about people.

Continue to care about people.
Do what you are obligated to do
Professionally, but
Do what you are able to do
Personally.

People need people.
People need people who will listen.
People need people who will understand.
People need people who will care.

Let people know
That you care about them.

Respond to the
Situation appropriately, but
Show the person
You care.

The situation may require
A response, but
The person requires
Someone who cares.

Choose to
Continue to care
About people.

SCRIPTURE ANALYSIS

Matthew 20: 29 - 34

29. And as they
- And as Jesus and his disciples

29. Departed from Jericho,
- Departed from [the city of] Jericho,

29. A great multitude followed him.
- A great multitude [of people] followed him.

30. And, behold, two blind men sitting
- And, behold, two blind men [were] sitting

30. By the way side,
- The NIV says: "By the roadside,"

30. When they
- When the two blind men

30. Heard that Jesus passed by,
- Heard that Jesus [was] passing by,

30. Cried out, saying,
- [The two blind men] cried out [to Jesus], saying,

30. Have mercy on us, O Lord, thou
- Have mercy on us, O Lord, you [who are a]

30. Son of David.
- Unger's Bible Dictionary states: " 'The Son of Man' is thus our Lord's racial name, as the 'Son of David' is distinctly his Jewish name and the 'Son of God' His divine name."
- (See: Matthew 1: 6-16 and Luke 2:4.)
- Son (descendent) of [King] David.

31. And the multitude
- And the multitude [of people following Jesus]

31. Rebuked them,
- Rebuked the two blind men,

31. Because they should
- Because [the multitude of people thought that] the two blind men should

31. Hold their peace:
- The NIV says: "Be quiet,"

119

31. But they cried
  - But the two blind men cried [out]

31. The more, saying,
  - [All] the more, saying,

31. Have mercy on us, O Lord, thou Son of David.
  - Have mercy on us, O Lord, you Son (descendant) of [King] David.

32. And Jesus stood still,
  - And [when] Jesus [heard the two blind men, he] stood still,

32. And called them, and said,
  - And called [out to] the two blind men, and said,

32. What will ye
  - What will you [have to be done]

32. That I shall do
  - That I can do

32. Unto you?
  - For you?

33. They say
  - The two blind men said

33. Unto him,
  - Unto Jesus,

33. Lord, that our eyes
  - Lord, [we ask] that our eyes

33. May
  - Would

33. Be opened.
  - Be opened [so that we can see.]

34. So Jesus had compassion
  - So, Jesus had [feelings of] compassion

34. On them,
  - For the two blind men,

34. And touched
  - And [Jesus] touched

34. Their eyes:
  - The two blind men's eyes:

34. And immediately their eyes

- And immediately <u>the two blind men's</u> eyes
34. Received <u>sight</u>,
    - Received <u>[their ability to have] sight,</u>
34. And <u>they</u>
    - And <u>the two [formerly] blind men</u>
34. Followed <u>him</u>.
    - Followed <u>[after] Jesus.</u>

CHOICE EXAMINATION

1. Why should some situations break your heart?

2. Why are supervisors, administrators, and people in authority especially susceptible to engaging an automatic defense mechanism in their minds which allows them to stop thinking of people as people?

3. Why is your job, no matter what your job is, all about people?

4. In the scripture, why was it appropriate for Jesus to detach himself from the multitude of people in order to minister to the two blind men?

5. Why did the multitude of people following Jesus rebuke the two blind men?

6. What choices do you need to make in order to *continue to care about people*?

BE WILLING TO FORGIVE OTHER PEOPLE

≈ 18 ≈

And when ye stand praying, forgive, if ye have ought against any: that your Father also which is in heaven may forgive you your trespasses. But if ye do not forgive, neither will your Father which is in heaven forgive your trespasses.

Mark 11: 25, 26

It was a really uncomfortable situation. Two people with a working relationship had a misunderstanding. The disagreement had become so sharp that a spouse of a store associate was asking me to get involved. It was a personal matter unrelated to store business, but maybe the influence of a store manager could help diffuse the situation. I told him I'd try to help.

I've endeavored to moderate numerous disagreements between people over the years. Sometimes there are obvious solutions to the problems. Quite often the greater challenge is finding ways to help people deal with their hurt feelings. This appeared to be one of those types of situations. All the two people really needed to do was to get together, state their feelings about the matter, and tell each other they were sorry. I was sure they could work it out.

I asked her to speak first. She said she was sorry for what she had done. She shouldn't have done it. She didn't intend for it to appear the way that it did. Would he please forgive her?

He said, "No."

She apologized again.

He still said, "No."

I spoke with him and encouraged him to forgive her.

He said, "No, I'll never forgive her."

I urged him to forgive her. "She can't undo what she did," I said. "It wasn't intended for the way it was perceived. She will try to never let it happen again. Her feelings are hurt, too. She just wants you to forgive her."

Again, he said, "No."

We spent several minutes in further discussion. I appealed to his common sense. "You'll both be happier after you forgive each other." I appealed to his sympathy. "Think of how she feels. It will be difficult for her to deal with this if you hold it against her." I appealed to his wisdom. "Is refusing to forgive her really going to benefit either one of you?" It was all to no avail. He still chose to not forgive her.

She quit her job soon after that.

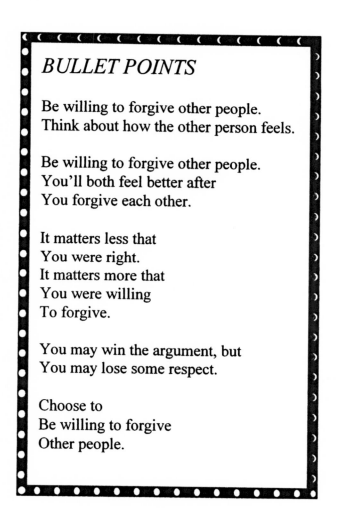

BULLET POINTS

Be willing to forgive other people.
Think about how the other person feels.

Be willing to forgive other people.
You'll both feel better after
You forgive each other.

It matters less that
You were right.
It matters more that
You were willing
To forgive.

You may win the argument, but
You may lose some respect.

Choose to
Be willing to forgive
Other people.

SCRIPTURE ANALYSIS

Mark 11: 25, 26

25. And when <u>ye</u>
   - And when <u>you</u>

25. <u>Stand</u>
   - From the Greek word *steko*, Strong's #4739: <u>to persevere [or] stand fast</u>.
   - <u>Stand fast, persevering</u>

25. <u>Praying,</u>
   - <u>[In] prayer,</u>

25. <u>Forgive,</u>
   - <u>Forgive [other people]</u>,

25. If you have <u>ought</u>
   - From the Greek word *tis*, Strong's #5100: <u>any thing</u>.
   - If you have <u>anything [you're holding]</u>

25. Against <u>any</u>:
   - Against <u>anyone</u>:

25. <u>That</u> your
   - <u>[So] that</u> your

25. Father also <u>which</u> is in heaven
   - Father <u>who</u> is in heaven, also

25. May forgive <u>you</u>
   - May forgive <u>you</u> [for]

25. Your <u>trespasses</u>.
   - From the Greek word *paraptoma*, Strong's #3900: <u>unintentional error or willful transgression [or] sin</u>.
   - Your <u>sins [including both] unintentional errors and willful transgressions</u>.

26. But if <u>ye</u>
   - But if <u>you</u>

26. Do not <u>forgive,</u>
   - Do not <u>forgive [other people]</u>,

26. Neither will your Father <u>which</u> is in heaven
   - Neither will your Father <u>who</u> is in heaven

26. <u>Forgive</u> your

- Forgive [you for] your
26. Trespasses.
- Sins [including both] unintentional errors and willful transgressions.

CHOICE EXAMINATION

1. Why is finding ways to help people deal with their hurt feelings often a greater challenge than finding a solution to the problem?

2. Why was it important to one person that her apology be accepted?

3. Why did the other person refuse to forgive her?

4. In the scripture, why is it important to forgive other people if you are holding anything against anyone?

5. Why does Jesus require us to forgive both unintentional errors and willful transgressions?

6. What choices do you need to make in order to *be willing to forgive other people*?

SPEAK WELL OF OTHER PEOPLE
≈ 19 ≈

For in many things we offend all. If any man offend not in word, the same is a perfect man, and able also to bridle the whole body.

Behold, we put bits in the horses' mouths, that they may obey us; and we turn about their whole body. Behold also the ships, which though they be so great, and are driven of fierce winds, yet are they turned about with a very small helm, whithersoever the governor listeth. Even so the tongue is a little member, and boasteth great things. Behold, how great a matter a little fire kindleth!

James 3: 2 - 5

I heard a good Christian woman tell this story about a lesson she learned while she was working at her job in a bank.

"This obnoxious family came into the bank. They were dirty; they smelled bad, and they were loud. No sooner had they left than several of we ladies got together to talk about them. 'Did you see what they did? Did you hear what they said? Did you notice how they smelled?' The insults were pouring freely out of our mouths until one young woman walked up and quietly said, 'They had nice teeth.' Nice teeth? Was that all she could say about them - *they had nice teeth*?

It's amazing how quickly four words can change the direction of a conversation. The insults stopped immediately. We knew what we were doing was wrong. While the rest of us were looking for something bad to say, she chose to look for something good. It surely took her some effort, but she found it. They had nice teeth."

BULLET POINTS

Speak well of other people.
We're all God's creation.

Speak well of other people.
Look for the good before
You look for the bad.

God loves everyone,
Not just people who are clean.

If the situation is obvious, it
Probably doesn't need to
Be told
Anyway.

If you look for
Something good to say,
You'll find it.
If you look for
Something bad to say,
You'll find that too.

Choose to
Speak well
Of other people.

SCRIPTURE ANALYSIS

James 3: 2 - 5

2. For <u>in</u> many
- For in [the] many

2. <u>Things</u> we offend
- <u>Things [we say]</u> we offend

2. <u>All</u>.
- [People in] all [kinds of ways].

2. If any man <u>offend not</u>
- If any man [does] not offend [people]

2. <u>In word</u>,
- <u>With [the]</u> words [he says],

2. <u>The same</u> is
- <u>That same [person]</u> is

2. A <u>perfect</u> man,
- From the Greek word *teleios*, Strong's #5046: <u>complete in moral character</u>.
- A man <u>[who is] complete in moral character</u>,

2. And <u>able</u> also
- And <u>[he is] able </u>also

2. To bridle <u>the</u> whole body.
- To bridle <u>his</u> whole body.

3. <u>Behold</u>,
- From the Greek word *idou*, Strong's #2400: <u>see</u>.
- <u>See [how]</u>,

3. We put bits in the horses' mouths, <u>that</u> they
- We put bits in the horses' mouths, <u>[so] that</u> they

3. <u>May</u> obey us;
- <u>Will</u> obey us;

3. And <u>we</u> turn about
- And <u>[because of the bits in the horses' mouths] we [are able to]</u> turn about

3. <u>Their</u> whole
- <u>The horses'</u> whole

3. <u>Body</u>.

- Bodies.

4. Behold also the ships,

    - See [how] also the ships,

4. Which though they be so great,

    - Which though they be so great [in size],

4. And are driven

    - And [they] are driven

4. Of

    - By

4. Fierce winds,

    - From the Greek word *skleros*, Strong's #4642: severe.

    - Severe winds,

4. Yet are they

    - Yet the ships are

4. Turned about

    - [Able to be] turned about

4. With a very small helm,

    - From the Greek word *pedalion*, Strong's #4079: rudder.

    - With a very small rudder,

4. Whithersoever

    - Wherever

4. The governor listeth.

    - The NIV says, "The pilot wants to go."

5. Even

    - From the Greek word *kai*, Strong's #2532: therefore.

    - Therefore

5. So

    - From the Greek word *houto*, Strong's #3779: after this manner.

    - After this manner

5. The tongue

    - The [human] tongue

5. Is a little member,

    - From the Greek word *melos*, Strong's #3196: a limb or part of the body.

    - Is a little part of the body,

5. And boasteth great things.

- And <u>boasts [of]</u> great things.
5. <u>Behold,</u>
- <u>See,</u>
5. How <u>great</u>
- How <u>great [of]</u>
5. A <u>matter</u>
- From the Greek word *hule*, Strong's #5208: <u>a forest</u>.
- A <u>forest [fire]</u>
5. A little fire <u>kindleth</u>!
- A little fire <u>kindles</u>!

CHOICE EXAMINATION

1. Why were the bank ladies sharing insults about the obnoxious family?

2. Why did one young woman say they had nice teeth?

3. In the scripture, what outward evidence tells us that a person is complete in moral character?

4. Why is it significant that the rudder turns the ship instead of the ship turning the rudder, also the bit turns the horse's body instead of the horse's body turning the bit?

5. How do great forest fires get kindled?

6. What choices do you need to make in order to *speak well of other people*?

ADJUST YOUR PERSPECTIVE

≈ 20 ≈

And why beholdest thou the mote that is in thy brother's eye, but considerest not the beam that is in thine own eye? Or how wilt thou say to thy brother, Let me pull out the mote out of thine eye; and, behold, a beam is in thine own eye?

Thou hypocrite, first cast out the beam out of thine own eye; and then shalt thou see clearly to cast out the mote out of thy brother's eye.

Matthew 7: 3 - 5

The old mama sow had thirteen baby pigs nursing her. She was lying on her side with her head placed underneath the front cross beam of the A-frame hog house. "That's an interesting place for her to lie down," I thought. I put out the feed and water and left the hog lot. The next morning, I found the mama sow in the same location, lying on her side with her head placed underneath the same board. "Wow, that must be her favorite spot!" I decided. I put out the feed and water again and headed back toward home. When day number three arrived, I found the old mama sow with the thirteen baby pigs *still* lying in the same spot. Her head was again placed underneath the front cross beam of the hog house. Finally, the realization hit me, "SHE'S STUCK!"

After waiting three full days to make this analysis, I sprang into immediate action! I ran to the corner of the hog house and tried to pick it up. I couldn't budge it! I turned and ran full speed toward the pickup, jumping over the hog lot fence at a full gallop, slid into the pickup seat, and drove like a maniac to the tool shed by the barn. I grabbed a six foot crowbar, spun the tires on the truck, and headed back to the hog lot. I stuck the end of the crow bar underneath the corner of the hog house, and with an adrenaline-filled heave, hoisted the hog house off the old mama sow.

"Boy, was she ever thirsty!" I told Barbie later that day. "The poor old sow raised herself up, then walked absolutely sideways, (I suppose three days on your side with thirteen baby pigs nursing you would throw off your equilibrium,) straight to the water trough. She gulped water for ten minutes, non-stop!"

I've been told that hogs are the most intelligent of all farm animals. That makes me wonder; what was the sow thinking when she saw me drive up each day? She surely thought that I would come to her rescue. She surely thought that her predicament should have appeared obvious to me. Instead to her surprise and agony, I had completely overlooked what was totally obvious for three full days.

I think that my lack of realization of the sow's predicament had something to do with my perspective. From my perspective, she appeared to be comfortable and relaxed because I was comfortable and relaxed. The sow, however, was stuck and extremely uncomfortable. Therefore, from the sow's perspective, the fact that she was stuck should have appeared obvious to anyone who saw her.

I moderated a dispute this week between two people who don't understand each other. One person is naturally aggressive and confrontational. The other person is naturally timid and non-confrontational. The aggressive person severely criticized the timid person for not forcefully taking charge of the issues that were affecting her life. The timid person refused to respond to the aggressive person's criticisms. The resulting outcome of the dispute was an arrogant victory from the one and bitter feelings from the other. These two people used to be best friends. Now, critical words have driven a wedge between their friendship, and they will be difficult to forget.

Why do some people choose to serve their harshest criticisms on the people they care about the most? I think it has something to do with their perspectives. It appears easy to solve another person's problems - *if you're not struggling with the same problems.*

I could have criticized the old mama sow for crawling underneath that board. I could have told her how to maneuver her legs and feet around to get herself unstuck. I think, however, that she was glad when instead of criticizing her I just chose to show up with a crowbar.

BULLET POINTS

Adjust your perspective.
Think about how the
Other person feels.

Adjust your perspective.
Think about what the
Other person needs.

Some needs are obvious, if
You look for them.

It appears easy to solve
Another person's problems,
If you're not struggling
With the same problems.

You may win
The argument, but
You may lose
The friend.

Try to understand
Your friend's
Point of view.

Choose to
Adjust your
Perspective.

SCRIPTURE ANALYSIS

Matthew 7: 3 - 5

3. And why beholdest thou
  - The NIV says: "Why do you look at"

3. The mote
  - From the Greek word *karphos*, Strong's #2595: A dry twig or straw.
  - The [piece of] a dry twig or straw

3. That is in thy brother's eye,
  - That is in your brother's eye,

3. But considerest not
  - But [do] not consider

3. The beam
  - From the Greek word *dokos*, Strongs #1385: A stick of timber.
  - The stick of timber

3. That is in thine own eye?
  - That is in your own eye?

4. Or how wilt thou say
  - Or [else] how will you [be able to] say

4. To thy brother,
  - To your brother,

4. Let me pull out the mote
  - Let me pull out the [piece of] a dry twig or straw [from]

4. Out of thine eye;
  - Out of your eye;

4. And, behold, a beam
  - And, behold, a stick of timber

4. Is in thine own eye?
  - Is in your own eye?

5. Thou hypocrite,
  - You hypocrite,

5. First
  - [The] first [thing you need to do is]

5. Cast out

- From the Greek word *ekballo*, Strong's #1544: <u>take</u>.
- <u>Take</u> out

5. The <u>beam</u>
- The <u>stick of timber [from]</u>

5. Out of <u>thine</u> own eye;
- Out of <u>your</u> own eye;

5. And then <u>shalt thou</u>
- And then <u>you shall</u> [be able to]

5. See clearly to <u>cast</u> out
- See clearly to <u>take</u> out

5. The <u>mote</u>
- The <u>[piece of] a dry twig or straw [from]</u>

5. Out of <u>thy</u> brother's eye.
- Out of <u>your</u> brother's eye.

CHOICE EXAMINATION

1. Why did the naturally aggressive person severely criticize the timid person for not forcefully taking charge of the issues that were affecting her life?

2. Why did the timid person not respond to the aggressive person's criticisms?

3. What needs to happen in order for the two people to renew and deepen their friendship?

4. In the scripture, why did Jesus say that taking the stick of timber from your own eye is the *first* thing that needs to be done?

5. What can a person see clearly to do after taking the stick of timber out of his own eye?

6. What choices do you need to make in order to *adjust your perspective?*

LET THE PEOPLE INVOLVED HELP MAKE THE DECISIONS

≈ 21 ≈

And it came to pass on the morrow, that Moses sat to judge the people: and the people stood by Moses from the morning unto the evening. And when Moses' father in law saw all that he did to the people, he said, What is this thing that thou doest to the people? why sittest thou thyself alone, and all the people stand by thee from morning unto even?

And Moses said unto his father in law, Because the people come unto me to enquire of God: When they have a matter, they come unto me; and I judge between one and another, and I do make them know the statutes of God, and his laws.

And Moses' father in law said unto him, The thing that thou doest is not good. Thou wilt surely wear away, both thou, and this people that is with thee: for this thing is too heavy for thee; thou art not able to perform it thyself alone. Hearken now unto my voice, I will give thee counsel, and God shall be with thee: Be thou for the people to God-ward, that thou mayest bring the causes unto God: And thou shalt teach them ordinances and laws, and shalt show them the way wherein they must walk, and the work that they must do. Moreover thou shalt provide out of all the people able men, such as fear God, men of truth, hating covetousness; and place such over them, to be rulers of thousands, and rulers of hundreds, rulers of fifties, and rulers of tens: And let them judge the people at all seasons: and it shall be, that every great matter they shall bring unto thee, but every small matter they shall judge: so shall it be easier for thyself, and they shall bear the burden with thee.

Exodus 18: 13 - 22

We had the worst stockroom in the district. It was terrible! By every measurement it was bad. Each day was a series of revolving events. Old freight would clog up the aisles. The receiving crew would push carts of freight to the sales floor so the department managers could work the merchandise onto the shelves. Next, the assistant managers would walk through their areas of the store and tell the department managers to clear off the sales floor. Then the department managers would simply push the carts back to the stockroom. The receiving area remained so congested that unloading the trucks was an extremely slow process. Wal-Mart's expectation was to unload and price 540 cases per hour. We were unloading only 265 cases per hour. I was the new assistant manager. I had been assigned to another area of the store. After I saw the situation in the receiving area, I wanted a chance to fix the big problem area of the store. I asked for, and got my chance.

"All right everyone, here's what we're going to do!" I proceeded to list off several specific directives. I had thought it through and had a definite plan on how to fix all our problems. I met with the store manager and told him I was going to force the other assistant managers to require their department managers to work up the existing carts of freight every morning so we could start each day with lots of space in the stockroom. I assigned jobs and duties to every individual on the unloading crew. I positioned myself in the process so that I would be able to watch every phase of the unloading operation. I visited with the district manager and developed an incentive plan: If our stockroom became the best stockroom in the district, the district manager would come to the store and cook steaks for all the store associates. "We're going to do this up right too! We will get one of those big chef's hats for him to wear!" I said. With all the plans in place, I was excited and totally confident. The next morning's early truck was going to mark our first big success story!

Morning arrived. We flipped on the computer to scan in the cases. "On your mark, get set, GO!" ... To my surprise, however, we didn't make our 540 cases per hour goal. We didn't even come close! I don't think we even improved on our current 265 case average. It was still terrible.

"They must need more motivation," I told Barbie when I returned home that evening. So the next morning I gave them a big pep talk. "I know we can do better than this! We're going to have the best receiving program in the district! Right?! It's going to be great! Now are you ready to try it again?! Come on, now, let's make this a good one! On your mark, get set, GO!"

Two hundred sixty-five.

Three or four days passed. I tried everything I could think of. I instructed people, I scolded people, I worked as hard as I could myself, but we made no improvement. What was I doing wrong? We had three trucks to unload. We had unloaded about half of the second truck when, totally out of frustration, I stopped the whole process. "Let's all go take a break. I'm going to buy each one of you a can of soda pop. Let's talk."

"Guys, I've done everything I know to do and we aren't getting any better. *What do you think we should do?*"

"Well, I think Clay should be standing beside the baler doing nothing but baling the cardboard boxes."

"And I think Garland should be cutting the boxes open."

"I think Tina should wait for the rollers to get filled, before she starts the case count."

"I think Beverly should help out with rollers number two and three. We can help her catch up with roller number four later."

…

I was amazed! They knew what to do! They all knew what to do! They had obviously all talked about what they needed to do among themselves, but I had never chosen to ask them what they thought. In reality, the procedure changes they had suggested were not much different from what I had outlined myself. The main difference was, we were talking about their ideas, not mine. Now they all had the desire to show me what they could accomplish, with *their* ideas.

We timed the next truck that we unloaded as usual. We processed 720 cases per hour. We never processed 265 cases per hour again. We never processed the company goal of 540 cases per hour either. We never got that low.

BULLET POINTS

Let the people involved
Help make the decisions.
They know what they need to do.

Let the people involved
Help make the decisions, and
They will respond in a positive manner.

People like to prove that
Their own ideas work.

Everyone has a good idea sometime.

If a person's important enough
For the job, then the
Person's ideas are
Important enough
To be solicited.

Deep down, everyone wants to be involved
In the decision making process.

You may be able to tell them what to do.
You must choose to ask them
What they think they should do.

Telling the right answer is a good choice.
Soliciting the right answer is a better choice.

Choose to
Let the people involved
Help make
The decisions.

SCRIPTURE ANALYSIS

Exodus 18: 13 - 22

13. And it came to pass on the <u>morrow</u>, that
   - From the Hebrew word *mochorath*, Stong's #4283: <u>next day</u>.
   - And it came to pass on the <u>next day</u>, that

13. Moses <u>sat to judge</u> the people:
   - The NIV says: "Moses <u>took his seat to serve as judge for</u> the people,"

13. And the people stood <u>by</u> Moses from the morning
   - And the people stood <u>[around, waiting for their turn]</u> with Moses from the morning

13. <u>Unto</u> the evening.
   - <u>Until</u> the evening.

14. And when Moses' father in law saw all that <u>he</u> did
   - And when Moses' father-in-law saw all that <u>Moses</u> did

14. <u>To</u> the people,
   - <u>For</u> the people,

14. <u>He</u> said,
   - <u>Moses' father-in-law</u> said,

14. What is this thing that <u>thou doest to</u> the people?
   - What is this thing that <u>you [are] doing for</u> the people?

14. Why <u>sittest thou thyself</u> alone,
   - Why <u>[are] you sitting [to judge the people by] yourself</u> alone,

14. <u>And</u>
   - <u>While</u>

14. All the people stand <u>by thee</u>
   - All the people stand <u>[around, waiting] for you</u>

14. From morning <u>unto even</u>?
   - From morning <u>until evening</u>?

15. And Moses said unto his father in law, Because the people come unto me to <u>enquire</u> of God:
   - And Moses said unto his father-in-law, Because the people come unto me to <u>inquire [about the statutes and laws]</u> of

God:

16. When they have a <u>matter</u>,

    - From the Hebrew word *dabar*, Strong's #1697: <u>a</u> <u>question</u>.

    - When they have a <u>question</u>,

16. They come unto me; and I <u>judge</u>

    - They come unto me; and I [<u>make a</u>] judgment

16. Between <u>one</u>

    - Between <u>one [person]</u>

16. And <u>another</u>,

    - And <u>another [person]</u>,

16. And I do make <u>them</u> know

    - And I do make [<u>sure that</u>] <u>they</u> know

16. The <u>statutes</u> of God,

    - From the Hebrew word *choq*, Strong's #2706: <u>an</u> <u>enactment, commandment, [or] ordinance</u>.

    - The <u>enactments, commandments and ordinances</u> of God,

16. And <u>his</u> laws.

    - And <u>God's</u> laws.

17. And Moses' father in law said unto <u>him</u>,

    - And Moses' father-in-law said unto <u>Moses</u>,

17. <u>The</u> thing

    - <u>This</u> thing

17. That <u>thou doest</u> is not good.

    - That <u>you [are] doing</u> is not good.

18. <u>Thou wilt</u>

    - <u>You will</u>

18. Surely wear <u>away</u>,

    - Surely wear [<u>yourself</u>] <u>away</u>,

18. Both <u>thou</u>,

    - Both <u>you</u>,

18. And <u>this</u> people

    - And <u>these</u> people

18. That <u>is</u>

    - That <u>are</u>

18. With <u>thee</u>:

    - With <u>you</u>:

18. For this thing

\   - For this [process of] making judgments between the people

18. Is too heavy

- Is too heavy [of a burden]

18. For thee;

- For you [to bear];

18. Thou art not

- You are not

18. Able to perform it

- Able to perform [these] duties [of making judgments between the people]

18. Thyself alone.

- Yourself alone.

19. Hearken now unto my voice,

- The NIV says: "Listen now to me"

19. I will give thee

- I will give you

19. Counsel,

- From the Hebrew word *yaats*, Strong's #3289: to advise.
- [Some] advice,

19. And God shall be with thee:

- And God shall be [in agreement] with you [on this]:

19. Be thou for the people

- You be for the people

19. To

- A

19. God-ward,

- The NIV says: "Representative before God

19. That thou mayest

- [So] that you may

19. Bring the causes unto God:

- Also From the Hebrew word *dabar*, Strong's #1697: a question. The same word was translated as *matter* in verse # 16.
- Bring the questions unto God:

20. And thou shalt

- And you shall

20. Teach <u>them</u> ordinances and laws,
- Teach <u>the people</u> ordinances and laws,

20. And <u>shalt</u>
- And [you] <u>shall</u>

20. Show <u>them</u>
- Show <u>the people</u>

20. The way <u>wherein they must walk,</u>
- The NIV says: "The way <u>to live</u>"

20. And the <u>work</u>
- The NIV says: "And the <u>duties</u>"

20. That <u>they</u> must do.
- That <u>the people</u> must do.

21. Moreover <u>thou shalt</u>
- Moreover <u>you shall</u>

21. <u>Provide</u>
- From the Hebrew word *chazah*, Strong's #2372: <u>look</u>.
- <u>Look [for people who can help you from]</u>

21. Out of all the <u>people</u>
- Out of all the <u>[many] people [you are responsible for]</u>

21. <u>Able</u> men,
- Men <u>[who are] able [to make good judgments]</u>

21. <u>Such as</u>
- <u>Such [men] as [these must]</u>

21. <u>Fear</u> God,
- From the Hebrew word *yare*, Strong's #3373: <u>reverent</u>.
- <u>[Have] reverence [for]</u> God,

21. <u>Men of truth,</u>
- <u>[They must be] men [who] are truthful,</u>

21. <u>Hating</u> covetousness;
- <u>[Who] hate [the thought of]</u> covetousness;

21. And <u>place such</u>
- And <u>[once you have chosen them] place such [men as these]</u>

21. Over <u>them,</u>
- Over <u>the people [you are responsible for]</u>,

21. To be <u>rulers</u> of thousands,
- From the Hebrew word *sar*, Strong's #8269: <u>a head</u>

person of any rank or class.
    - To be head persons [in charge] of thousands,
21. And rulers of hundreds,
    - And head persons [in charge] of hundreds,
21. Rulers of fifties,
    - Head persons [in charge] of fifties,
21. And rulers of tens:
    - And head persons [in charge] of tens:
22. And let them judge the people
    - And let the head people [whom you have placed in charge], judge the people
22. At all seasons:
    - From the Hebrew word *eth*, Strong's #6256: time.
    - At all times:
22. And it shall be, that every great matter
    - And it shall be that every question [of] great [importance]
22. They shall
    - They shall [be required to]
22. Bring unto thee,
    - Bring unto you,
22. But every small matter
    - But every question [of] small [importance]
22. They
    - The head people [whom you have placed in charge]
22. Shall judge:
    - Shall judge [themselves]:
22. So shall it
    - So shall the judging process
22. Be easier for thyself,
    - Be easier for you,
22. And they
    - Because the people [whom you have placed in charge]
22. Shall bear the burden
    - Shall bear the burden [of judging the people]
22. With thee.
    - With you.

CHOICE EXAMINATION

1. Why did the store associates not respond to Galen's initial directions for improving the stockroom?

2. Why did the store associates respond better to their own ideas?

3. Why did Galen initially neglect to ask the store associates for ideas?

4. In the scripture, why did Moses try to take on the entire responsibility of judging the people by himself?

5. Why was Moses' father-in-law more able to recognize the need to organize the judging process than Moses was?

6. What choices do you need to make in order to *let the people involved help make the decisions*?

VISIT PEOPLE WHO ARE LONELY
≈ 22 ≈

Pure religion and undefiled before God and the Father is this, To visit the fatherless and widows in their affliction, and to keep himself unspotted from the world.

James 1: 27

"I finally decided that I had a choice to make. I could sit at home and feel sorry for myself, or I could get up and see what I could do to help somebody else. I go by the rest home now every time I buy groceries."

After my dad passed away, Mother struggled with feelings of loneliness. I can only imagine how difficult the adjustments to her life have been after fifty-seven years of marriage! All of us in the family spent additional time visiting Mother in her home. She appreciated the company and she enjoyed frequent visits to our homes too. But something just didn't feel right. Her entire adult life had been consumed with involvements and service to other people. Suddenly, in one day's time, other people were focused on serving her, and she wasn't focused on serving other people. She needed to regain a purpose for her life. That's when she came up with the idea.

"They all really look forward to my visits. Some of them will grab my hand and say, 'Please come back and visit us again soon.' I always tell them what day I'll be back. I don't usually stay long, but I visit once or twice a week."

Mother's visits to the rest home have been a blessing to the residents there. They have been a blessing to Mother, too.

BULLET POINTS

Visit people who are lonely.
They will enjoy
Visiting with you.

Visit people who are lonely.
You will enjoy
Visiting with them too.

A lonely person is still a
person.

Loneliness is curable.

People who are old
Like to visit,
The same as
People who are young.

You can sit at home and
Feel sorry for yourself, or
You can get up, and
See what you can do
To help somebody else.

Choose to
Visit people
Who are lonely.

SCRIPTURE ANALYSIS

James 1: 27

27. Pure
- [An example of] pure
27. Religion
- Religious [service]
27. And
- Which [is]
27. Undefiled
- From the Greek word *amiantos*, Strong's #283: pure [or] unsoiled.
- [Considered] pure and unsoiled
27. Before
- To
27. God and the Father is this,
- God [who] is the [heavenly] Father is this,
27. To visit

- From the Greek word *episkeptomai*, Strong's #1980: <u>look out [or] visit</u>.
  - To <u>visit and look out [for]</u>

27. The <u>fatherless</u>
  - The <u>[children who are] fatherless</u>

27. And <u>widows</u>
  - And <u>[to visit and look out for] widows</u>

27. <u>In</u> their affliction,
  - <u>[While they are] in [the midst of]</u> their affliction,

27. And to keep <u>himself</u>
  - And to keep <u>yourself</u>

27. <u>Unspotted</u>
  - From the Greek word *aspilos*, Strong's #784: <u>unblemished (phys. or mor.)</u>.
  - <u>Morally unblemished</u>

27. <u>From</u> the world.
  - <u>From [the sinful nature of]</u> the world.

CHOICE EXAMINATION

1. Why did the mother decide to visit people in the rest home each week?

2. Why did the visits from family members not feel right to her?

3. How have the rest home visits been a double blessing?

4. In the scripture, why does God consider visiting and looking out for widows and children who are fatherless while they are in the midst of their affliction, to be pure?

5. How does keeping yourself morally unblemished from the sinful nature of the world relate to visiting and looking out for widows and children who are fatherless while they are in the midst of their affliction?

6. What choices do you need to make in order to *visit people who are lonely*?

CHOOSE TO TAKE CARE OF YOUR SOUL

FIND A PLACE TO PRAY EVERY DAY

≈ 23 ≈

And when thou prayest, thou shalt not be as the hypocrites are: for they love to pray standing in the synagogues and in the corners of the streets, that they may be seen of men. Verily I say unto you, They have their reward. But thou, when thou prayest, enter into thy closet, and when thou hast shut thy door, pray to thy Father which is in secret; and thy Father which seeth in secret shall reward thee openly. But when you pray, use not vain repetitions, as the heathen do: for they think that they shall be heard for their much speaking. Be not ye therefore like unto them: for your Father knoweth what things ye have need of, before ye ask him. After this manner therefore pray ye:

> Our Father which art in heaven,
> Hallowed be thy name.
> Thy kingdom come.
> Thy will be done
> in earth, as it is in heaven.
> Give us this day our daily bread.
> And forgive us our debts,
> as we forgive our debtors.
> And lead us not into temptation,
> but deliver us from evil:
> For thine is the kingdom, and the power,
> and the glory, forever. Amen.

Matthew 6: 5 - 13

The hog lot was my favorite place. It didn't smell good... but it was convenient. It was located in a secluded spot in the woods, about a half mile from the house. I used to stop there on my way home from work each day - to pray.

I've always sought out private locations for prayer. When I

pray, I want to feel completely uninhibited. If I want to shout for joy to God, I can do it. If I want to sing praises to God, I can do it. If I want to fall humbly on my face before God with feelings of reverence and admiration, I can do it. If I need to make confessions to God, to repent of my sins, I can do it. If I need to seek God for guidance for a decision in my life, I can do it. If I need to believe God for a miracle for a need in my life, I can do it. But, I can't make any of these expressions to God sufficiently unless I can feel uninhibited to do so. That's why the hog lot was so important to me. That's where I first learned how to *really* pray.

For eight years I kept hogs up in those woods. For eight years that was my favorite place to pray. Even if I worked late into the night, I'd stop at the hog lot and spend thirty to forty-five minutes in prayer and praise before I drove the rest of the way home. Oh, what joy, what peace of mind, what reassurance I felt coming home each evening after spending time in God's presence. It didn't matter how stressful the pressures of the day had been, by the time I arrived home, it was already in God's hands. I'm certain that my wife and children met a better husband and father at the door each evening because of those daily times of prayer.

Sound evidently travels fairly well through the woods. My brother and his family live in the woods about a quarter of a mile straight north of the old hog lot. One day, while praying - loudly - I heard David's voice shout in my direction, "Hey Galen, when you're done praying, come on over to my house. I need to talk to you about something." ...(Oops?!)... (I had no idea that my voice was carrying to his house.) Despite this revelation about sound and distance, I still chose to keep praying at the hog lot. I did, however, lower the volume of my voice... slightly.

A few months later, I learned that one of my neighbors who lived through the woods straight west of the old hog lot got saved and started attending a church!!

I guess sound travels in all directions.

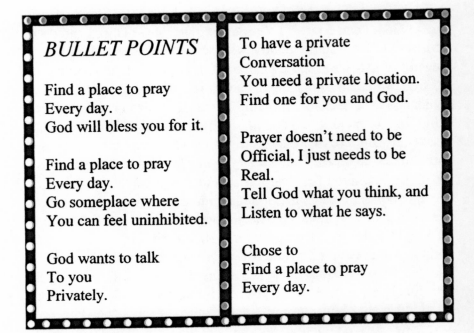

BULLET POINTS

Find a place to pray
Every day.
God will bless you for it.

Find a place to pray
Every day.
Go someplace where
You can feel uninhibited.

God wants to talk
To you
Privately.

To have a private
Conversation
You need a private location.
Find one for you and God.

Prayer doesn't need to be
Official, I just needs to be
Real.
Tell God what you think, and
Listen to what he says.

Chose to
Find a place to pray
Every day.

SCRIPTURE ANALYSIS

Matthew 6: 5 - 13

5. And when <u>thou prayest</u>,
    - And when <u>you pray</u>,
5. <u>Thou shalt</u> not be
    - <u>You shall</u> not be
5. As the <u>hypocrites</u> are:
    - From the Greek word *hupokrites,* Strong's #5273: <u>an actor</u>
<u>under an assumed character</u>.
    - As the <u>[people who] are acting under an assumed</u>
<u>character</u>:
5. For <u>they</u>
    - For <u>[the] people [who are acting under an assumed</u>
<u>character]</u>
5. Love to pray <u>standing</u>
    - Love to pray <u>[while] standing</u>
5. In the <u>synagogues</u>

- The Unger's Bible Dictionary states: "The general direction of affairs was committed to elders, while special officers were appointed for special purposes. But the peculiarity here is that … for the acts proper to public worship - the reading of the Scriptures, preaching and prayer - no special officials were appointed. These acts were, on the contrary, in the time of Christ still freely performed in turn by members of the congregation."

- In the <u>synagogues, [praying publicly in front of the congregation,]</u>

5. And <u>in</u> the corners of the streets,

- And [they also like to pray while standing] on the corners of the streets,

5. <u>That</u>

- [So] that

5. They <u>may</u> be seen

- They <u>will</u> be seen

5. <u>Of</u> men.

- <u>By [other]</u> men

5. <u>Verily</u> I say unto you,

- From the Greek word *amen*, Strong's #281: <u>surely [or] so be it.</u>

- <u>Surely</u> I say unto you,

5. <u>They have</u> their reward.

- <u>The people [who pray while acting under an assumed character] have [received all of]</u> their reward.

6. But <u>thou,</u>

- But <u>you,</u>

6. When <u>thou prayest,</u>

- When <u>you pray,</u>

6. Enter into <u>thy</u>

- Enter into <u>your</u>

6. <u>Closet,</u>

- From the Greek word *tameion,* Strong's #5009: <u>secret chamber.</u>

- <u>Secret chamber,</u>

6. And when <u>thou hast</u>

- And when <u>you have</u>

6. Shut <u>thy</u> door,
> - Shut <u>the</u> door,

6. Pray to <u>thy</u> Father
> - Pray to <u>your [heavenly]</u> Father

6. <u>Which is</u>
> - <u>Who is [revealed to you]</u>

6. In <u>secret</u>;
> - From the Greek word *kruptos*, Strong's #2927: <u>private</u>.
> - In <u>[your] private [times of prayer]</u>;

6. And <u>thy</u> Father
> - And <u>your [heavenly]</u> Father

6. <u>Which seeth</u>
> - <u>Who sees [you praying]</u>

6. In <u>secret</u>
> - In <u>private [times of prayer]</u>

6. Shall reward <u>thee</u> openly.
> - Shall reward <u>you</u> openly.

7. <u>But</u>
> - <u>And</u>

7. When <u>ye</u> pray,
> - When <u>you</u> pray,

7. Use <u>not</u>
> - <u>[Do] not</u> use

7. <u>Vain repetitions</u>,
> - *Vain* comes from the Greek word *maten*, Strong's #3155: <u>to no purpose</u>.
> - <u>Repetitious [words, spoken] to no purpose</u>,

7. As the <u>heathen</u> do:
> - As the <u>heathen [people]</u> do:

7. For <u>they</u>
> - For <u>the heathen [people]</u>

7. Think that they shall be <u>heard</u>
> - Think that they shall be <u>heard [by God]</u>

7. <u>For their much speaking</u>.
> - The NIV says: "<u>Because of their many words</u>."

8. Be not <u>ye</u> therefore
> - Therefore, <u>you [do]</u> not be

8. Like <u>unto them</u>:

    - Like <u>they are</u>:

8. For your <u>Father knoweth</u>

    - For your [heavenly] <u>Father knows</u>

8. What things <u>ye have</u> need of,

    - What things <u>you are [in]</u> need of,

8. Before <u>ye</u> ask him.

    - Before <u>you</u> ask him.

9. After <u>this manner</u>

    - After <u>the [following]</u> manner

9. Therefore pray <u>ye</u>:

    - Therefore, <u>you [should] pray</u>:

9. Our Father <u>which art</u> in heaven,

    - Our Father <u>who is</u> in heaven,

9. <u>Hallowed</u>

    - From the Greek word *hagiazo*, Strong's #37: <u>to make holy</u>.

    - <u>Holy</u>

9. <u>Be thy</u> name.

    - <u>Is your</u> name.

10. <u>Thy kingdom come</u>.

    - <u>[We acknowledge that] your kingdom [has] come [to us]</u>.

10. <u>Thy will</u> be done

    - <u>[And we pray that] your will [shall]</u> be done

10. In <u>earth</u>,

    - From the Greek word *ge*, Strong's #1093: <u>world</u>.

    - In <u>[this] world</u>,

10. As <u>it is</u> in heaven.

    - As <u>your will is [done]</u> in heaven.

11. Give us <u>this</u> day

    - Give us <u>[for] this</u> day

11. Our daily <u>bread</u>.

    - From the Greek word *artos*, Strong's #740: <u>bread (as raised) or a loaf</u>.

    - Our daily <u>loaf of bread</u>.

12. And forgive us <u>our debts</u>,

    - And forgive us <u>[for] our debts [to you]</u>,

12. As <u>we</u> forgive our debtors.

- As <u>we [also]</u> forgive our debtors.

13. And lead us <u>not</u> into temptation,

- And lead us [<u>so that we will</u>] not [<u>fall</u>] into temptation,

13. But <u>deliver</u> us from evil:

- From the Greek word *rhuomai*, Strong's #4606: <u>rescue</u>.

- But <u>rescue</u> us from evil:

13. For <u>thine is</u>

- For <u>you are</u>

13. The <u>kingdom,</u>

- <u>The [ruler of your] kingdom</u>

13. <u>And</u> the power,

- <u>With</u> the power,

13. And the <u>glory,</u> forever.

- And the <u>glory [that lasts]</u> forever.

13. <u>Amen.</u>

- From the Greek word *amen*, Strong's #281: <u>surely [or] so be it</u>. The same word was translated as *verily*, in verse #5.

- <u>So be it</u>.

CHOICE EXAMINATION

1. Why did Galen like to pray at the hog lot?

2. What expressions was Galen able to make to God while praying at the hog lot?

3. Why was it important for Galen to feel uninhibited while he was praying?

4. In the scripture, why were the hypocrites prayers ineffective?

5. Why did Jesus say to enter a secret chamber and shut the door for times of prayer?

6. What choices do you need to make in order to *find a place to pray every day*?

STUDY THE BIBLE EVERY DAY

≈ 24 ≈

Study to shew thyself approved unto God, a workman that needeth not to be ashamed, rightly dividing the word of truth. But shun profane and vain babblings: for they will increase unto more ungodliness.

II Timothy 2: 15, 16

I got it for Christmas. It was a children's edition. The book itself was large in size. It had large printed words and it had lots of pictures. It was full of stories, Bible stories. My guess is that I was eight or nine years old when I received my first Bible. I started reading a chapter from the Bible every day. I no longer read from a children's Bible of course, but the habit I chose to develop as a young child has continued throughout my adult life. I still read from the Bible daily.

I can only imagine what benefit I have gained from reading the Bible. When I was a teenager I wasn't a dedicated Christian. I quit attending church and I scarcely ever prayed. I involved in some things of which I'm not proud now. Even so, I continued reading from the Bible daily. I'm certain that my behavior was influenced by the many Bible stories I read, and they helped me avoid participating in some regrettable sins.

Our church recently purchased two hundred Bibles. We distributed them throughout our classrooms. We determined that it was important for children and adults to learn to study the Bible for themselves. Using a Bible to teach someone is good, but teaching someone to use a Bible is better.

The first time I was asked to teach a Sunday school class I said, "yes" without hesitation. I'm sure I wasn't very effective with my initial attempt at teaching. Although, I was a faithful Bible *reader*, I hadn't yet learned how to be a faithful Bible *studier*. I asked a friend of mine to give me some suggestions. When he arrived at our home, I assumed we would read and study a chapter from the Bible. Instead, we spent an entire hour studying one verse! I remember some of what he taught me about the message in that verse, but more importantly, I remember a basic concept he taught me about Bible study:

Look at every word in the verse, and consider each individual word to be imperative to the message in the verse.

When the Bible says God <u>wilt</u>, that doesn't mean God <u>might</u>. When the Bible says thou <u>shalt</u>, that doesn't mean thou <u>should</u>. When you study the Bible, remember this:

It says exactly what it means, and *you can depend on <u>every</u> word.*

He had an expensive Bible. He always left his Bible in the front seat of his car while he was at work. He often left the windows rolled down. One day I asked him, "Aren't you afraid someone will steal your Bible?"

"Oh, not really," he said. "I figure if someone steals a Bible, they need to read it."

Actually they need to study it. They need to study *every word.*

BULLET POINTS

Study the Bible every day.
It says exactly what it means.

Study the Bible every day.
You can depend on every word.

Look at every word in the verse and
Consider each individual word to be
Imperative to the message in the verse.

Using a Bible to teach someone is
Good, but
Teaching someone to use a Bible is
Better.

Give your child
A children's Bible.
His behavior will be influenced by
The many stories he reads.

Choose to
Study the Bible
Every day.

SCRIPTURE ANALYSIS

II Timothy 2: 15, 16

15. Study
  - Study [the Bible]
15. To shew
  - From the Greek word *paristemi*, Strong's #3936: prove.
  - To prove
15. Thyself
  - Yourself
15. Approved unto God,
  - From the Greek word *dokimos*, Strong's #1384: acceptable.
  - Acceptable unto God,
15. A workman
  - From the Greek word *ergates*, Strong's #2040: teacher.
  - A teacher
15. That needeth not
  - Who [does] not need
15. To be ashamed,
  - To be ashamed [of his lack of knowledge],
15. Rightly
  - From the Greek word *orthos*, Strong's #3723: correctly.
  - Correctly
15. Dividing
  - From the Greek word *orthotomeo*, Strong's #3718: to dissect.
  - Dissecting [the Bible to find]
15. The word of truth.
  - The word of truth [that's found in the Bible scriptures].
16. But shun
  - From the Greek word *periistemi*, Strong's #4026: avoid.
  - But avoid
16. Profane
  - From the Greek word *bebelos*, Strong's #952: wicked.
  - Wicked

16. And vain

    - From the Greek word *kenophonia*, Strong's #2757: fruitless discussion.

    - And fruitless

16. Babblings:

    - Also from the Greek word *kenophonia*, Strong's #2757: fruitless discussion.

    - Discussions:

16. For they

    - For people [who participate in fruitless discussions]

16. Will increase

    - From the Greek word *prokopto*, Strong's #4298: advance.

    - Will [continue to] advance [their opinions]

16. Unto more ungodliness.

    - [And that will lead] unto more ungodliness.

CHOICE EXAMINATION

1. Why did the parents purchase a children's Bible for their child?

2. Why did the church distribute two hundred Bibles throughout the classrooms?

3. Why is it important to consider each individual word in a verse to be imperative to the message in the verse?

4. In the scripture, why is it important for a teacher to study the Bible?

5. Why is it important to avoid wicked and fruitless discussions?

6. What choices do you need to make in order to *study the Bible every day*?

ASK JESUS TO FORGIVE YOUR SINS

≈ 25 ≈

Therefore I will judge you, O house of Israel, every one according to his ways, saith the Lord GOD. Repent, and turn yourselves from all your transgressions; so iniquity shall not be your ruin. Cast away from you all your transgressions, whereby ye have transgressed; and make you a new heart and a new spirit: for why will ye die, O house of Israel? For I have no pleasure in the death of him that dieth, saith the Lord GOD: wherefore turn yourselves, and live ye.

Ezekiel 18: 31 - 32

He was sitting right next to me. Our associate pastor, Brother Richard, was preaching that day. When Richard asked if anyone wanted to repent of their sins, Ken chose to respond. When Richard led Ken in a prayer of repentance, the whole church repeated it with him. When Ken sat back down, he was crying softly. Everyone in the church clapped their hands and smiled. When the service was over, numerous people came by and shook hands with Ken. Several people told Ken they loved him and they were proud of him. Barbie and I drove Ken home that day. When we dropped him off at his house, he was still crying softly. "I've needed to do this for a long time," he said. He's getting baptized next Sunday.

John did baptize in the wilderness, and preach the baptism of repentance for the remission of sins.
Mark 1: 4

Now after that John was put in prison, Jesus came into Galilee, preaching the gospel of the kingdom of God, and saying, The time is fulfilled, and the kingdom of God is at hand: repent ye,

and believe the gospel.
Mark 1: 14, 15

And he spake this parable unto them saying, What man of you, having an hundred sheep, if he lose one of them, doth not leave the ninety and nine in the wilderness, and go after that which is lost, until he find it? And when he hath found it, he layeth it on his shoulders, rejoicing. And when he cometh home, he calleth together his friends and neighbours, saying unto them, Rejoice with me; for I have found my sheep which was lost. I say unto you, that likewise joy shall be in heaven over one sinner that repenteth, more than over ninety and nine just persons, which need no repentance.
Luke 15: 3-7

And when they were come to the place, which is called Calvary, there they crucified him, and the malefactors, one on the right hand, and the other on the left. Then said Jesus, Father, forgive them; for they know not what they do.
Luke 23: 33, 34

SCRIPTURE ANALYSIS

Ezekiel 18: 30 - 32

30. Therefore I will <u>judge</u> you,
   - From the Hebrew word *shaphat*, Strong's #8199: <u>to vindicate or punish.</u>
   - Therefore I will <u>vindicate or punish</u> you,
30. O <u>house</u> of Israel,
   - From the Hebrew word *bayith*, Strong's #1004: <u>family.</u>
   - O [members of the] <u>family</u> of Israel,
30. Everyone according to his <u>ways</u>,
   - From the Hebrew word *derek*, Strong's #1870: <u>a course of life or mode of action.</u>

- Everyone according to his <u>course of life and mode of</u>
<u>action,</u>

30. <u>Saith</u> the Lord GOD.

   - <u>Says</u> the Lord God.

30. <u>Repent,</u>

   - From the Hebrew word *shuwb*, Strong's #7725: <u>turn</u>
<u>away</u>.

   - <u>Turn away [from your sins],</u>

30. And <u>turn</u> yourselves from

   - Also from the Hebrew word *shuwb*, Strong's #7725: <u>turn</u>
<u>away</u>.

   - And <u>turn</u> yourselves <u>away</u> from

30. All your <u>transgressions;</u>

   - From the Hebrew word *pesha*, Strong's #6588: <u>rebellion</u>
<u>[or] sin</u>.

   - All your <u>rebellion [against the Lord God]</u>;

30. So <u>iniquity</u> shall not be

   - From the Hebrew word *avon*, Strong's #5771: <u>sin</u>.

   - So [that] <u>sin</u> shall not be

30. Your <u>ruin.</u>

   - The NIV says, "Your <u>downfall</u>."

31. Cast away from <u>you</u>

   - Cast away from <u>yourself</u>

31. All your <u>transgressions,</u>

   - All your <u>sins and rebellions [against the Lord God]</u>,

31. <u>Whereby</u>

   - From the Hebrew word *asher*, Strong's #834: <u>which</u>.

   - <u>Which</u>

31. <u>Ye</u>

   - <u>You</u>

31. Have <u>transgressed;</u>

   - From the Hebrew word *pasha*, Strong's #6586: <u>rebel</u>.

   - Have <u>rebelled [against the Lord God]</u>;

31. And <u>make</u>

   - From the Hebrew word *asah*, Strong's #6213: <u>get</u>.

   - And <u>get</u>

31. <u>You</u>

- <u>Yourself</u>

31. A new <u>heart</u>

- From the Hebrew word *leb*, Strong's #3820: <u>the feelings, the will and even the intellect.</u>
- Webster's Dictionary defines *will* as: <u>desire.</u>
- A new [set of] <u>feelings and desires</u>

31. And a new <u>spirit</u>:

- From the Hebrew word *ruwach*, Strong's #7307: <u>life</u>.
- And a new <u>life</u>:

31. For why <u>will ye die</u>,

- For why <u>would you [choose to]</u> die,

31. O <u>house</u> of Israel?

- O [<u>members of the</u>] <u>family</u> of Israel?

32. For I <u>have</u> no pleasure

- The NIV says: "For I <u>take</u> no pleasure"

32. In the death of him that <u>dieth, saith</u> the Lord GOD:

- In the death of him that <u>dies, says</u> the Lord God:

32. <u>Wherefore</u>

- From the Hebrew word *ken*, Strong's #3651: <u>so</u>.
- <u>So</u>

32. Turn <u>yourselves</u>,

- Turn [<u>away from</u>] your [<u>sins</u>],

32. And live <u>ye</u>.

- And <u>you [will]</u> live.

Mark 1: 4

4. John did <u>baptize</u> in the wilderness,

- The Unger's Bible Dictionary states: "The baptism of John was not Christian, but Jewish. It was, however, especially a baptism 'unto repentance.' The only faith that it expressed concerning Christ was that his coming was close at hand. They who confessed and repented of their sins and were baptized by John were thus obedient to his call to 'prepare the way of the Lord.'"

- John did <u>baptize [a Jewish baptism symbolizing repentance in preparation of the coming of the Christ]</u> in the wilderness,

4. And preach the baptism of <u>repentance</u>

    - From the Greek word *metanoia*, Strong's #3341: <u>reversal of another's decision</u>.

    - Unger's Bible Dictionary states: "Although faith alone is the condition for salvation (Eph. 2:8-10; Acts 16:31), repentance is bound up with faith and inseparable from it, since without some measure of faith no one can truly repent, and repentance never attains to its deepest character till the sinner realizes through saving faith how great is the grace of God against whom he has sinned. On the other hand there can be no saving faith without true repentance. Repentance contains as essential elements (1) a genuine sorrow toward God on account of sin (II Cor. 7:9, 10; Matt. 5:3, 4; Psa 51). (2) An inward repugnance to sin necessarily followed by the actual forsaking of it (Matt. 3:8; Acts 26:20; Heb. 6:1). (3) Humble self-surrender to the will and service of God (see Acts 9:6, as well as scriptures above referred to)."

    - And preach the baptism of <u>reversing the decision [to sin]</u>

4. <u>For</u>

    - <u>For [the purpose of]</u>

4. The <u>remission</u>

    - From the Greek word *aphesis*, Strong's #859: <u>deliverance</u>.

    - The <u>deliverance [from the penalty]</u>

4. <u>Of</u> sins.

    - <u>Of [committing]</u> sins.

Mark 1: 14, 15

14. Now after that John was put in <u>prison,</u>

    - Unger's Bible Dictionary states: "Herod Antipas had taken Herodias, his brother Phillip's wife, and when John reproved him for this and other sins (Luke 3:19), Herod cast him in prison, the castle of Machaerus, on the eastern shore of the dead sea."

    - Now after that John was put in <u>prison [by Herod Antipas, as retribution for John reproving him for his sins]</u>,

14. Jesus came into <u>Galilee,</u>

    - Unger's Bible Dictionary states: Palestine was divided into three provinces - Judea, Samaria, and Galilee. There are many scripture references to it [Galilee]. The first three gospels are occupied largely with Christ's ministry in Galilee. Of his thirty two parables nineteen were spoken in Galilee, and twenty five of his thirty three great miracles were performed in Galilee. In this province the Sermon on the Mount was spoken. Here our Lord was transfigured."

    - Jesus came into [the province of] Galilee.

14. Preaching the <u>gospel</u> of the kingdom of God,

    - From the Greek word *euaggelion*, Strong's #2098: <u>a good message</u>.

    - Preaching the <u>good message</u> of the kingdom of God,

15. And saying, The time is fulfilled, <u>and</u>

    - And saying, The time is fulfilled, <u>and [therefore]</u>

15. The kingdom of God is <u>at hand</u>:

    - *Hand* is from the Greek word *eggizo*, Strong's #1448: <u>near</u>.

    - The kingdom of God is <u>near to [you]</u>:

15. <u>Repent ye,</u>

    - *Repent* is from the Greek word *metanoeo*, Strong's #3340: <u>reconsider</u>.

    - <u>You [must] reconsider [your status in the kingdom of God]</u>

15. And believe the <u>gospel</u>.

    - And believe the <u>good message [of the kingdom of God]</u>.

Luke 15: 3 - 7

3. And <u>he spake</u>

    - And <u>Jesus spoke</u>

3. This <u>parable</u>

    - From the Greek word *parabole*, Strong's #3850: <u>fictitious narrative of common life conveying a moral</u>.

    - This <u>fictitious narrative of common life conveying a moral</u>

3. Unto <u>them</u>, saying,

    - Unto <u>the Pharisees and scribes (see verse #2)</u>, saying,

4. What man <u>of</u> you,

    - What man [such as one] of you,

4. Having <u>an</u> hundred sheep,

- Having <u>one</u> hundred sheep,

4. If he <u>lose</u>
   - If he <u>loses</u>

4. One of <u>them</u>,
   - One of [his] sheep,

4. <u>Doth</u> not leave
   - <u>Does</u> not leave

4. The ninety <u>and nine</u>
   - The ninety <u>nine</u> [sheep]

4. In the wilderness, and go <u>after that</u> which is lost,
   - In the wilderness, and go [<u>searching</u>] <u>after the</u> [<u>one sheep</u>] which is lost,

4. Until he <u>find it</u>?
   - Until he <u>finds the lost sheep</u>?

5. And when <u>he hath</u>
   - And when <u>the sheep's owner has</u>

5. Found <u>it</u>,
   - Found <u>the lost sheep</u>,

5. <u>He layeth it</u> on his shoulders,
   - <u>The sheep's owner lays the lost sheep</u> on his shoulders,

5. <u>Rejoicing</u>.
   - <u>Rejoicing [as he carries the lost sheep back to rejoin the flock</u>].

6. And when <u>he cometh</u> home,
   - And when <u>the sheep's owner comes</u> home,

6. <u>He calleth</u> together his friends and neighbours,
   - <u>The sheep's owner calls</u> together his friends and neighbors,

6. Saying unto <u>them</u>, rejoice with me; for I have found my sheep which was lost.
   - Saying unto <u>his friends and neighbors</u>, rejoice with me; for I have found my sheep which was lost.

7. I say unto <u>you</u>,
   - I say unto <u>you</u> [scribes and Pharisees],

7. That likewise joy shall be in heaven <u>over</u> one sinner
   - From the Greek word *epi*, Strong's #1909: <u>on behalf of</u>.
   - That likewise joy shall be in heaven <u>on behalf of</u> one

sinner
7. That <u>repenteth,</u>
- That <u>repents [of his sins]</u>,
7. More than <u>over</u>
- More than <u>[joy shall be found in heaven]</u> on behalf of
7. Ninety <u>and nine</u>
- Ninety <u>nine</u>
7. <u>Just</u> persons,
- From the Greek word *dikaios*, Strong's #1342: <u>righteous</u>.
- <u>Righteous</u> persons,
7. <u>Which</u> need no repentance.
- <u>Who</u> need no repentance.

Luke 23: 33, 34

33. And when <u>they</u> were come to the place
- And when <u>the great company of people (verse #27), including women who bewailed and lamented Jesus (verse #27), chief priests and scribes (verse #10), Herod's men of war (verse #11), rulers of the people (verse #13), two malefactors (verse #32), and Jesus</u> were come to the place
33. Which is called <u>Calvary,</u>
- From the Greek word *kranion*, Strong's #2898: <u>skull</u>.
- Unger's Bible Dictionary states: "[Calvary is] the place where Christ was crucified, designated as the place of a skull (Golgotha), either because of the shape of the mound or elevation or because [it was] a place of execution."
- Which is called <u>skull</u>,
33. There they crucified <u>him,</u>
- There they crucified <u>Jesus</u>,
33. <u>And</u>
- <u>And [they also crucified]</u>
33. The <u>malefactors,</u>
- From the Greek word *kakourgos*, Strong's #2557: <u>criminal</u>.
- The <u>[two] criminals</u>,
33. <u>One</u>
- <u>One [criminal was crucified]</u>

33. On the right <u>hand</u>,
- On the right <u>hand [side of Jesus]</u>

33. And the <u>other</u>
- And the <u>other [criminal was crucified]</u>

33. On he <u>left</u>.
- On the <u>left [hand side of Jesus]</u>.

34. Then said Jesus, <u>Father</u>,
- Then said Jesus, <u>Father [God]</u>,

34. Forgive <u>them</u>;
- Forgive <u>all the people of the world (see John 11:49-52)</u>

34. For they know <u>not</u>
- For they <u>[do] not</u> know

34. What they <u>do</u>.
- What they <u>[are] doing</u>.

CHOICE EXAMINATION

1. How did numerous people respond to Ken after the service was over?

2. In the scripture, why were the members of the family of Israel told to turn away from their rebellion against the Lord God?

3. What did John's baptism symbolize?

4. Why shall joy be found in heaven on behalf of one sinner that repents of his sins more than for ninety nine righteous persons who need no repentance?

5. Whom did Jesus ask the Father [God] to forgive?

6. What choice do you need to make in order to *ask Jesus to forgive your sins*?

ACCEPT JESUS AS YOUR SAVIOUR
≈ 26 ≈

FOR the kingdom of heaven is like unto a man that is an householder, which went out early in the morning to hire labourers into his vineyard. And when he had agreed with the labourers for a penny a day, he sent them into his vineyard. And he went out about the third hour, and saw others standing idle in the market place, And said unto them; Go ye also into the vineyard, and whatsoever is right I will give you. And they went their way. Again he went out about the sixth and ninth hour, and did likewise. And about the eleventh hour he went out, and found others standing idle, and saith unto them, Why stand ye here all the day idle?

They say unto him, Because no man hath hired us.

He saith unto them, Go ye also into the vineyard; and whatsoever is right, that shall ye receive.

So when even was come, the lord of the vineyard saith unto his steward, Call the labourers, and give them their hire, beginning from the last unto the first.

And when they came that were hired about the eleventh hour, they received every man a penny. But when the first came, they supposed that they should have received more; and they likewise received every man a penny. And when they had received it, they murmured against the goodman of the house, Saying, These last have wrought but one hour, and thou hast made them equal unto us, which have borne the burden and heat of the day.

But he answered one of them, and said, Friend, I do thee no wrong: didst not thou agree with me for a penny? Take that thine is, and go thy way: I will give unto this last, even as unto thee.

Matthew 20: 1-14

He was eighty-eight years old when he died. Mother wanted her three boys to be involved in the funeral. My younger brother, David, read the obituary and the previous referenced scripture. My older brother, Gary, shared fond memories of our dad. I preached the following sermon:

"My brothers have spoken to you of events concerning our dad's life. I will take my turn now and speak to you about our dad's death and the days leading up to our dad's death. I have a portion of scripture to read to you from the second chapter of II Kings.

AND it came to pass, when the LORD would take up Elijah into heaven by a whirlwind, that Elijah went with Elisha from Gilgal. And Elijah said unto Elisha, Tarry here, I pray thee; for the LORD hath sent me to Bethel. And Elisha said unto him, As the LORD liveth, and as thy soul liveth, I will not leave thee. So they went down to Bethel.

And the sons of the prophets that were at Bethel came forth to Elisha, and said unto him, Knowest thou that the LORD will take away thy master from thy head to day?

And he said, Yea, I know it; hold ye your peace.

And Elijah said unto him, Elisha, tarry here, I pray thee; for the LORD hath sent me to Jericho. And he said, As the LORD liveth and as thy soul liveth, I will not leave thee. So they came to Jericho.

And the sons of the prophets that were at Jericho came to Elisha, and said unto him, Knowest thou that the LORD will take away thy master from thy head to day?

And he answered, Yea, I know it; hold ye your peace.

And Elijah said unto him, Tarry, I pray thee, here; for the LORD hath sent me to Jordan.

And he said, As the LORD liveth, and as thy soul liveth, I will not leave thee. And they two went on.

And fifty men of the sons of the prophets went, and stood to view afar off: and they two stood by Jordan. And Elijah took his mantle, and wrapped it together, and smote the waters, and they were divided hither and thither, so that they

two went over on dry ground. And it came to pass, when they were gone over, that Elijah said unto Elisha, Ask what I shall do for thee, before I be taken away from thee.

And Elisha said, I pray thee, let a double portion of thy spirit be upon me.

And he said, Thou hast asked a hard thing: nevertheless, if thou see me when I am taken from thee, it shall be so unto thee; but if not, it shall not be so.

And it came to pass, as they still went on, and talked, that, behold, there appeared a chariot of fire, and horses of fire, and parted them both asunder; and Elijah went up by a whirlwind into heaven. And Elisha saw it, and he cried, My father, my father, the chariot of Israel, and the horsemen thereof.

The fifteenth of the month was significant for my father. He was born on August 15. He died on March 15. But the most important fact that I will share with you today is that he was saved, accepted Jesus as his Savior, on February 15, thirty days prior to his death. If you knew my dad well, you know this was truly a miracle. Dad was a self-proclaimed agnostic. His official religious claim was that he did not know if God existed. He had worked out in his mind that since he hadn't seen God, nor heard God, nor touched God, he therefore could not verify the existence of God. Since he could not verify the existence of God, he therefore would not humble himself to pray to a god who might not exist.

Dad suffered with Parkinson's disease for many years. Mother was quite attentive in her efforts to care for him. About two years ago, it was discovered that Dad also had cancer. He was too frail to survive the surgery that was needed to eradicate the disease. We all knew his time for continued life was limited.

Everyone in the family talked to Dad about his need to accept Jesus as his Savior. We told him, 'Dad, there's going to come a time when you will be departing this life, and it will be important for you to know that you are right with God.' But it was hard for Dad to accept the existence of God. He had spent his entire life refusing to acknowledge God, and he didn't want to change his beliefs now.

Dad never joined a church. He only attended services two

times a year, Easter and Christmas. He always wanted to see his children or grandchildren in the church plays and the choir presentations. I think he enjoyed the fellowship, but he never accepted the doctrine of the church. I remember being a small child when Dad came to watch me in an Easter program. The pastor asked everyone to stand and bow their heads for a word of prayer. I opened my eyes to peek at my dad. His eyes weren't closed and his head wasn't bowed. He refused to pray to a god whom he could not verify existed.

Dad's health declined. We knew he wouldn't live long. He became interested in talking about the possibility of the existence of God, but nothing more. He still wasn't ready to humble himself before God and accept Jesus as his Savior. 'God may not exist,' he told me, 'and Jesus may have been just a normal man.'

Salvation is a personal matter. We could not accept Jesus as Savior in place of our dad, and we could not force Dad to accept Jesus as his Savior. If he was to be saved, he would have to choose to accept Jesus as his Savior for himself.

Last month, on February 15, Mother left the house to go grocery shopping. At that time, we were able to leave Dad unattended for only brief periods of time. I was assigned the job of checking on Dad while Mother was away. As I walked into the house, the phone was ringing. Dad's sister, Aunt Madge, was calling. When I answered the phone Madge said, 'Galen, I know this is a silly thing to ask, but would you ask Walter if he ever found that spoon he was looking for?'

'I don't know if I ever got back with you Madge; [I was speaking to Madge while addressing the congregation,] but in case you were still wondering about it, he did find the spoon.'

'I've been talking with Walter for quite a while,' Madge said. 'He's concerned. He knows he's going to die. He doesn't know if there's a heaven to go to and he doesn't know if he will be going there if it does exist.'

'I'll go talk to him,' I said.

I walked into his room and knelt down beside his hospital bed, a bed which the hospice organization had provided for him. 'Dad,' I said, 'Aunt Madge said you've been talking to her about God. Would you like to talk some more?'

He said, 'Yes'.

I shared some personal testimony with him about my relationship with God. Then he asked me, 'How can we know that there actually is a God?'

'Well,' I said, 'You just have to look for evidence. Consider for instance, God's Word, the Bible. Did you know that the Bible was written over a period of 1600 years by forty different authors. Did you know that from the first chapter of the first book of the Bible, to the last chapter of the last book of the Bible, there is a single continuous message presented to us. That message is that God loves us and He wants a relationship with us, but sin has separated us from God. That's why God sent His Son, Jesus, to die on a cross and thereby pay for the penalty of our sins. Through faith in Jesus' sacrifice, we can be blessed with a relationship with God. The Old Testament points to that message. The New Testament verifies that message. Another piece of evidence in God's Word is fulfillment of prophesy. Some things prophesied, or in other words, predicted in some portions of scripture are fulfilled in other portions of scripture. There are literally thousands of fulfilled specific prophesies scattered throughout the Bible. Considering the time span involved in the writing of the Bible, the number of people involved, the fulfillment of prophesy, and the continuity of the message presented to us in the Bible, the Bible itself is a miracle. It's evidence of the existence of God.'

Then he said, 'But nobody's ever seen God. How do you know that there is a God when you can't see him?'

'But you've seen miracles,' I replied. 'You've seen miracles happen within your family's lives. You've seen miracles in *my* life. There have been times in my life when you've seen me receive miraculous healing, and you know that. You saw me when I was sick, and yet you know that I am now healed. Remember when I was diagnosed with an incurable disease called essential tremors.' [The disease has symptoms similar to Parkinson's disease.] 'I suffered with it for almost three years, yet God has delivered me from it. I no longer take medication for it, and I no longer have any symptoms of the disease. You know that the doctors said there was no cure for essential tremors, yet you know also that I'm healed. You may not see God, but you do see evidence of God when you see miracles.

'It's just so hard to accept,' he said.

'Well, let's just take a look at someone in the Bible who also was skeptical and had a difficult time accepting the reality of the things of God.' I turned to the third chapter of John and read to my dad the story of a man named Nicodemus.

THERE was a man of the Pharisees, named Nicodemus, a ruler of the Jews: The same came to Jesus by night, and said unto him, Rabbi, we know that thou art a teacher come from God: for no man can do these miracles that thou doest, except God be with him.

Jesus answered and said unto him, Verily, verily, I say unto thee, Except a man be born again, he cannot see the kingdom of God.

Nicodemus saith unto him, How can a man be born when he is old? can he enter the second time into his mother's womb, and be born?

Jesus answered, Verily, verily, I say unto thee, Except a man be born of water and of the Spirit, he cannot enter into the kingdom of God.

I stopped reading so I could try to explain this portion of scripture to my dad. 'It takes a flesh birth, a born of water birth, to enter natural life. My daughter-in-law, Lauren, is pregnant with twin babies right now. The two babies are currently living in their mother's womb. In every pregnant mother's womb there is embryonic fluid; Jesus called it water, which is necessary to protect and grow the baby, or babies, until they are ready to be born. This, the natural pregnancy and birth process, is what I believe Jesus was referring to when he said, '**Except a man be born of water.**' But Jesus also said that we must be born '**of the Spirit**', or else, '**he cannot enter into the kingdom of God.**'

Dad, like Nicodemus, understood the flesh birth, the born of water birth. But, Dad, like Nicodemus, did not understand the spiritual birth. So I read further.

'**That which is born of the flesh is flesh; and that which is born of the Spirit is spirit. Marvel not that I say unto thee, Ye must be born again.**'

'Do you see this Dad? When Jesus said, 'Ye must be born

again,' He wasn't referring to a natural / flesh birth. He was referring to a *spiritual* birth. That's why he said you must be born *again*. Let's read further.'

'The wind bloweth where it listeth, and thou hearest the sound thereof, but canst not tell whence it cometh, and whither it goeth: so is every one that is born of the Spirit.'

I explained, 'When you walk outside, and you see the leaves on the trees moving, you're seeing evidence of the wind. You can't see the wind itself because air is invisible to us, but you know the wind is blowing because you see the evidence. That's a reference to the spiritual aspect of being born again. When you get saved, Jesus doesn't come down and physically shake your hand and God doesn't hand you a document to put in a frame and hang on the wall. But you know a change has taken place because you can feel it. You don't see anything tangible happen, but you know something is different because you feel it. You do, however, see results from being born of the Spirit. When the wind blows the leaves, each leaf's movement is a result of the wind blowing. When a person accepts Jesus as his Savior, the lifestyle changes and the attitude changes that occur are also a result of being born of the Spirit. Let's read some more.'

'Nicodemus answered and said unto him, How can these things be?'

'Jesus answered and said unto him, Art thou a master of Israel, and knowest not these things? Verily, verily, I say unto thee, We speak that we do know, and testify that we have seen; and ye receive not our witness. If I have told you earthly things, and ye believe not, how shall ye believe, if I tell you of heavenly things? And no man hath ascended up to heaven, but he that came down from heaven, even the Son of man which is in heaven. And as Moses lifted up the serpent in the wilderness, even so must the Son of man be lifted up:'

I stopped again to explain. 'When the children of Israel were traveling to the promised land, they got distracted and they rebelled against God. Even though God had miraculously provided for them all along their journey, they chose to give up on God by questioning God's motives. God, however, didn't give up on them. They had traveled far from Egypt, and they were headed toward the

177

promised land. They needed God's protection from all the enemies that surrounded them. God had to re-focus their attention back to him, so he sent fiery serpents among the people. Then, when the people were bitten by the serpents, they repented of their sin and cried out to God for help. So often that's what people do. When things are going well, they ignore God. But when a time of need arises, they repent and cry out to God. So God told Moses to make a serpent of brass and put it on a pole. Everyone who suffered with a snake bite from one of the fiery serpents was required to stare at the serpent of brass, on the pole. After focusing their attention on the serpent of brass, they received their physical healing. Let's understand what Jesus was talking about when he said, '**As Moses lifted up the serpent in the wilderness, even so must the Son of man be lifted up.**' When Jesus said *Son of man*, He was referring to Himself. When Jesus said, '**Even so must the Son of man be lifted up,**' He was referring to the cross on which He would be crucified. The children of Israel had to *focus their attention* on the serpent of brass in order to receive their physical healing. We have to *focus our attention* on Jesus, in order to receive our spiritual healing, or in other words, our salvation.' I continued reading.

'**That whosoever believeth in him should not perish, but have eternal life. For God so loved the world, that he gave his only begotten Son, that whosoever believeth in him should not perish, but have everlasting life. For God sent not his Son into the world to condemn the world; but that the world through him might be saved.**'

'Here's an important part, Dad.'

'**He that believeth on him is not condemned: but he that believeth not is condemned already, because he hath not believed in the name of the only begotten Son of God.**'

I explained a critical concept to my Dad at this time. 'Dad, do you understand, being a good person is not good enough. You've been a good person your whole life. But you're in condemnation if you don't believe in the Son of God; if you don't accept Jesus as your Savior.' Then I turned directly to him and said, 'Dad, would you like to be saved?'

He said, 'Yes.'

Then I said, 'Would you like to pray a sinner's prayer of

repentance, and ask Jesus to forgive you of your sins?'

He said, 'Yes, but I don't know how to pray.'

He was a man who had lived eighty-eight years, but never in his life had he prayed. Remember his refusal to bow his head at the Easter service. I suppose that if you had an opportunity to talk to the most wicked scoundrel in the country, you'd probably find out that at some time in his life, he had gotten into trouble and had cried out to God. But that's not true of my Dad. He never prayed. He didn't even know how to pray.

I said, 'It's easy. Just talk to God.'

He said, 'I just don't know if I can do it.'

I said, 'Would you like me to pray with you? You can just repeat after me.'

He said, 'Yes.'

I walked over to the hospital bed. I knelt down beside him. I held his hand. I opened my mouth and started to pray. All of a sudden, the phone rang. I didn't want to let the moment pass so I ignored it for about three rings. Then I decided that it was too much distraction. I answered the phone. It was Diane, Gary's wife.

She said, 'I was just checking on Walter. How's he doing?'

I said, 'Diane, he's about to pray through to salvation *right now.*'

'Oh! I'll hang up the phone.'

We both hung up the phone. I walked back to the bedroom. I visited with Dad a little bit more, then I said, 'Are you ready, again, to pray?'

He said, 'Yes.'

I knelt down beside him again. I held his hand. I closed my eyes. I opened my mouth to begin praying when, once again, the phone rang. This time I didn't wait for three rings. I got up immediately and walked into the next room to answer the phone. As I was walking to the phone, the door swung open, and into the house walked my daughter Amy. She was one step ahead of me, so she answered the phone before I could get to it. I was thinking, 'I can't let this opportunity pass.' I turned around and walked back to the bedroom again. I got to the same spot, bypassing any discussion this time. I got down on one knee. I grabbed hold of my dad's hand. I closed my eyes and opened my mouth to pray when... into the room walked my wife, Barbie, and Amy.

'Hi, Granddad! How are you doing!?'

They immediately realized something significant and personal was happening and they backed out of the room with an 'Oh! We're sorry. We'll come back later.'

There had been a lot of distractions, but, it appeared now that we had our opportunity to pray. I turned to my dad and said, 'Dad, are you ready to pray a sinner's prayer of repentance, to ask Jesus to forgive you of your sins, now?'

He looked at me and said, 'No.'

No?! All I could think was... 'Awwwwwwwwgh!!!'

Then he said, 'I've been thinking about it. I think I'd like my family to be here for this.'

'Oh ....well... Ok! Great idea!'

He then said, 'I want to get *all* my family here!'

I said, 'Well, Kayla [David's daughter] is in Weatherford, Oklahoma. I don't know if we can get her here.' I was thinking that we shouldn't put this off for a week. 'But I can get my brothers and some of our children here. Would that be all right?'

He said, 'Yes.'

I contacted my brothers, told them what was happening, and asked them to bring as many of their children as were available. I called my children. My mother arrived home, found out what was happening, and then she started calling people and telling them to pray for this event.

That evening, we all met at Mother and Dad's house at seven o'clock. We gathered around the kitchen table. We shared some personal testimony about our salvation experiences and our relationships with God. We read the scripture about the story Jesus told concerning the laborers who went to the field at different times of the day; yet when it came time for them to receive their wages, they all received the same payment. Gary said, 'You see Dad, it doesn't matter that you are waiting until you're eighty-eight years old to get saved. The payment is still the same. You'll go to heaven the same as you would if you would have accepted Jesus as your Savior when you were a young person.'

Someone said, 'Are you ready to pray?'

He said, 'Yes,' and *'I hope Jesus can forgive me of my*

sins.'

We all spoke at once. 'Oh yes, Dad! Jesus can forgive you! Absolutely, Dad! Jesus will forgive you!'

Karissa [David's daughter] had a written-out prayer of repentance. Here's what it said:

Heavenly Father, I have sinned against you.
I want forgiveness for all my sins.
I believe that Jesus died on the cross for me and arose
again.
Father, I give you my life to do with as you wish.
I want Jesus to come into my life and into my heart.
This I ask in Jesus' name.
Amen.

David was sitting next to Dad. He read the words of this prayer, one line at a time, and Dad repeated every word. It was his first prayer. He repeated each line with emotion and in a strong voice. When it came time for Amen, he almost shouted out - 'AMEN!'

Dad was never an affectionate person, but he felt emotional at the time. He wanted to express it to us in some way. When he finished praying, we were all still sitting around the table smiling at each other. Dad said, 'I'd like to shake everyone's hand!' We all stood up, lined up in a row, and each one of us took our turn shaking his hand. No sooner had we finished shaking Dad's hand and offering our congratulations that he spoke to us again and said, 'I want to give everyone a hug!' We all lined up, again, and allowed him to give each one of us a hug. Once this was completed, and we had all sat back down, Dad said, 'I want you all to know that *I love you very much.*'

I'm forty-nine years old. That was the first time I can ever remember hearing my father say that he loved me. I knew that he surely did, but he never shared things like that. Dear friends, can you see the change that takes place, immediately in people's lives, when they allow Jesus to take the load of the sin that they've been carrying and they allow God to replace sin's burden with his love! Dad was never able to express to his children that he loved them, because he never knew that God loved him. Once Dad chose to accept Jesus as his Savior, the shackles of sin were released, and he was free to receive love and free to express love.

We had about a week to rejoice. Dad had about a week of mental clarity before his mind started failing him. But during that week, his mind was alert and rational. He participated in Bible study every day. He had prayer before each meal, and he had a time of personal prayer to God each day. His demeanor took on a sweetness that we had never seen before. The change in his life was truly amazing.

After about a week, as Dad's mind began to fail him, he was no longer able to have conversations or think rationally. His body began shutting down and the dying process took over.

Remember the scripture that I started with today: **Elijah went up by a whirlwind into heaven, and Elisha saw it.**

We had some hospice nurses attending to Dad for the last few weeks of his life. They were quite helpful. We appreciate them very much. Mother's favorite nurse was a lady named Suzy. About 4:00 A.M. on the morning that my dad was to pass away, Mother called hospice, and Suzy came to assist the family. Suzy had seen death many times. That's what she does for a living. She assists patients and their families with the dying process. We three boys were taking turns staying with Dad in his final days. Gary refused to leave, but David and I took turns each night. It was my night off. Dad's health had deteriorated. He was suffering terribly. At about 6:45 A.M., there was a call at my house. Barbie answered the phone. Mother said, 'Tell Galen to get over here right now!'

I jumped up and got into my clothes. As I was putting on my shirt, a button popped off. I fumbled with the button situation for about fifteen to twenty seconds. Barbie scolded me, 'Don't worry about that button, just go!' I ran out the door and drove quickly down the road to my mother and dad's house. At the same instant that I was opening the door and taking my first step to enter the house, Dad breathed his last breath, and Suzy pronounced him to be dead.

I walked into the bedroom. Everyone was sitting around the bed facing the body of my father. I could immediately tell that life was gone from my father's face. I had been watching him almost constantly for the last couple of days, not being sure at any time if life was going to continue to the next breath. But seeing him now, it was easy to recognize that life was gone. He just looked different. Something about a person's appearance changes when life has left the body. They began to share with me what had happened. They said that Dad had suffered terribly throughout the night. But, in that last few minutes of Dad's life, a peaceful look had come across his face. They said he had died *peacefully*. Sometime during that last few minutes, when the peaceful look was on his face, Suzy had turned to my brothers and my mother and said, 'Your father / your husband, *is viewing the Promised Land* right now.'

Elijah went up by a whirlwind into heaven, and Elisha saw it.

I can only imagine what my father was seeing as he was viewing the Promised Land.

We were all standing around the hospital bed. Dad's body was still warm and we were all touching his arms or holding his hand. Someone turned the light on and Mother said 'Turn the light off. Walter never liked it shining in his eyes.' He was gone, but Mother was acting like he was still alive. As I stood there by the bed, looking at my dad, all I could see was *death*. But, from my father's perspective, he was viewing the Promised Land, and all he could see was *life*!

Elijah went up by a whirlwind into heaven, and Elisha saw it!

Dear friends! If only we could see what our loved ones see as they leave this life and enter the Promised Land. When Elijah entered heaven by the whirlwind, Elisha saw it! I was viewing the body, and all I could see was death. But Dad was viewing the Promised Land, and all he could see was life.

I can only imagine what was taking place at that time. I remembered the last words my dad said before he prayed the sinner's prayer: '*I hope Jesus can forgive me of my sins.*' I can imagine that at the very moment we were gathered around the bed, viewing the body which used to contain my father, Dad was at that moment standing at the entrance gate to Heaven. I can imagine my dad turning to the gate keeper and repeating those same words, ' *I hope Jesus can forgive me of my sins.*' I would presume that the first person to step out and greet the new arrival would be Jesus himself. I can imagine Jesus hearing my dad say those words, 'I hope Jesus can forgive *me* of *my* sins,' and Jesus himself stepping out from behind a gate post, reaching out his hand and saying 'Welcome, Walter. Yes, I can forgive you... I just did... I just did."

For all have sinned and come short of the glory of God. Romans 3:23

But God commendeth his love toward us, in that, while we were yet sinners, Christ died for us. Romans 5: 8

For the wages of sin is death; but the gift of God is eternal life through Jesus Christ our Lord. Romans 6:23

That if thou shalt confess with thy mouth the Lord Jesus, and shalt believe in thine heart that God hath raised him from the dead, thou shalt be saved. For with the heart man believeth unto righteousness; and with the mouth confession is made unto salvation. Romans 10:9-10

SCRIPTURE ANALYSIS

Matthew 20: 1 - 14

1. FOR the kingdom of heaven is <u>like</u> unto
- From the Greek word *homoios*, Strong's #3664: <u>similar in appearance or character</u>.
- For the kingdom of heaven is <u>similar</u> unto

1. A man <u>that</u> is
- A man <u>who</u> is

1. <u>An</u>
- <u>The</u>

1. Householder,
- From the Greek word *oikodespotes*, Strong's #3617: <u>master of the house</u>.
- <u>Master of the house,</u>

1. <u>Which</u> went out early in the morning
- <u>Who</u> went out early in the morning

1. To hire labourers <u>into</u> his vineyard.
- To hire laborers [to work] <u>in</u> his vineyard.

2. And when <u>he</u>
- And when <u>the master of the house</u>

2. Had <u>agreed</u> with the labourers
- Had [made an] agreement with the laborers

2. <u>For</u>
- <u>For</u> [them to work for]

2. <u>A penny</u> a day,
- Unger's Bible Dictionary states: From the parable of the laborers in the vineyard it would seem that a denarius [penny] was then the ordinary pay for a day's labor [comparable to] about fifteen cents [today].
- [The normal wage of] a penny a day,

2. <u>He</u> sent
- <u>The master of the house</u> sent

2. <u>Them</u> into his vineyard.
- <u>The laborers</u> into his vineyard.

3. And <u>he</u> went out

- And <u>the master of the house</u> went out

3. <u>About</u>
- <u>[At]</u> about

3. <u>The third hour,</u>
- <u>Nine o'clock A.M.,</u>

3. And saw <u>others</u> standing idle in the marketplace,
- And saw <u>other [laborers]</u> standing idle in the marketplace,

4. And <u>said</u>
- And <u>[the master of the house] said</u>

4. Unto <u>them</u>;
- Unto <u>the laborers [who were standing idle in the marketplace]</u>;

4. Go <u>ye</u> also
- <u>You</u> go also

4. <u>Into</u> the vineyard,
- <u>[To work] in</u> the vineyard,

4. And <u>whatsoever</u> is right
- And <u>whatever [payment]</u> is right

4. I will <u>give you.</u>
- I will <u>give [that pay to]</u> you.

4. And <u>they</u>
- And <u>the laborers [who had been standing idle in the marketplace]</u>

4. Went <u>their way.</u>
- Went <u>[on] their way [to the vineyard to work]</u>.

5. <u>Again</u>
- <u>[And] again</u>

5. <u>He</u> went out
- <u>The master of the house</u> went out

5. <u>About</u>
- <u>[At] about</u>

5. <u>The sixth and ninth hour,</u>
- <u>Noon and three o'clock P.M.,</u>

5. And did <u>likewise.</u>
- And did <u>likewise, [hiring laborers for his vineyard]</u>.

6. And <u>about</u>
- And <u>[at] about</u>

6. The eleventh hour
- Five o'clock P.M.

6. He went out,
- The master of the house went out,

6. And found others standing idle,
- And found other [laborers] standing idle,

6. And saith
- And [the master of the house] said

6. Unto them,
- Unto the laborers,

6. Why stand ye here
- Why [are] you standing here

6. All the day idle?
- All [of] the day idle?

7. They say
- The laborers said

7. Unto him,
- Unto the master of the house

7. Because no man hath hired us.
- Because no man has hired us.

7. He saith
- The master of the house said

7. Unto them,
- Unto the laborers,

7. Go ye also
- You go also

7. Into the vineyard;
- [To work] in the vineyard;

7. And whatsoever is right,
- And whatever [payment] is right,

7. That shall
- That [amount of pay] shall

7. Ye receive.
- You receive.

8. So when even was come,
- So when evening had come,

8. The lord of the vineyard

- From the Greek word *kurios*, Strong's #2962: <u>supreme in authority</u>
- The [<u>master of the house who had</u>] <u>supreme authority</u> of the vineyard

8. <u>Saith</u> unto
- <u>Said</u> unto

8. His <u>steward</u>,
- From the Greek word *epitropos*, Strong's #2012: <u>domestic manager</u>.
- His <u>domestic manager</u>;

8. Call the labourers, and give <u>them</u>
- Call the laborers, and give <u>the laborers</u>

8. Their <u>hire</u>,
- From the Greek word *misthos*, Strong's #3408: <u>wages</u>.
- Their <u>wages</u>,

8. Beginning <u>from</u>
- Beginning <u>with</u>

8. The <u>last</u>
- The <u>last [laborer hired]</u>

8. <u>Unto</u>
- The NIV says, "<u>And going on to</u>"

8. The <u>first</u>.
- The <u>first [laborer hired]</u>.

9. And when <u>they</u> came
- And when <u>the laborers</u> came

9. <u>That</u> were hired
- <u>Who</u> were hired

9. <u>About</u>
- [<u>At</u>] <u>about</u>

9. <u>The eleventh hour</u>,
- <u>Five o'clock P.M.</u>

9. <u>They</u>
- <u>The laborers [who were hired at five o'clock P.M.]</u>

9. Received <u>every</u> man
- Received [<u>the same as</u>] every [<u>other</u>] man

9. <u>A</u> penny.
- [<u>The normal wages of</u>] <u>a</u> penny.

10. But when the <u>first</u>
> - But when the <u>first [laborers hired]</u>

10. <u>Came</u>,
> - <u>Came [to receive their pay]</u>,

10. <u>They</u>
> - <u>The laborers [who were hired first]</u>

10. Supposed <u>that they</u>
> - <u>[Assumed] that they [were]</u> supposed

10. <u>Should</u> have received
> - <u>To</u> have received

10. <u>More</u>;
> - <u>More [pay than the laborers who were hired later in the day]</u>;

10. <u>And they</u> likewise
> - <u>But, the laborers [who were hired first]</u> likewise

10. Received <u>every</u> man
> - Received <u>[the same as]</u> every <u>[other]</u> man

10. <u>A</u> penny.
> - <u>[The normal wages of]</u> a penny.

11. And <u>when they</u>
> - And <u>after the laborers [who were hired first]</u>

11. Had received <u>it</u>,
> - Had received <u>their pay</u>,

11. <u>They</u> murmured against
> - <u>The laborers [who were hired first]</u> murmured against

11. The <u>goodman</u> of the <u>house</u>,
> - Both *Goodman* and *house* are translated from the Greek word *oikodespotes*, Strong's #3617: <u>master of the house</u>. The same word was translated as *householder* in verse #1.
> - The <u>master of the house [who had hired them]</u>,

12. Saying, These <u>last</u>
> - Saying, these <u>last [people hired]</u>

12. Have <u>wrought</u>
> - From the Greek word *poieo*, defined by Strong's Concordance as: <u>work</u>.
> - Have <u>worked</u>

12. <u>But</u> one hour,

- <u>Only</u> one hour,
12. And <u>thou hast</u>
- And <u>you have</u>
12. Made them <u>equal</u> unto us,
- Made them <u>[to be paid an amount]</u> <u>equal</u> unto us,
12. <u>Which</u> have
- <u>Who</u> have
12. <u>Borne</u> the burden and heat of the day.
- From the Greek word *bastazo*, Strong's #941: <u>endure</u>.
- <u>Endured</u> the burden and heat of the day.
13. But <u>he</u> answered
- But the <u>master of the house</u> answered
13. One of <u>them</u>,
- One of <u>the laborers [who was hired first and had endured the burden and heat of the day]</u>
13. And said, Friend, I <u>do thee no wrong</u>:
- And said, Friend, I <u>[am]</u> doing nothing wrong <u>[to]</u> you:
13. <u>Didst</u> not
- <u>Did</u> not
13. <u>Thou agree</u> with me
- <u>You [make an] agreement</u> with me
13. <u>For</u> a penny?
- <u>[To work] for</u> a penny?
14. Take <u>that thine is</u>,
- Take <u>[the pay] that is yours</u>,
14. And go <u>thy</u> way:
- And go <u>[on] your</u> way:
14. I will give unto this <u>last</u>,
- I will give unto this <u>last [group of laborers hired]</u>,
14. <u>Even</u> as
- <u>[The] same [wages]</u> as
14. Unto <u>thee</u>.
- Unto <u>you</u>.

Romans 3: 23

23. For all
- For all [people]

23. Have sinned,
- From the Greek word *hamartano*, Strong's #264: to miss the mark and so not share in the prize.
- Have missed the mark [before God] and therefore can not share in the prize [of eternal life],

23. And come short
- From the Greek word *hustereo*, Strong's #5302: to fall short [or] be deficient.
- And [have been found] deficient and fallen short

23. Of the glory of God;
- From the Greek word *doxa*, Strong's #1391: glory as very apparent.
- Webster's Dictionary defines glory as: praise, honor, or distinction extended by common consent.
- Of the very apparent praise honor and distinction of God;

Romans 5: 8

8. But God commendeth
- From the Greek word *sunistao*, Strong's #4921: to introduce favorably [or] to exhibit.
- The NIV says, "Demonstrates"
- But God favorably introduces and demonstrates

8. His love toward us,
- From the Greek word *eis*, Strong's #1519: to.
- His love to us,

8. In that,
- By this [example]

8. While we were yet sinners, Christ died for us.
- While we were still sinners, Christ died for us.

Romans 6: 23

23. For the <u>wages</u>
> - From the Greek word *opsonion*, Strong's #3800: <u>rations for a soldier, pay [or] wages</u>
> - For the <u>rations or payment a soldier [receives]</u>

23. <u>Of</u>
> - <u>For</u>

23. <u>Sin</u> is death;
> - From the Greek word *hamartia*, Strong's #266: <u>offence</u>.
> - <u>[Committing an] offence</u> is death;

23. But the <u>gift</u>
> - From the Greek word *charisma*, Strong's #5486: <u>deliverance from danger or passion, a spiritual endowment [or] free gift</u>.
> - But the <u>free spiritual deliverance from danger</u>

23. <u>Of</u> God
> - <u>[Which is given to you]</u> by God

23. Is eternal life <u>through</u> Jesus Christ our Lord.
> - Is eternal life <u>[which is accomplished] through</u> Jesus Christ our Lord.

Romans 10: 9, 10

9. That if <u>thou shalt</u>
> - That if <u>you shall</u>

9. <u>Confess</u>
> - From the Greek word *homologeo*, Strong's #3670: <u>acknowledge</u>.
> - <u>Acknowledge</u>

9. With <u>thy</u> mouth
> - With <u>your</u> mouth

9. <u>The</u>
> - <u>[That]</u>

9. <u>Lord Jesus,</u>
> - Jesus <u>[is your] Lord</u>

9. And <u>shalt</u> believe
> - And <u>shall</u> believe

9. In <u>thine</u>
> - In <u>the</u>

9. Heart
    - From the Greek word *kardia*, Strong's #2588: the thoughts or feelings (mind).
    - Thoughts and feelings [of your] mind

9. That God hath raised him from
    - That God has raised Jesus [back to life] from

9. The dead,
    - His dead [body],

9. Thou shalt
    - You shall

9. Be saved.
    - Unger's Bible dictionary states: "In the New testament salvation is regarded almost exclusively as [freedom] from the power and dominion of sin. And of this Jesus Christ is the author (see Matt. 1:21; Acts 4:12; Heb. 2:10; 5:9, et al). It is freely offered to all men, but is conditioned upon repentance and faith in Christ (see John 3:16; Heb. 2:3, et al)."
    - Be saved [from your sins].

10. For with the heart
    - For with the thoughts and feelings [of a man's] mind

10. Man believeth
    - [Is how a] man believes

10. Unto
    - [And] becomes

10. Righteousness;
    - From the Greek word *dikaiosune*, Strong's #1343: equity of character or act.
    - [Qualified as] equal in character [to God];

10. And with the mouth
    - And with your mouth

10. Confession is made
    - Acknowledgement [that Jesus is your Lord] is made

10. Unto
    - [Which brings you] unto [the state of]

10. Salvation.
    - Salvation [from your sins].

CHOICE EXAMINATION

1. Why was the father a self proclaimed agnostic?

2. Why do you think the father wanted his family to be with him when he accepted Jesus as his savior?

3. Why was the father never able to tell his children he loved them before he accepted Jesus as his savior?

4. In the scripture, why did the master of the house pay every laborer the same amount?

5. What steps for accepting Jesus as your savior are outlined in Romans 3:23, 5:8, 6:23, and 10:9-10?

6. What choices do you need to make in order to *accept Jesus as your savior*?

RECEIVE GOD'S POWER
≈ 27 ≈

But ye shall receive power, after that the Holy Ghost is come upon you: and ye shall be witnesses unto me both in Jerusalem, and in all Judea, and in Samaria, and unto the uttermost part of the earth.

Act 1: 8

"Read the four Gospels: Matthew, Mark, Luke and John, and see what Jesus had to say about the Holy Ghost. Read the book of Acts and see what happened to members of the early church. Pay attention as you read the rest of the New Testament."

It wasn't a very fulfilling answer. I was working at my first job as a clerk in a convenience store. I had started attending a Pentecostal church. I had heard some people praying in tongues and I didn't understand what was happening. I just wanted to know what was going on. A local minister had entered the store to make a purchase. I had asked him for an explanation of this activity. Basically, he had told me to look it up for myself!

I took his advice. I decided the answers to my questions were all located in the Bible. I determined to read it without any preconceived notions. It was probably a year later before I came to the following five conclusions.
The Bible claims:

(1.) There is a gift which Jesus promised he would send to us.
(2.) This gift indeed arrived, on the day of Pentecost.
(3.) Evidence of this gift is found throughout the New Testament.
(4.) This gift is still available today.
(5.) This gift is the power of the Holy Ghost.
I started seeking God for it.

People probably got tired of praying with me. I spent the

next two years frequenting the front of the church during altar call time, seeking God for the power of the Holy Ghost. Invariably, some of the faithful men and women of the church would lay hands on me praying that I would receive this gift from God. Each time would end with the same response. Nothing would happen.

One day I came home upset about a situation at work. (It's discussed in chapter #51.) When I arrived home the house was empty. The only available source to sound off to was God. I decided to pray. "Lord, it's not fair!" I said. "This shouldn't be happening to me! I don't deserve this! Don't you see what's happening? Shouldn't you get involved and change this situation? Why aren't you doing something about this?!"

Suddenly, a realization hit me. "Galen, this is God you're talking to. Get control of yourself and put this in its proper perspective." I paused for a few seconds, gathered my thoughts and calmed down. I resumed praying. "Lord, I apologize to you. I realize that I've taken a relatively small situation and blown it out of proportion. I realize, Lord, that I'm just a small speck in a giant universe, and this situation at work really isn't all that significant. Lord, I want the right perspective…. and *that's why I want the power of the Holy Ghost*."

During times of prayer at the church's altar, seeking God for the power of the Holy Ghost, I've sometimes had people give me instructions. "God will anoint you, but you still have to speak. Open your mouth and pray out loud." I'm sure I was receiving appropriate instructions. However, when God filled me with the Holy Ghost, right there in my house, I didn't have to think about the process. God took over! An overwhelming presence of God's Spirit encompassed me and I started praying in tongues. The petty things of this life which had caused me to be upset, only moments before, suddenly felt like minor inconveniences. All I wanted was more of God's Spirit, God's Holy Spirit. I continued praying in tongues for several minutes.

I heard a car drive up. It was Barbie arriving home from shopping. I ran outside to tell her. "Barbie, I've just received the power of the Holy Ghost! Quickly, come inside and pray with me!" We knelt down by the couch in the living room. I felt self-conscious about praying in tongues. "I'm just going to pray in normal English and thank the Lord for anointing me," I said. I started praying, "Dear Lord I ...." I couldn't stop it. I started praying in tongues again.

It's been twenty-eight years since I received that initial infilling of God's Holy Spirit. I continue to pray in tongues daily. God's presence has blessed me with comfort in times of sorrow, strength in times of adversity, and boldness in my witness to others.

I wanted more. I read in the Bible in I Corinthians, chapter twelve, that there were spiritual gifts available. Verse thirty-one says **"But covet earnestly the best gifts."**

"I'm going to dedicate an hour a day for prayer to seek God for a spiritual gift," I told Barbie. I prayed daily for about a month without receiving any indications of a response from God. Then one day, while praying in normal English, I felt the presence of God descend upon me. "This is it!" I thought. I became increasingly excited in anticipation of what God was going to do. I began praying more loudly, praising God and firmly believing that he was going to anoint me with a spiritual gift. Just as God's presence seemed to be the strongest, I began, without effort from my part, forcefully and distinctly praying in tongues.

I was confused. I thought God had used the tongues to stop me. "Lord" I said, "Why did you stop me when I was getting so close?"

Immediately, a voice spoke to me (for one of only two times in my life) and said, *"Man, I didn't stop you. That's when I filled you."* I didn't know what doors this encounter with God had opened, but I knew that God had done a work in my life. The work had been enabled, because I had received the gift of the power of the Holy Ghost.

For several years I had suffered from a reoccurring moderate pain in my abdomen. This time, however, the pain was severe. I was standing at the cash register in the Sporting Goods department, taking a man's money for a fishing reel he was purchasing. The pain hit me so quickly and severely that I wasn't sure I'd be able to hand his change back to him. I finished the transaction and immediately started walking toward the associate lounge. An assistant manager saw me. "What's wrong?" he said.

"You look like you're in pain." Someone drove me to the hospital emergency room while another person called my wife.

The doctor was speaking to me. "It appears that you have a kink in your colon. You know how a garden hose can get kinked and restrict the water pressure. Your colon may have enough kink in it to build up a gas pressure and cause you this pain."

Several months later I was at my favorite prayer location, the hog lot, praying. A spirit of praise had fallen upon me. I spent about thirty minutes just singing and praising God. It was late at night and I needed to go home. I shifted the pickup into reverse and started backing out of the hog lot. As I was backing up, I remembered that I had this pain in my abdomen, and it was hurting at that time. I prayed these words: "Lord, I thank you for healing me of this pain, in Jesus name. Hallelujah!!" The instant I said the word - "Hallelujah!" - *I felt a hand reach into my abdomen, make a twisting motion, and come back out.* I have never had any kind of surgery. I had never thought of this fact before; I could feel the hand touching my internal organs. I didn't realize that our internal organs had the sense of touch. I had been touched literally by the hand of God or one of God's messengers. The problem which had caused the pain in my abdomen had been corrected. I was instantly healed. The pain has never reoccurred. A miracle healing had occurred because I had received a gift of healing enabled by the power of the Holy Ghost.

Some time later I made an agreement to go into management training with Wal-Mart. The company was opening up a lot of stores in California and they needed people with store experience to move to that area of the country. Barbie and I were sitting in a pew at church listening to a song someone was singing. Suddenly, I heard a voice speak to me (this was the second occasion I referred to) and say, "Wal-Mart's not the way for you to go." I immediately turned to Barbie as she simultaneously turned to me. When the church service was over, I told Barbie, "I heard the Lord speak to me while Loretta was singing tonight."

"I heard a voice, too!" she said. "What did God tell you?"

"He said 'Wal-Mart's not the way for you to go'. What did He tell you?"

"He said 'It will be all right'. "

A direction had been issued for my life from God. I learned that the focus of my work at Wal-Mart must not be career success, but ministry success, serving the needs of associates and customers with a Christian witness. I cancelled my plans to enter the management program for Wal-Mart at that time. A few years later, I joined the management team at Wal-Mart and became the manager of a small store within driving distance of my house and farm. This gift of guidance was able to be issued to me, because Barbie and I had received power from the Holy Ghost.

We live a mile down a dirt road. Joshua was only a toddler at the time. He was sitting in our driveway playing in the dirt. I heard a truck rumbling down the road, perhaps a half mile away. A terrifying fear came upon me. I ran to Joshua, picked him up, and carried him into the yard. About thirty seconds later, the big truck roared right off the dirt road and onto our driveway! I'm certain that Joshua would have been killed if I had not moved him. I received the gift of saving Joshua's life, because I had received power from the Holy Ghost.

I wasn't paying attention. I stopped for some fast food on my way home from work. In the middle of the driveway, exiting the Taco Mayo, I suddenly began speaking rapidly and distinctly in tongues. "That was a surprising experience," I thought as I pulled onto the highway ... right into the path of a fast approaching car. The driver of the car slammed on his brakes, squealed his tires and came to a complete stop only a couple of inches from my driver's side door. My life, or at least severe injury, was spared because the Holy Ghost had prayed through me to warn the oncoming driver. I received this gift of protection because I had received power from the Holy Ghost.

I was on my way to work. About a mile out of town I started speaking in tongues. Oh no, I thought. I wonder what's waiting for me now? (By this time I had learned that God was always preparing me for something when he ministered to me this way.) No sooner had I entered the door than one of the ladies was there, waiting for me, upset and crying. I had just the right words to say to her. I had been anointed with the gift of the right words to speak to her, because I had received power from the Holy Ghost.

It seems strange to me that many people who believe in

God are skeptical when they hear of miraculous power. In essence, they are saying, I believe God exists, but I don't believe he does anything.

I've thought about what the local minister had to say when I questioned him about the gift of the power of the Holy Ghost. His basic answer of - go look it up yourself - was just what I needed. I chose to listen to his advice. I also chose to believe God's Word and to respond to it.

And it shall come to pass afterward, that I will pour out my spirit upon all flesh; and your sons and your daughters shall prophesy, your old men shall dream dreams, your young men shall see visions: And also upon the servants and upon the handmaids in those days will I pour out of my spirit.
Joel 2: 28, 29

Nevertheless I tell you the truth; It is expedient for you that I go away: for if I go not away, the Comforter will not come unto you; but if I depart, I will send him unto you.
John 16: 7

But the Comforter, which is the Holy Ghost, whom the Father will send in my name, he will teach you all things, and bring all things to your remembrance, whatsoever things I have said unto you.
John 14: 26

AND when the day of Pentecost was fully come, they were all with one accord in one place. And suddenly there came a sound from heaven as of a rushing mighty wind, and it filled all the house where they were sitting. And there appeared unto them cloven tongues like as of fire, and it sat upon each of them. And they were all filled with the Holy Ghost, and began to speak with other tongues, as the Spirit gave them utterance.
Acts 2: 1 - 4

Then Peter said unto them, Repent and be baptized every one of you in the name of Jesus Christ for the remission of sins, and ye shall receive the gift of the Holy Ghost. For the promise is unto you, and to your children, and to all that are afar off, even as many as the Lord our God shall call.
Acts 2: 38, 39

SCRIPTURE ANALYSIS

Acts 1: 8

8. But ye shall
>   - But you shall
8. Receive power,
>   - From the Greek word *dunamis*, Strong's #1411:
miraculous power.
>   - Receive miraculous power,
8. After that the
>   - As [soon] as the
8. Holy Ghost
>   - From the Greek word *pneuma*, Strong's #4151: spirit.
>   - Holy Spirit
8. Is come upon you:
>   - Has come upon you:
8. And ye shall
>   - And you shall
8. Be witnesses
>   - Become witnesses
8. Unto me
>   - Of me
8. Both in Jerusalem,
>   - The Unger's Bible Dictionary states: "Jerusalem [was] the
first city of Palestine. 'The Holy City' for three great world
religions: Christianity, Judaism and Islam. The history of
Jerusalem from the time of Joshua to its destruction by Titus, a

period of fifteen centuries, is a succession of changes, revolutions, sieges, surrenders, famines, each followed by restorations and rebuilding. After the death and resurrection of Christ, Jerusalem became the scene of the most stirring events connected with Christianity, beginning with the day of Pentecost and including much of the history contained in the Acts of the Apostles."

- Both in [the city of] Jerusalem,

8. And in all Judea,

- The Unger's Bible Dictionary states: "Judea [is] the name of the southern-most Roman division of Palestine. Judea is very small…fifty-five miles long, from Bethlehem to Beer-sheba, and from twenty five to thirty miles broad. Judea was the seat of the one enduring dynasty of Israel, the site of their temple, the platform of their chief prophets.

- And in all [of] Judea,

8. And in Samaria,

- The Unger's Bible Dictionary states: "[The] city of Samaria [is] an important place in central Palestine, noted as the capital of the northern kingdom, [and] as giving name to the region about."

- And in [the region of] Samaria,

8. And unto the uttermost part of the earth.

- The NIV says. "And to the ends of the earth.

Joel 2: 28, 29

28. And it shall come to pass afterward,

- And it shall come to pass afterwards,

28. That I

- That I (God, see 2:27)

28. Will pour out my spirit upon all flesh;

- From the Hebrew word basar, Strong's #1320: mankind.
- Will pour out my Spirit upon all [of] mankind;

28. And your sons and your daughters shall prophesy,

- From the Hebrew word naba, Strong's #5012: speak (or sing) by inspiration in prediction or simple discourse.

- And you sons and your daughters shall speak and sing by inspiration [from my (God's) Spirit] in prediction and simple discourse,

28. Your old men shall dream <u>dreams</u>,

    - Your old men shall dream <u>dreams [which are inspired by my (God's) Spirit]</u>,

28. Your young men shall see <u>visions</u>:

    - From the Hebrew word *chizzayown*, Strong's #2384: <u>a revelation</u>.

    - Your young men shall see <u>revelations [which are inspired by my (God's) Spirit]</u>:

29. And also upon the <u>servants</u>

    - From the Hebrew word *ebed*, Strong's #5650: <u>bondman</u>.

    - Webster's Dictionary defines *bondman* as: <u>slave</u>.

    - And also upon the [male] <u>slaves</u>

29. And upon the <u>handmaids</u>

    - From the Hebrew word *shiphchah*, Strong's #8198: <u>a female slave</u>.

    - And upon the <u>female slaves</u>

29. In those <u>days</u>

    - In those <u>days [which are coming afterwards]</u>

29. Will <u>I</u> pour out my spirit.

    - Will <u>I (God)</u> pour out my Spirit.

John 16: 7

7. Nevertheless <u>I</u> tell you the truth;

    - Nevertheless <u>I (Jesus, see14:23)</u> tell you the truth;

7. It is <u>expedient</u> for you

    - From the Greek word *sumphero*, Strong's #4851: <u>advantage</u>.

    - It is <u>advantageous</u> for you

7. That I <u>go</u> away:

    - That I [am] going away:

7. For if I go <u>not</u> away,

    - For if I [do] not go away,

7. The <u>Comforter</u> will not come unto you;

    - From the Greek word *parakletos*, Strong's #3875: <u>an intercessor</u>.

    - The Unger's Bible Dictionary states: "[Some different

names referring to the Comforter are:] (the Holy Ghost or the Holy Spirit). Frequently the term is simply 'the Spirit,' or 'the Spirit of the Lord,' or 'the Spirit of God,' or 'the Spirit of Jesus Christ.' The prevailing doctrine may be thus summed up: (1.)The Holy Ghost is the same in substance and equal in power and glory with the Father and the Son. (2.) He is, nevertheless, as to his mode of subsistence and operation, subordinate to both the Father and the Son, as [or since] he proceeds from them and is sent by them, and they operate through him.

- The <u>Intercessor [(see note above, also see John 14:26) who is the Holy Spirit]</u> will not come unto you;

7. But <u>if</u> I depart,
- But <u>when</u> I depart,
7. I will send <u>him</u> unto you.
- I will send <u>the Holy Spirit</u> unto you.

John 14: 26

26. But the Comforter, <u>which</u> is
- But the Comforter, <u>who</u> is
26. The Holy <u>Ghost</u>,
- From the Greek word *pneuma*, Strong's #4151: <u>spirit</u>.
- The Holy <u>Spirit</u>,
26. Whom the <u>Father</u>
- Whom the <u>Father (God)</u>
26. Will send in <u>my</u> name,
- Will send in <u>my (Jesus')</u> name,
26. He shall teach you <u>all</u> things,
- He shall teach you [about] all [spiritual] things,
26. And bring <u>all</u> things to your remembrance,
- And bring <u>all</u> [spiritual] things to your remembrance,
26. <u>Whatsoever</u> things I have said unto you.
- [<u>In accordance to</u>] whatever things I have said unto you.

Acts 2: 1 - 4

1. AND when the day of <u>Pentecost</u>
- The Unger's Bible Dictionary states: "Pentecost [is] the

second of the three great annual festivals, the others being the Passover and Tabernacles. This festival is called (1.) The Feast of Weeks... because it was celebrated seven complete weeks, or fifty days, after the Passover. (2.) The Feast of Harvest... because it concluded the harvest of the later grains. (3.) The day of first fruits... because the first loaves made from the new grain was then offered on the alter. The Pentecost was essentially linked to the Passover - that festival which, above all others, expressed the fact of a race chosen and separated from other nations - and was the solemn termination of the consecrated period.

- And when the day of [the festival of] Pentecost's [scheduled time]

1. Was fully come,
- Had fully come,

1. They
- The 120 disciples [of Jesus (see 1: 4, 5, 15)]

1. Were all
- Were all [gathered]

1. With one accord in one place.
- From the Greek word *homothumadon*, Strong's #3661: unanimously.
- With one unanimous [purpose, together] in one place.

2. And suddenly there came a sound from heaven
- From the Greek word *ouranos*, Strong's #3772: the sky
- And suddenly there came a sound from the sky

2. As of
- That [sounded] like

2. A rushing mighty wind,
- The NIV says, "The blowing of a violent wind"

2. And it filled all the house where they were sitting.
- And it filled all the house where the 120 disciples [of Jesus] were sitting.

3. And there appeared unto them
- And there appeared unto the 120 disciples [of Jesus]

3. Cloven tongues
- From the Greek word *diamerizo*, Strong's #1266: divide.
- Divided tongues

3. Like as of fire,

- [That looked] like [they were made] of [a substance such] as fire,

3. And it
- And the divided tongues [that looked like they were made of fire]

3. Sat upon each of them.
- From the Greek word *kathizo*, Strong's #2523: to settle.
- Settled upon each of them.

4. And they were all
- And the 120 disciples [of Jesus] were all

4. Filled with the Holy Ghost,
- Filled with the Holy Spirit,

4. And began
- And [the 120 disciples of Jesus] began

4. To speak with
- To speak in

4. Other tongues,
- From the Greek word *glossa*, Strong's #1100: a language.
- Other languages,

4. As the Spirit
- As the [Holy] Spirit

4. Gave them utterance.
- Gave the 120 disciples [of Jesus the] utterance [to do so].

Acts 2: 38 - 39

38. Then Peter said unto them,
- Then Peter said unto about three thousand people (see 2:41),

38. Repent,
- Repent [of your sins],

38. And be baptized
- And be baptized [in water]

38. Every one of you in the name of Jesus Christ for the remission
- From the Greek word *aphesis*, Strong's #859: forgiveness.
- Everyone of you in the name of Jesus Christ for the

forgiveness
38. Of sins,
        - Of [your] sins,
38. And ye shall
        - And you shall
38. Receive the gift
        - Receive this gift
38. Of
        - From
38. The Holy Ghost.
        - From the Greek word *pneuma*, Strong's #4151: spirit.
        - The Holy Spirit.
39. For the promise
        - For the promise [in Joel 2: 28 - 32 (see 2:17 - 21)]
39. Is unto you, and to your children, and to all that are
        - Is unto you, and to your children, and to all who are
39. Afar off,
        - [Living in lands] far off,
39. Even as many as
        - Even [to] as many [people] as
39. The Lord our God shall call.
        - From the Greek word *proskaleomai*, Strong's #4341: to
call toward oneself.
        - The Lord our God shall call [to himself].

CHOICE EXAMINATION

1. Why did the local minister basically tell Galen to look it up for himself?

2. Why did Galen seek God's power for a spiritual gift?

3. In the scripture, why did God pour his Spirit upon all of mankind?

4. Why was it advantageous for Jesus to go away?

5. Why was it important that the 120 disciples of Jesus were gathered together with one unanimous purpose in one place?

6. What choices do you need to make in order to *receive God's power*?

TELL PEOPLE ABOUT JESUS

≈ 28 ≈

There cometh a woman of Samaria to draw water: Jesus saith unto her, Give me to drink. (For his disciples were gone away unto the city to buy meat.)

Then saith the woman of Samaria unto him, How is it that thou, being a Jew, asketh drink of me, which am a woman of Samaria? for the Jews have no dealings with the Samaritans.

Jesus answered and said unto her, If thou knewest the gift of God, and who it is that saith to thee, Give me to drink; thou wouldest have asked of him, and he would have given thee living water.

The woman saith unto him, Sir, thou hast nothing to draw with, and the well is deep: from whence then hast thou that living water? Art thou greater than our father Jacob, which gave us the well, and drank thereof himself, and his children, and his cattle?

Jesus answered and said unto her, Whosoever drinketh of this water shall thirst again: But whosoever drinketh of the water that I shall give him shall never thirst; but the water that I shall give him shall be in him a well of water springing up into everlasting life.

The woman saith unto him, Sir, give me this water, that I thirst not, neither come hither to draw. The woman saith unto him, I know that Messias cometh, which is called Christ: when he is come, he will tell us all things.

Jesus saith unto her, I that speak unto thee am he.

John 4: 7 - 15, 25, 26

He said there was some terribly vulgar graffiti written about me on the wall of stall number one. I wasn't surprised. Erasing graffiti from the restroom walls was a daily chore. I was the store's co-manager, and therefore, a likely target for someone's misguided expression. I grabbed a cloth and some powerful restroom cleaner. The graffiti at stall number one was soon erased.

A few weeks later I was *pleasantly* surprised when I saw the latest installment of graffiti at stall number one. I liked it so much that I came back with a notebook and *copied it down*! Here's what it said:

"Too many people on drugs, who have fried their brains, think everything they see when they are high is real. It makes them crazy, paranoid, and insane. It's too bad that we live, work, and drive around these people who are making many of the world's decisions, rules, and laws for us. What a horrible and sad shape the world is in. In the 1960's, people took drugs to make the world seem weird. Now, the world we live in is weird, and people take prescription drugs to help them make the world seem normal. Drugs are not the answer to the world's problems. Jesus is the answer to the world's problems. Choose Jesus, not drugs. He loves you so much that he died for you; and he will set you free!"

I didn't hurry off to the maintenance room to get a cloth and some powerful restroom cleaner. I wasn't in a hurry to erase the graffiti from the wall of stall number one - not this time. "One of the maintenance people can take care of it when they get around to it," I thought.

I couldn't help but notice… it was several days before they got around to it.

How beautiful upon the mountains are the feet of him that bringeth good tidings, that publisheth peace; that bringeth good tidings of good, that publisheth salvation; that saith unto Zion, Thy God reigneth!
Isaiah 52: 7

And there was delivered unto him the book of the prophet Esaias. And when he had opened the book, he found the place where it was written, The Spirit of the Lord is upon me, because he hath anointed me to preach the gospel to the poor; he hath sent me to heal the broken hearted, to preach deliverance to the captives, and recovering of sight to the blind, to set at liberty them that are bruised, To preach the acceptable year of the Lord.
Luke 4: 17, 18

And he said unto them, Go ye into all the world, and preach the gospel to every creature. He that believeth and is baptized shall be saved; but he that believeth not shall be damned.
Mark 16: 15, 16

And they, continued daily with one accord in the temple, and breaking bread from house to house, did eat their meat with gladness and singleness of heart, Praising God, and having favour with all the people. And the Lord added to the church daily such as should be saved.
Acts 2: 46, 47

SCRIPTURE ANALYSIS

John 4: 7 - 15, 25, 26

7. There **cometh** a woman
- There came a woman
7. **Of** Samaria
- From Samaria
7. To draw **water:**
- To draw water [from Jacob's well (see verse #6)]:
7. Jesus **saith**
- Jesus said
7. Unto **her,**
- Unto the woman [from Samaria],

7. Give me <u>to</u> drink.
> - Give me [some water] to drink.

8. (For <u>his</u> disciples
> - (For <u>Jesus'</u> disciples

8. Were gone away unto the <u>city</u>
> - Were gone away unto the <u>city of Sychar (see verse # 5)</u>

8. To buy <u>meat</u>.)
> - From the Greek word *trophe*, Strong's #5160: <u>food</u>.
> - To buy <u>food</u>.)

9. Then <u>saith</u>
> - Then <u>said</u>

9. The woman <u>of</u> Samaria
> - The woman <u>from</u> Samaria

9. Unto <u>him</u>,
> - Unto <u>Jesus</u>,

9. <u>How</u> is it
> - <u>Why</u> is it

9. That <u>thou</u>, being a Jew,
> - That <u>you</u>, being a Jew,

9. <u>Asketh drink</u>
> - [Are] asking [for a] drink [of water]

9. <u>Of</u> me,
> - <u>From</u> me,

9. <u>Which</u> am a woman
> <u>Who</u> am a woman

9. <u>Of</u> Samaria?
> - <u>From</u> Samaria?

9. For the Jews <u>have</u> no dealings with the Samaritans.
> - For the Jews <u>[usually] have</u> no dealings with the
Samaritans.

10. Jesus answered and said unto <u>her</u>,
> - Jesus answered and said unto <u>the woman [from Samaria]</u>,

10. If <u>thou knewest</u> the gift
> - If <u>you knew</u> the gift

10. <u>Of God</u>,
> - <u>That God [was willing to give to you]</u>,

10. And who <u>it</u> is

- And who <u>this</u> is

10. That <u>saith</u>

- That [is] saying

10. To <u>thee</u>,

- To <u>you</u>,

10. Give me <u>to</u> drink;

- Give me [some water] to drink;

10. <u>Thou wouldst</u>

- <u>You would</u>

10. Have <u>asked</u>

- Have <u>asked [for water]</u>

10. <u>Of him</u>,

- <u>From me [instead]</u>,

10. And <u>he</u>

- And <u>I</u>

10. Would have given <u>thee</u> living water.

- Would have given <u>you</u> living water.

11. The woman <u>saith</u>

- The woman <u>said</u>

11. Unto <u>him</u>,

- Unto <u>Jesus</u>,

11. Sir, <u>thou hast</u> nothing

- Sir, <u>you have</u> nothing

11. To <u>draw</u> with,

- To <u>draw [water]</u> with,

11. And the well is deep: from <u>whence</u> then

- And the well is deep: from <u>what [source]</u> then

11. <u>Hast thou</u> that living water?

- <u>[Do] you have</u> that living water?

12. <u>Art thou</u> greater

- <u>Are you</u> greater

12. Than our <u>father</u>

- From the Greek word *pater*, Strong's #3962: <u>a father (lit. or fig., near or more remote)</u>.

- Than our <u>forefather</u>

12. Jacob, <u>which</u> gave us

- Jacob, <u>who</u> gave us

12. The well,
- This well,

12. And drank thereof himself,
- And [who] drank thereof himself,

12. And his children, and his cattle?
- And [likewise] his children, and his cattle?

13. Jesus answered and said unto her,
- Jesus answered and said unto the woman [from Samaria],

13. Whosoever drinketh of
- Whoever drinks from

13. This water
- This water [in this well]

13. Shall thirst again:
- Shall [become] thirsty again:

14. But whosoever drinketh of the water
- But whoever drinks from the water

14. That I shall give him
- That I shall [be willing to] give him

14. Shall never thirst;
- Shall never [become] thirsty;

14. But the water that I shall give him
- But the water that I shall [be willing to] give him

14. Shall be in him
- Shall become to him

14. A well of water springing up into everlasting life.
- From the Greek word *aionios*, Strongs #166: eternal.
- A well of water springing up into eternal life.

15. The woman saith
- The woman said

15. Unto him, Sir,
- Unto Jesus, Sir,

15. Give me this water,
- Give me [some of] this water,

15. That I
- [So] that I

15. Thirst not
- [Will] not [become] thirsty,

15. Neither

    - [And] neither [will I have to]

15. Come hither

    - Come here

15. To draw.

    - To draw [water].

25. The woman saith

    - The woman [from Samaria] said

25. Unto him,

    - Unto Jesus,

25. I know that Messias cometh,

    - I know that [the] Messiah [is] coming,

25. Which is called Christ:

    - Who is called Christ:

25. When he is come,

    - When Christ has come,

25. He will

    - Christ will [be able to]

25. Tell us all things.

    - Tell us [about] all things.

26. Jesus saith

    - Jesus said

26. Unto her,

    - Unto the woman [from Samaria],

26. I that speak

    - I[,the person] who [is] speaking

26. Unto thee

    - Unto you

26. Am he.

    - Am Christ, the Messiah.

Isaiah 52: 7

7. How beautiful upon the mountains are the feet of him that bringeth good tidings,

    - All three words are translated from the Hebrew word *basar*, Strong's #1319: to announce glad news.

-How beautiful upon the mountains are the feet of him that announces glad news,

7. That <u>publisheth</u> peace;
- From the Hebrew word *shama*, Strong's #8085: <u>proclaim</u>.
- That <u>proclaims</u> peace;

7. That <u>bringeth good tidings</u>
- That <u>announces glad news</u>

7. <u>Of</u>
- <u>About</u>

7. <u>Good</u>,
- From the Hebrew word *towb*, Strong's #2896: <u>a good or good thing</u>.
- <u>A good thing [that is happening]</u>,

7. That <u>publisheth</u> salvation;
- That <u>proclaims</u> salvation;

7. That <u>saith</u>
- That <u>says</u>

7. Unto <u>Zion</u>,
- Unger's Bible Dictionary states: "Zion has a threefold significance in the Bible apart from it's original historical significance. In the [old testament] Zion refers to Jerusalem, the city that David conquered and made a capital of the United Kingdom of Israel. In a prophetic sense, Zion has reference to Jerusalem as the future capital city of the nation Israel in the kingdom age. Amillennial theologians deny this equation and spiritualize the term to mean the Christian church of this age. The [new testament] also refers Zion to the New Jerusalem, the eternal city into which the church will be received."
- Unto <u>Zion[, referring to Jerusalem and symbolic of Christian people]</u>,

7. <u>Thy</u> God
- <u>Your</u> God

7. <u>Reigneth</u>!
- From the Hebrew word *malak*, Strong's #4427: <u>to ascend the throne</u>.
- <u>[Has] ascended to the throne</u>!

Luke 4: 17, 18

17. And there was <u>delivered</u>
- From the Greek word *epididomi*, Strong's #1929: <u>to give over by hand</u>.
- And there was <u>handed</u>

17. Unto <u>him</u>
- Unto <u>Jesus</u>

17. The book of the prophet <u>Esaias</u>.
- The book of the prophet <u>Isaiah</u>.

17. And when <u>he</u> had opened the book,
- And when <u>Jesus</u> had opened the book,

17. <u>He</u> found the place where it was written,
- <u>Jesus</u> found the place where it was written,

18. The Spirit of the <u>Lord</u>
- The spirit of the <u>Lord [God] (see Isaiah 61: 1)</u>

18. Is upon me, because <u>he hath</u>
- Is upon me, because <u>the Lord [God] has</u>

18. <u>Anointed</u> me
- From the Greek word *chrio*, Strong's #5548: <u>to consecrate to an office or religious service</u>.
- Webster's Dictionary defines *consecrate* as: <u>dedicated to a sacred purpose</u>.
- <u>Dedicated me to [do] religious service [with] a sacred purpose</u>

18. To <u>preach</u>
- From the Greek word *euaggelizo*, Strong's #2097: <u>to announce good news</u>.
- To <u>announce</u>

18. The <u>gospel</u>
- Also from the Greek word *euaggelizo*, Strong's #2097: <u>to announce good news</u>.
- The <u>good news</u>

18. To the <u>poor</u>;
- To the <u>[people who are] poor</u>;

18. <u>He hath</u> sent me
- The <u>Lord [God] has</u> sent me

18. To heal the <u>broken hearted</u>,
- To heal the <u>[people who are] broken-hearted</u>,

18. To preach
- From the Greek word *kerusso*, Strong's #2784: proclaim.
- To proclaim

18. Deliverance
- [A message of] deliverance

18. To the captives,
- From the Greek word *aichmalotos*, Strong's #164: a prisoner of war.
- To the prisoners of [spiritual] war,

18. And recovering of sight
- And [to proclaim a message of] recovering of sight

18. To the blind,
- To the [people who are] blind,

18. To set at liberty
- To set [free] to liberty

18. Them that are
- People who are

18. Bruised,
- From the Greek word *thrauo*, Strong's #2352: to crush [or] bruise.
- The NIV says, "Oppressed,"
- Bruised, crushed, or oppressed.

18. To preach
- To proclaim [to people that this is]

18. The acceptable year of the Lord.
- The NIV says: "The year of the Lord's favor."

Mark 16: 15, 16

15: And he said
- And Jesus said

15. Unto them,
- Unto the eleven disciples (see verse #14)

15. Go ye into
- You [must] go into

15. All the world,
- All [areas of] the world,

15. And <u>preach</u>
  - From the Greek word *kerusso*, Strong's #2784: <u>proclaim</u>.
  - And <u>proclaim</u>

15. The <u>gospel</u>
  - From the Greek word *euaggelion*, Strong's #2098: <u>a good message</u>.
  - The <u>good message</u>

15. To <u>every creature</u>.
  - The NIV says: "To <u>all creation</u>."

16. He <u>that believeth</u>
  - He <u>who believes</u>

16. And is <u>baptized</u>
  - The Unger's Bible Dictionary states: "[Baptism is] the application of water as a rite of purification or initiation; a Christian sacrament. Symbolizing regeneration through union with Christ, baptism portrays not only Christ's death and resurrection and their purpose in atoning for sin in delivering sinners from its penalty and power, but also betokens the accomplishments of that purpose in the person baptized. (Rom. 6: 3-5; Gal. 3:27; Col 3:3). By the external rite the believer professes his death to sin and resurrection to spiritual life.
  - And is <u>baptized [as a profession of his death to sin and resurrection to spiritual life]</u>

16. Shall be <u>saved</u>;
  - The Unger's Bible Dictionary states: "In the New Testament salvation is regarded almost exclusively as [freedom] from the power and dominion of sin. And of this Jesus Christ is the author (see Matt. 1:21; Acts 4:12; Heb. 2:10; 5:9, et al). It is freely offered to all men, but is conditioned upon repentance and faith in Christ (see John 3:16; Heb. 2:3; et al)."
  - Shall be <u>saved [from his sins]</u>;

16. But he <u>that believeth</u> not
  - But he <u>who [does]</u> not <u>believe</u>

16. Shall be <u>damned</u>.
  - From the Greek word *katakrino*, Strong's #2632: <u>to judge against, sentence [or] condemn</u>.
  - Shall be <u>judged, condemned and sentenced</u>.

Acts 2: 46 - 47

46. And they,
- And the people of the church (see verse #47),
46. Continuing daily
- From the Greek word *proskartereo*, Strong's #4342: be constantly diligent.
- Being constantly diligent [met together] daily
46. With one accord in the temple,
- From the Greek word *homothumadon*, Strong's #3661: unanimously [or] with one accord (mind).
- With one unanimous mindset in the temple,
46. And breaking bread
- From the Greek word *artos*, Strong's #740: bread (as raised) or a loaf.
- And breaking [apart] loaves of bread
46. From house to house,
- [With each other, going] from house to house.
46. Did eat
- [They] did eat
46. Their meat
- From the Greek word *trophe*, Strong's #5160: food.
- Their food
46. With
- With [feelings of]
46. Gladness and singleness of heart,
- The NIV says: "Glad and sincere hearts."
47. Praising God, and having favour with all the people.
- Praising God and having [the] favor of all the people.
47. And the Lord added to the church daily
- And the Lord added [people] to the church daily
47. Such as should be saved.
- The NIV says: "Who were being saved."

CHOICE EXAMINATION

1. Why did the graffiti author identify drug usage as evidence of people searching in wrong places for answers to the world's problems?

2. In the scripture, why did Jesus use water as an object lesson to tell the woman from Samaria that he was Christ, the Messiah?

3. Why did Isaiah proclaim that the person who announces the good news that God has ascended the throne has beautiful feet?

4. Where did Jesus tell the eleven disciples to go to proclaim the good message?

5. What evident factors helped influence people who were being saved to be added to the church daily?

6. What choices do you need to make in order to *tell people about Jesus*?

GIVE YOUR POSSESSIONS TO GOD

≈ 29 ≈

And, behold, one came and said unto him, Good Master, what good thing shall I do, that I may have eternal life?

And he said unto him, Why callest thou me good? there is none good but one, that is, God: but if thou wilt enter into life, keep the commandments.

He saith unto him, Which?

Jesus said, Thou shalt do no murder, Thou shalt not commit adultery, Thou shalt not steal, Thou shalt not bear false witness, Honour thy father and thy mother: and, Thou shalt love thy neighbor as thyself.

The young man saith unto him, All these things have I kept from my youth up: what lack I yet?

Jesus said unto him, If thou wilt be perfect, go and sell that thou hast, and give to the poor, and thou shalt have treasure in heaven: and come and follow me.

But when the young man heard that saying, he went away sorrowful: for he had great possessions.

Matthew 19: 16 - 22

It was probably the only opportunity we would have to purchase the neighbor's farm in our entire lifetime. Barbie and I drove to the neighbor's house as soon as we saw the "FOR SALE" sign go up.

I asked, "Why are you selling? How much are you asking? Has anyone else expressed interest in your farm yet? Would you give us an opportunity to purchase it first?"

The answers were similar to: "We're tired, too much, not yet," and "yes."

That evening I started walking through the fields and praying. I prayed one of the most intense and *goofiest* prayers I have ever prayed.

"Lord, if it would be pleasing to you to bless your servant with that property, then in Jesus' name, don't let anyone else purchase it! Nevertheless, Lord, if you don't want the property to go to me, then I pray that your will be done. However Lord, if you don't really care either way, then I request that you would bless me with that property, instead of someone else. However, again Lord, if you have some great plan where someone else is to purchase that property, and the other person will do some great ministry for you because of the purchase of that property, then I understand and I will submit to your will. On the other hand Lord, if that property will otherwise be purchased by someone who will not honor you with it, then in Jesus' name, I believe for you to bless me with that property instead of someone else who will not honor you with it. Lord, if there's any reason that you don't want me to have that property, then don't let me have it. But likewise Lord, if there's not any reason for you to not want me to have that property, then in Jesus' name, bless me Lord, with that property. LORD, I WANT THAT PROPERTY! I WANT THAT PROPERTY BAD! I BELIEVE FOR YOU LORD, IN JESUS' NAME, TO BLESS ME WITH THAT PROPERTY! If that's all right with you, of course. Amen."

By the time I had finished praying I was a half mile away from the house, out in the middle of a field, and totally exhausted. I had prayed my heart out. I didn't sense a definite answer from God in regard to him allowing Barbie and me to purchase that property. I did know, however, that I had told God everything that was in my heart.

A multi-millionaire owns land on the other side of the neighbor's farm. He bought the property. It was sold at an auction. The new owner didn't go to the trouble to attend the auction. He just sent one of his hired hands to the auction with his checkbook.

It's been four years since I prayed that prayer about the neighbor's farm. I haven't noticed any spiritual revivals breaking loose. I'm not aware of any plans for the property which will produce a great ministry. I have been blessed, however, with some great new neighbors and the new owner has been kind and gracious to Barbie and me.

I've thought about how I prayed when I asked God to bless me with that property. I realize now that God wasn't as interested in what I was saying about the neighbor's farm as much as he was interested in what I was saying about my priorities. I think that God actually blessed me by giving me an opportunity to choose to give up what was at that time, my most sought after possession - the neighbor's farm.

A couple of years ago we had a dry fall and we ran out of pasture for the cattle. I asked my new neighbor to find out if the owner would allow our cattle to graze in one of his fields. I offered to pay for the privilege. His answers were: "yes," and "no charge."

I guess God found a way to bless us with that property after all.

Lay not up for yourselves treasures upon earth, where moth and rust doth corrupt, and where thieves break through and steal: But lay up for yourselves treasures in heaven, where neither moth nor rust doth corrupt, and where thieves do not break through nor steal: For where your treasure is, there will your heart be also.
Matthew 6: 19 - 21

No man can serve two masters: for either he will hate the one, and love the other; or else he will hold to the one, and despise the other. Ye cannot serve God and mammon. Therefore I say unto you, Take no thought for your life, what you shall eat, or what you shall drink; nor yet for your body, what ye shall put on. Is not the life more than meat, and the body than raiment? Behold the fowls of the air: for they sow not, neither do they reap, nor gather into barns; yet your heavenly father feedeth them. Are ye not much better than they?
Matthew 6: 24 - 26

But seek ye first the kingdom of God, and his righteousness; and all of these things shall be added unto you.
Matthew 6: 33

SCRIPTURE ANALYSIS

Matthew 19: 16 - 22

16. And, behold, <u>one</u> came
- And, behold, <u>a young man [who had a great amount of possessions (see verse #22)]</u> came

16. And said unto <u>him</u>,
- And said unto <u>Jesus</u>,

16. Good <u>Master</u>,
- From the Greek word *didaskalos*, Strong's #1320: <u>teacher</u>.
- Good <u>teacher</u>,

16. What good thing shall <u>I</u> do,
- What good thing shall <u>I [be required to]</u> do

16. <u>That</u> I may
- <u>[So] that</u> I may

16. <u>Have</u>
- <u>Have [an opportunity to obtain]</u>

16. Eternal <u>life</u>?
- Eternal <u>life [in heaven]</u>?

17. And <u>he</u> said
- And <u>Jesus</u> said

17. Unto <u>him</u>,
- Unto <u>the young man [who had a great amount of possessions]</u>,

17. Why <u>callest thou</u> me
- Callest, comes from the Greek word *lego*, Strong's #3004: <u>ask</u>.
- Why <u>[are] you asking</u> me

17. <u>Good</u>?
- From the Greek word *agathos*, Strong's #18: <u>good [or] good things</u>.
- <u>[About doing a]</u> good thing?

17. There is <u>none good</u>
- There is <u>no [requirement for doing a] good thing</u>

17. <u>But</u> one,
- <u>Except [for]</u> one,

17. <u>That</u> is,

- [And] that is,
17. God:
- [to obey (see verse #20)] God:
17. But if thou wilt
- But if you will
17. Enter into life,
- Enter into [heaven, so that you can have eternal] life,
17. Keep the commandments.
- Keep the [ten] commandments (see Exodus 20: 3 - 17)
18. He saith
- The young man [who had a great amount of possessions] said
18. Unto him,
- Unto Jesus,
18. Which?
- Which [of the ten commandments am I required to keep]?
18. Jesus said, Thou shalt
- Jesus said, You shall
18. Do no murder,
- Do no [act of] murder
18. Thou shalt not commit adultery,
- You shall not commit adultery,
18. Thou shalt not steal,
- You shall not steal,
18. Thou shalt not
- You shall not
18. Bear
- From the Greek word *pseudomartureo*, Strong's #5576: to be an untrue testifier.
- Be an untrue testifier [of]
18. False witness,
- Also from the Greek word *pseudomartureo*, Strong's #5576: to be an untrue testifier. (The same Greek word translated as *bear*, earlier in this verse, is translated as *witness*, in this instance.)
- False testimony,
19. Honour thy father

- Honor your father
19. And thy mother:
 - And your mother:
19. And, Thou shalt
 - And, you shall
19. Love thy neighbor
 - Love your neighbor
19. As thyself.
 - As [if you were loving] yourself.
20. The young man saith
 - The young man said
20. Unto him,
 - Unto Jesus,
20. All these things
 - All these things [which you've quoted from the ten commandments]
20. Have I kept
 - From the Greek word *phulasso*, Strong's #5442: obey.
 - Have I obeyed
20. From my youth
 - From [the time of] my youth
20. Up:
 - Up [to now]:
20. What lack I yet?
 - What [do] I lack yet?
21. Jesus said unto him,
 - Jesus said unto the young man [who had great possessions],
21. If thou wilt be
 - If you will be
21. Perfect,
 - From the Greek word *teleios*, Strong's #5046: complete.
 - Complete,
21. Go and sell that thou hast,
 - Go and sell [the possessions] that you have,
21. And give
 - And give [your possessions]

21. To the <u>poor</u>,
- To the [people who are] poor,

21. And <u>thou shalt</u>
- And <u>you shall</u>

21. Have <u>treasure</u> in heaven:
- Have [a spiritual] <u>treasure</u> [located] in heaven:

21. And <u>come</u> and follow me.
- And [then,] <u>come</u> and follow me.

22. But when the young man heard <u>that</u> saying,
- But when the young man heard [the words] that [Jesus was] saying,

22. <u>He</u> went away
- <u>The young man</u> went away

22. <u>Sorrowful</u>:
- <u>Sorrowfully</u>:

22. For <u>he</u> had
- For <u>the young man</u> had

22. <u>Great</u> possessions.
- [A] <u>great</u> [amount of] possessions.

Matthew 6: 19 - 21

19. <u>Lay not up</u> for yourselves
- The NIV says: "<u>Do not store up</u> for yourselves"

19. <u>Treasures</u>
- From the Greek word *thesauros*, Strong's #2344: <u>wealth</u>.
- <u>Wealth</u>

19. Upon <u>earth</u>,
- Upon [the] <u>earth</u>,

19. Where <u>moth</u>
- Where <u>moths</u>

19. And rust <u>doth</u>
- And rust <u>can</u>

19. <u>Corrupt</u>,
- From the Greek word *aphanizo*, Strongs #853: <u>consume</u>.
- <u>Consume</u> [your wealth],

19. And where thieves <u>break through</u>
- And where thieves [can] <u>break in</u>

19. And steal:

    - And steal [your wealth]:

20. But lay up for yourselves

    - But [instead,] store up for yourselves

20. Treasures in heaven,

    - Wealth in heaven,

20. Where neither moth nor rust doth corrupt,

    - Where neither moth nor rust can consume [your wealth],

20. And where thieves do not break through

    - And where thieves do not break into [it]

20. Nor steal.

    - Nor [are they able to] steal [your wealth].

21. For where

    - For wherever

21. Your treasure is,

    - Your wealth is [stored],

21. There will

    - There will [the focus of]

21. Your heart

    - From the Greek word *kardia*, Strong's #2588: the thoughts or feelings.

    - The thoughts and feelings [of] your heart

21. Be also.

    - Be [found] also.

Matthew 6: 24 - 26

24. No man can serve two masters: for either he

    - No man can serve two masters: for either the servant

24. Will hate the one,

    - Will hate the one [master],

24. And love the other;

    - And love the other [master];

24. Or else he

    - Or else the servant

24. Will hold to

    - The NIV says: "Will be devoted to"

24. The one,

- The <u>one</u> [master],

24. And despise the <u>other</u>.

- And despise the <u>other</u> [master].

24. <u>Ye</u> cannot

- <u>You</u> cannot

24. <u>Serve</u> God

- <u>Serve</u> [both] God

24. And <u>mammon</u>.

- From the Greek word *mammonas*, Strong's #3126: <u>wealth</u>.

- And <u>wealth</u>.

25. Therefore I say unto <u>you</u>,

- Therefore I say unto <u>you</u> [who are trying to serve both God and wealth],

25. <u>Take no thought for</u> your life,

- The NIV says: "<u>Do not worry about</u> your life,

25. <u>What</u>

- From the Greek word *tis*, Strong's #5101: <u>what</u> [or] <u>how</u>.

- [<u>Concerning things such as</u>] what or how

25. <u>Ye</u> shall eat,

- <u>You</u> shall eat,

25. Or <u>what ye</u> shall drink;

- Or <u>what or how you</u> shall drink;

25. Nor <u>yet</u> for your body,

- Nor <u>even</u> for your body,

25. What <u>ye</u> shall put on.

- What [<u>clothing</u>] you shall put on.

25. Is not the <u>life</u>

- From the Greek word *psuche*, Strong's #5590: <u>soul</u>.

- Is not the <u>soul</u> [of a man]

25. <u>More</u>

- <u>More</u> [important]

25. Than <u>meat</u>,

- From the Greek word *trophe*, Strong's #5160: <u>food</u>.

- Than <u>food</u>.

25. <u>And</u>

<u>And</u> [is not]

25. The <u>body</u> than
    - The <u>body</u> [more important] than
25. <u>Raiment</u>?
    - From the Greek word *enduma*, Strong's #1742: <u>clothing</u>.
    - <u>Clothing</u>?
26. <u>Behold</u>
    - From the Greek word *emblepo*, Strong's #1689: <u>observe</u>.
    - <u>Observe</u>
26. The <u>fowls</u>
    - From the Greek word *peteinon*, Strong's #4071: <u>bird</u>.
    - The <u>birds</u>
26. <u>Of</u>
    - <u>In</u>
26. The <u>air</u>:
    - From the Greek word *ouranos*, Strong's #3772: <u>sky</u>.
    - The <u>sky</u>:
26. For <u>they</u>
    - For [the] birds
26. <u>Sow not</u>,
    - [Do] not sow [crops and therefore],
26. Neither do they <u>reap</u>,
    - Neither do they <u>reap [a harvest]</u>,
26. Nor <u>gather</u>
    - Nor <u>gather [food items]</u>
26. Into <u>barns</u>;
    - Into <u>barns [for storage]</u>;
26. Yet your heavenly Father <u>feedeth them</u>.
    - Yet your heavenly Father <u>feeds the birds</u>.
26. Are <u>ye</u> not
    - Are <u>you</u> not
26. <u>Much</u>
    - [Of] <u>much</u>
26. <u>Better</u>
    - From the Greek word *diaphero*, Strong's #1308: <u>be of more value</u>.
    - <u>More value</u>
26. Than <u>they</u>?

- Than the birds?

Matthew 6: 33

33. But seek ye
- But you [must] seek
33. First the kingdom of God,
- [As your] first [priority] the kingdom of God,
33. And his righteousness;
- And God's righteousness;
33. And all these things
- And food, drink, and clothing (see verse #31)
33. Shall be added unto you.
- From the Greek word *prostithemi*, Strong's #4369: give more [or] to place additionally.
- Shall be given additionally unto you.

CHOICE EXAMINATION

1. Why did Galen pray about the sale of the neighbor's farm in such an indecisive manner?

2. Why did Galen think he was actually blessed by having the opportunity to give up his most sought after possession?

3. In the scripture, why did Jesus omit the commandments dealing with man's relationship with God in his initial instructions to the young man who had a great amount of possessions?

4. Why did Jesus say it was important for our wealth to be stored in heaven?

5. Why did Jesus say to not worry about our lives concerning things such as what we shall eat, drink, or even what clothing we shall put on?

6. What choices do you need to make in order to *give your possessions to God*?

GIVE YOUR CHILDREN TO GOD
≈ 30 ≈

So Hannah rose up after they had eaten in Shiloh, and after they had drunk. Now Eli the priest sat upon a seat by a post of the temple of the LORD. And she was in bitterness of soul, and prayed unto the LORD, and wept sore. And she vowed a vow, and said, O LORD of hosts, if thou wilt indeed look on the affliction of thine handmaid, and remember me, and not forget thine handmaid, but wilt give unto thine handmaid a man child, then I will give him unto the LORD all the days of his life, and there shall no razor come upon his head.

Then Eli answered and said, Go in peace: and the God of Israel grant thee thy petition that thou hast asked of him.

Wherefore it came to pass, when the time was come about after Hannah had conceived, that she bare a son, and called his name Samuel, saying, Because I have asked him of the LORD.

And when she had weaned him, she took him up with her, with three bullocks, and one ephah of flour, and a bottle of wine, and brought him unto the house of the LORD in Shiloh: and the child was young.

And they slew a bullock, and brought the child to Eli. And she said, Oh my lord, as thy soul liveth, my lord, I am the woman that stood by thee here, praying unto the LORD. For this child I prayed; and the LORD hath given me my petition which I asked of him: Therefore also I have lent him to the LORD; as long as he liveth he shall be lent to the LORD.

And he worshiped the LORD there.

I Samuel 1: 9 - 11, 17, 20, 24 - 28

―――――――――――――

I started praying some variation of this prayer as soon as I learned that Barbie was pregnant with our first child. I've prayed it almost daily now for twenty-six years. It goes like this: "Lord, I give my children to you. Are they missionaries? Are they pastors? Are they Sunday school teachers? Do they work at Wal-Mart? Do they teach school? Lord, whatever they are, whatever they do, they're yours. I give them to you. You do with them what you want. They belong to you."

Parenting is a difficult task. We, like all parents, have faced a number of challenges in raising our children. Of course, not everything has been perfect in our children's lives. Even now, despite our best yet sometimes flawed efforts, our children choose for themselves how to deal with the struggles and temptations they face in life. I believe, however, that our children naturally avoided involvement in many difficult issues because they knew their parent's primary focus for them was always on service to God.

I still pray that prayer. Now I'm praying it for our grandchildren, too.

And he took a child, and set him in the midst of them: and when he had taken him in his arms, he said unto them, Whosoever shall receive one of such children in my name, receiveth me: and whosoever shall receive me, receiveth not me, but him that sent me.
Mark 9: 36, 37

And whosoever shall offend one of these little ones that believe in me, it is better for him that a millstone were hanged about his neck, and he were cast into the sea.
Mark 9: 42

And they brought young children to him, that he should touch them: and his disciples rebuked those that brought them. But when Jesus saw it, he was much displeased, and said unto them, Suffer the little children to come unto me, and forbid them not: for of such is the kingdom of God. Verily I say unto you, Whosoever shall not receive the kingdom of God as a little

child, he shall not enter therein.
Mark 10: 13 - 15

And, ye fathers, provoke not your children to wrath: but bring
them up in the nurture and admonition of the Lord.
Ephesians 6: 4

SCRIPTURE ANALYSIS

I Samuel 1: 9 - 11, 17, 20, 24 - 28

9. So Hannah rose up after <u>they</u> had
    - So Hannah rose up after <u>she and Elkanah [her husband
(see verse #8)]</u>, had
9. <u>Eaten</u>
    - [Finished] eating
9. In <u>Shiloh,</u>
    - The Unger's Bible Dictionary states that Shiloh is: "The
site of Israel's early sanctuary in the time of the Judges. It was the
focal point of Israel's amphictyonic [Defined by Webster's
Dictionary as: An association of neighboring states in ancient
Greece to defend a common religious center.] organization before
the establishment of the kingdom."
    - In [the religious sanctuary of] Shiloh,
9. And after <u>they</u> had
    - And after <u>Hannah and Elkanah</u> had
**9. <u>Drunk</u>. Now Eli the priest sat upon a seat by a post of the
temple of the LORD.**
    - [Finished] drinking. Now Eli the priest sat upon a seat by
a post of the temple of the Lord.
10. And <u>she</u>
    - And <u>Hannah</u>
10. Was <u>in</u> bitterness
    - Was [having feelings] of bitterness
10. <u>Of</u>
    - From [the]

10. Soul,
 - From the Hebrew word *nephesh*, Strong's #5315: <u>heart</u>.
 - Webster's Dictionary defines *heart* as: <u>One's innermost character, feelings, or inclinations.</u>
 - <u>Innermost feelings of her heart,</u>

10. And <u>prayed</u> unto the LORD,
 - And [Hannah] prayed unto the Lord,

10. <u>And</u>
 - And [she]

10.Wept <u>sore</u>.
 - The NIV says, "Wept <u>much</u>."

11. And <u>she</u> vowed a vow, and said,
 - And <u>Hannah</u> vowed a vow, and said,

11. O LORD of <u>hosts</u>,
 - From the Hebrew word *tsaba*, Strong's #6635: <u>a mass of persons</u>.
 - O Lord of <u>the masses of people,</u>

11. If <u>thou wilt</u> indeed
 - If <u>you will</u> indeed

11. Look <u>on</u> the affliction
 - Look <u>at</u> the affliction

11. Of <u>thine</u>
 - Of <u>your</u>

11. <u>Handmaid</u>,
 - From the Hebrew word *amah*, Strong's #519: <u>a maid servant</u>.
 - <u>Maid servant,</u>

11. And <u>remember</u> me,
 - From the Hebrew word *zakar*, Strong's #2142: <u>be mindful</u>
 - And <u>be mindful [of]</u> me,

11. And not forget <u>thine handmaid</u>,
 - And not forget [<u>this request from</u>] <u>your maid servant,</u>

11. But <u>wilt</u> give unto
 - But <u>will</u> give unto

11. <u>Thine handmaid</u>
 - <u>Your maid servant</u>

11. A <u>man child</u>,

- The NIV says: "A <u>son</u>,"

11. Then I will give <u>him</u>

    - Then I will give <u>my son</u>

11. Unto <u>the</u> LORD all the days of his life,

    - Unto <u>you</u>, Lord all the days of his life,

11. And there shall no <u>razor</u>

    - The Unger's Bible Dictionary states: "Long flowing hair was worn only by youth's in more ancient times, and by Nazarites (One of either sex who was bound by a vow of a peculiar kind to be set apart from others for the service of God) during the term of their vow."

    - And there shall no <u>razor [as a symbol of this vow be allowed to]</u>

11. Come upon <u>his</u> head.

    - Come upon <u>my son's</u> head.

17. Then <u>Eli</u>

    - Then <u>Eli [the priest]</u>

17. <u>Answered</u> and said,

    - <u>Answered [Hannah]</u> and said,

17. <u>Go in peace:</u>

    - <u>[You may] go with [a feeling of] peacefulness</u>:

17. <u>And</u> the God of Israel

    - <u>And [may]</u> the God of Israel

17. Grant <u>thee thy</u> petition

    - Grant <u>you the</u> petition

17. That <u>thou hast</u> asked of him.

    - That <u>you have</u> asked of him.

20. Wherefore it came to pass, when the <u>time was</u> come about

    - Wherefore it came to pass, when the <u>[proper amount of] time had</u> come about

20. After Hannah had conceived, that she bare a son and called his name <u>Samuel</u>,

    - From the Hebrew word *shmuwel*, Strong's #8050: <u>heard of God</u>.

    - After Hannah had conceived, that she bare a son and called his name <u>Samuel, [which means: heard of God]</u>

20. <u>Saying,</u>

- <u>Saying, [I have given Samuel this name]</u>

20. Because I have <u>asked</u> him

    - Because I have <u>asked [for]</u> him

20. <u>Of</u> the LORD.

    - <u>From</u> the Lord.

24. And when <u>she</u> had

    - And when <u>Hannah</u> had

24. Weaned <u>him</u>,

    - Weaned <u>Samuel</u>,

24. <u>She</u> took

    - <u>Hannah</u> took

24. <u>Him up</u> with her,

    - <u>Samuel [back] up [to Shiloh]</u> with her,

24. With three <u>bullocks</u>,

    - From the Hebrew word *par*, Strong's #6499: <u>young bull</u>.

    - With three <u>young bulls</u>,

24. And <u>one ephah</u> of flour,

    - And <u>1.1 bushel</u> of flour,

24. And a <u>bottle</u> of wine,

    - From the Hebrew word *nebel*, Strong's #5035: <u>a skin-bag for liquids</u>.

    - And a <u>skin-bag</u> of wine,

24. And brought <u>him</u> unto the house of the LORD in Shiloh:

    - And brought <u>Samuel</u> unto the house of the Lord in Shiloh:

24. And <u>the child</u> was young.

    - And <u>Samuel</u> was young.

25. And <u>they</u>

    - And <u>Elkanah and Hannah</u>

25. <u>Slew</u>

    - From the Hebrew word *shachat*, Strong's #7819: <u>kill</u>.

    - <u>Killed</u>

25. A <u>bullock</u>,

    - A <u>bull [for a sacrifice]</u>,

25. And brought <u>the child</u>

    - And brought <u>Samuel</u>

25. To <u>Eli</u>.

    - To <u>Eli [the priest]</u>.

26. And <u>she</u> said,
- And <u>Hannah</u> said,
26. Oh my <u>lord</u>,
- Oh my <u>lord (Eli)</u>,
26. As <u>thy</u> soul
- As <u>[surely as] your</u> soul
26. <u>Liveth</u>,
- <u>[Is] alive</u>,
26. My <u>lord</u>,
- My <u>lord (Eli)</u>,
26. I am the woman <u>that</u>
- I am the woman <u>who</u>
26. Stood by <u>thee</u> here, praying unto the LORD.
- Stood by <u>you</u> here, praying unto the Lord.
27. For this <u>child</u> I prayed;
- For this <u>child (Samuel)</u> I prayed;
27. And the LORD <u>hath</u> given me
- And the Lord <u>has</u> given me
27. <u>My</u> petition which I asked of him:
- <u>The</u> petition which I asked of him.
28. Therefore also I have <u>lent</u>
- From the Hebrew word *shaal*, Strong's #7592: <u>lend</u>.
- Therefore also I have <u>loaned</u>
28. <u>Him</u> to the LORD;
- <u>Samuel</u> to the Lord;
28. <u>As</u> long
- <u>[For] as</u> long
28. As he <u>liveth</u>
- As he <u>lives</u>
28. <u>He</u> shall be
- <u>Samuel</u> shall be
28. <u>Lent</u> to the LORD.
- <u>[On] loan</u> to the Lord.
28. And <u>he</u> worshipped the LORD there.
- And <u>Samuel</u> worshipped the Lord there.

Mark 9: 36, 37

36. And <u>he</u> took a child,
- And <u>Jesus</u> took a child

36. And set <u>him</u>
- And set <u>the child</u>

36. In the midst of <u>them</u>:
- In the midst of <u>his twelve disciples (see verse #35)</u>:

36. And when <u>he</u> had
- And when <u>Jesus</u> had

36. Taken <u>him</u> in his arms,
- Taken <u>the child</u> in his arms,

36. <u>He</u> said
- <u>Jesus</u> said

36. Unto <u>them</u>,
- Unto <u>the twelve disciples,</u>

37. <u>Whosoever</u>
- <u>Whoever</u>

37. Shall <u>receive</u>
- From the Greek word *dechomai*, Strong's #1209: <u>accept</u>.
- Shall <u>accept</u>

37. One of <u>such children</u> in my name,
- One of [a person's] <u>children such [as this child]</u> in my name,

37. <u>Receiveth</u> me:
- [Is also] <u>accepting</u> me:

37. And <u>whosoever</u>
- And <u>whoever</u>

37. Shall <u>receive</u> me,
- Shall <u>accept</u> me,

37. <u>Receiveth not</u> me,
- <u>Accepts not</u> [just] me,

37. But <u>him that</u> sent me.
- But [also] <u>God who</u> sent me.

Mark 9: 42

42. And <u>whosoever</u>

- And <u>whoever</u>

42. Shall **offend**
- From the Greek word *akandalizo*, Strong's #4624: <u>entice</u>
<u>to sin</u>.
- Shall <u>entice to sin</u>

42. One of these little **ones**
- One of these little <u>children</u>

42. <u>That</u>
- <u>Who</u>

42. <u>Believe</u>
- From the Greek word *pisteuo*, Strong's #4100: <u>to have</u>
<u>faith in</u>.
- <u>Has faith</u>

42. In <u>me,</u>
- In <u>me (Jesus)</u>,

42. It <u>is</u> better
- It <u>would [be]</u> better

42. For <u>him</u>
- For <u>the person [who entices a child to sin]</u>

42. <u>That</u> a
- <u>If</u> a

42. <u>Millstone</u>
- The Unger's Bible Dictionary states: "The mills of the
ancient Hebrews probably differed but little from those at present
in use in the East. These consist of two circular stones, about
eighteen inches or two feet in diameter, the lower of which is fixed,
and has it's upper surface slightly convex, fitting into a
corresponding concavity in the upper stone. The [upper stone] has
a hole in it through which the grain passes, immediately above a
pivot or shaft which rises from the center of the lower stone. The
upper stone is turned by means of an upright handle fixed near the
edge."
- <u>Millstone[,eighteen inches to two feet in diameter,]</u>

42. <u>Were hanged</u>
- <u>Was hung</u>

42. <u>About</u> his neck,
- From the Greek word *peri*, Strong's #4012: <u>around</u>.

- <u>Around</u> his neck,

42. And <u>he</u>
   - And <u>the person [who entices a child to sin]</u>

42. <u>Were</u> cast into the sea.
   - <u>Was</u> cast into the sea.

Mark 10: 13 - 15

13. And <u>they</u>
   - And <u>people (see verse #1)</u>

13. Brought young children to <u>him</u>,
   - Brought young children to <u>Jesus</u>,

13. <u>That he should</u>
   - <u>[So] that Jesus could</u>

13. Touch <u>them</u>:
   - Touch <u>the young children</u>:

13. And <u>his</u> disciples
   - And <u>Jesus'</u> disciples

13. Rebuked <u>those</u>
   - Rebuked <u>the people</u>

13. That brought <u>them</u>.
   - That brought <u>the children</u>.

14. But when Jesus saw <u>it</u>,
   - But when Jesus saw <u>[his disciples] rebuking the children</u>,

14. <u>He</u>
   - <u>Jesus</u>

14. Was <u>much</u> displeased,
   - Was <u>[very] much</u> displeased,

14. And <u>said</u>
   - And <u>[Jesus] said</u>

14. Unto <u>them</u>,
   - Unto <u>his disciples</u>,

14. <u>Suffer</u> the little children
   - From the Greek word *aphiemi*, Strong's #863: <u>let</u>.

- Let the little children

14. To come unto me,
- [Be allowed] to come unto me,

14. And forbid them not:
- And [do] not forbid the little children [from coming to me]:

14. For of such is the kingdom of God.
- For the kingdom of God is [passed on to children] such as [these].

15. Verily I say unto you,
- From the Greek word *amen*, Strong's #281: surely.
- Surely I say unto you,

15. Whosoever shall not
- Whoever does not

15. Receive the kingdom of God
- From the Greek word *dechomai*, Strong's #1209: accept.
- Accept the kingdom of God

15. As
- [In the same way] that

15. A little child,
- A little child [can accept the kingdom of God],

15. He shall not enter
- He shall not [be able to] enter

15. Therein.
- From the Greek word *eis*, Strongs #1519: into. And, from the Greek word *autos*, Strongs #846: it.
- Into it.

Ephesians 6: 4

4. And, ye fathers,
- And, you fathers,

4. Provoke not your children
- *Provoke* comes from the Greek word *parorgizo*, Strong's #3949: to anger alongside.
- [Do] not get angry alongside [of] your children

4. To

- [And, thereby, influence them] to

4. Wrath:
- Also from the Greek word *parorgizo*, Strong's #3949: <u>to anger alongside</u>. (The same Greek word translated as *provoke*, earlier in the verse, is translated as *wrath* in this instance).
- <u>Get angry alongside [of you]</u>:

4. But bring
- From the Greek word *ektrepho*, Strong's #1625: <u>to rear up to maturity, to cherish or train</u>.
- But <u>cherish, and train</u>

4. Them up in
- <u>Your children up [to maturity] with</u>

4. The nurture
- From the Greek word *paideia*, Strong's #3809: <u>disciplinary correction</u>.
- The <u>disciplinary correction</u>

4. And admonition
- From the Greek word *nouthesia*, Strong's #3559: <u>calling attention to by mild rebuke or warning</u>.
- And <u>mild rebukes and warnings</u>

4. Of the Lord.
- [That are] of the Lord.

CHOICE EXAMINATION

1. How did the children's knowledge that their parent's primary focus for them was always on service to God, help them naturally avoid many difficult issues?

2. In the scripture, what effect did the story of Hannah's prayer, the meaning of Samuel's name, and the symbol of the vow, have on Samuel's attitude toward God?

3. Why did Jesus say that accepting a child in his name is also accepting him?

4. Why did Jesus say that the kingdom of God must be accepted in the same way that a little child can accept the kingdom of God?

5. Why is it important for fathers to not get angry alongside of their children?

6. What choices do you need to make in order to *give your children to God*?

TAKE YOUR CHILDREN TO CHURCH WITH YOU

≈ 31 ≈

Let us hold fast the profession of our faith without wavering; (for he is faithful that promised;) And let us consider one another to provoke unto love and unto good works: Not forsaking the assembling of ourselves together, as the manner of some is; but exhorting one another: and so much the more, as ye see the day approaching.

Hebrews 10: 23 - 25

I heard an evangelist tell this story on himself:

"My dad was a pastor when I was a child. My parents used to *drag* me to church. I was an energetic boy. I was interested in all kinds of fun stuff. I didn't think I should have to take time out of my busy day to attend the church services. One day when I was a little older, I got the bright idea to sneak outside just before the end of the service. That way I could get a head start on having some fun. I thought no one would notice. A few minutes later someone ran outside and found me. I thought the church service had ended.

'You need to get back inside the church right now! Your dad sent me to get you.'

I figured I was in trouble, but I didn't expect to see this! The whole church congregation was still sitting quietly in their pews waiting. As soon as I seated myself, my dad, the pastor, said, 'And now, my son will close us in prayer.' He didn't have to scold me. I learned my lesson really well."

The most zealous Christian man I have ever met used to be a really ornery young boy. His parents *dragged* him to church too! He didn't have the option to decide if he wanted to go to church or not. His parents chose for him. As soon as he reached adulthood he quit attending church. He was free, he thought. No one could make him go to church. He started involving in all kinds of debauchery.

He surely found some temporary pleasure, but he knew something was missing in his life. A day came when he found himself in more trouble than he could get himself out of, and then he remembered what he had learned in church. He knew what was missing in his life. He needed a relationship with God. He chose to start attending church services again, but this time because he wanted to.

These were good parents. Both sets of parents had their children's best interests in mind. They both understood that it would be unrealistic to expect their young children to make responsible decisions in a rational manner. As parents of young children they were obligated for their children's protection and development. They surely cautioned their children to look both ways before crossing the street, to wash their hands before they ate their dinner, and to not climb into a car with a stranger. They surely required their children to develop good habits such as completing their homework on time, eating healthy foods, and showing respect to their elders. They taught these important behaviors to their children because they were the responsible adults. It was their duty, as parents, to make these decisions for their children. After the children became adults, then they would have the responsibility of choosing to continue, or to not continue, with the responsible behaviors their parents had taught them.

Including church attendance.

BULLET POINTS

Take your children to
Church
With you.
Go as a family.

Take your children to
Church
With you.
You're obligated for
Your children's
Protection and development.

Teach your children
Good behaviors
While they are young.
When they become adults
They can choose for
Themselves.

Church attendance is not
Optional if
Your parents tell you to
Go and
You're still a child.

Sending your children to
Church
With someone else
Is good, but
Taking your children to
Church with you
Is better.

Choose to
Take your children
To church
With you.

SCRIPTURE ANALYSIS

Hebrews 10: 23 - 25

23. Let us <u>hold</u>
- Let us <u>hold [onto and]</u>
23. <u>Fast</u>
- From the Greek word *katecho*, Strong's #2722: <u>keep in memory</u>.
- <u>Keep in [our] memory</u>

23. The <u>profession</u>

 - From the Greek word *homologia*, Strong's #3671: <u>acknowledgement</u>.

 - The <u>acknowledgement</u>

23. Of our <u>faith</u>

 - From the Greek word *elpis*, Strong's #1680: <u>to anticipate usually with pleasure</u>.

 - Of our <u>pleasurable anticipation [of a holy relationship with God due to the sacrifice made for us by Jesus (see verse #19 & 20)]</u>.

23. <u>Without wavering;</u>

 - The NIV says: "<u>Unswervingly</u>"

23. (For <u>he</u>

 - (For <u>God</u>

23. Is faithful <u>that promised</u>;)

 - <u>Who promised [to remember our sins no more (see verse #17)]</u> is faithful;)

24. And let us <u>consider</u>

 - From the Greek word *katanoeo*, Strong's #2657: <u>to observe fully</u>.

 - And let us <u>fully observe</u>

24. One <u>another</u>

 - One <u>[and] another [person's actions]</u>

24. To provoke <u>unto</u> love

 - To provoke <u>[each other] to [do actions of]</u> love

24. And <u>to</u> good works:

 - And <u>to [do actions of]</u> good works:

25. Not forsaking the assembling of ourselves together, as the <u>manner</u>

 - From the Greek word *ethos*, Strong's #1485: <u>a usage prescribed by habit or law</u>.

 - Not forsaking the assembling of ourselves together, as the <u>habit</u>

25. Of some <u>is</u>;

 - Of some <u>[people] is</u>;

25. But <u>exhorting</u>

 - From the Greek word *parakaleo*, Strong's #3870: <u>invite [or] exhort</u>.

- Webster's Dictionary defines *exhort* as: <u>to make urgent</u> <u>appeals</u>.
    - But [rather] <u>inviting [with urgent appeals]</u>
25. One <u>another</u>:
    - One [and] <u>another persons [to assemble with us]</u>:
25. <u>And</u>
    - <u>And [invite people]</u>
28. So much the <u>more</u>,
    - So much the <u>more [urgently]</u>,
25. As you see the <u>day</u> approaching.
    - As you see the <u>day [of the Lord (see I Thessalonians 5: 1-</u> <u>11)]</u> approaching.

CHOICE EXAMINATION

1. How did both sets of parents instill the importance of church attendance to their children?

2. Why was the man who had involved in all kinds of debauchery such a zealous Christian now?

3. Why did both sets of parents feel that it was their responsibility to teach important behaviors to their children, including church attendance?

4. In the scripture, why are we supposed to fully observe one and another's actions?

5. Why are we supposed to invite people with urgent appeals?

6. What choices do you need to make in order to *take your children to church with you?*

BLESS OTHERS ANONYMOUSLY

≈ 32 ≈

TAKE heed that ye do not your alms before men, to be
seen of them: otherwise ye have no reward of your Father
which is in heaven. Therefore when thou doest thine alms, do
not sound a trumpet before thee, as the hypocrites do in the
synagogues and in the streets, that they may have glory of men.
Verily I say unto you, They have their reward. But when thou
doest alms, let not thy left hand know what thy right hand
doeth: That thy alms may be in secret: and thy Father which
seeth in secret himself shall reward thee openly.

Matthew 6: 1-4

She waited until nobody was around. She knew her sister
would be coming soon and Charity always stopped by the mailbox
on her way home. She placed three hundred dollars in an envelope,
wrote Charity's name on it, and left quickly. Charity didn't know
who had left the money. She only knew that she had been blessed.

Amy is careful with her money. Her first job was at a bank.
Most of her first paychecks were routinely deposited into a savings
account, rather than a checking account. I remember one of the
first checks she ever wrote. It was to the Full Gospel Church. She
was paying her ten percent tithe. Amy understands the importance
of saving and investing. She also understands the importance of
giving.

For Charity it was the opportunity of a lifetime. Missouri
Southern State College was offering to send her to one semester of
classes in Cambridge, England. The college would pay for her
tuition, meals, and lodging. Transportation and miscellaneous
expenses would be her responsibility. Charity and her husband,
Jon, were both attending college classes and working part-time
jobs. They could pay their bills, but they had very little left over. It
would be difficult to come up with the money needed to make the

trip to England. They couldn't afford the burden of borrowed money, and they didn't think it would be appropriate to ask for help from their parents. Charity wanted to go, but it appeared that she might have to pass up this exciting opportunity.

I remember a time when Barbie went into Amy's room to help her organize her dresser. You can imagine Barbie's surprise when she found a pile of coins and cash stashed in the corner of one of the drawers. "Galen, I had no idea she had accumulated this much money," she told me later that evening. "This is the money she has earned from picking walnuts each fall. Instead of spending it, she's just been sticking it in her drawer. She's been collecting this money since she was a little girl."

"How much was in there?" I asked.

"About three hundred dollars."

I've thought a lot about what Amy did. She could have spent that money on herself. That three hundred dollars could have turned into something pretty, something fun, or even something useful. But, instead, Amy chose to turn it into something blessed. She gave it to her sister... anonymously.

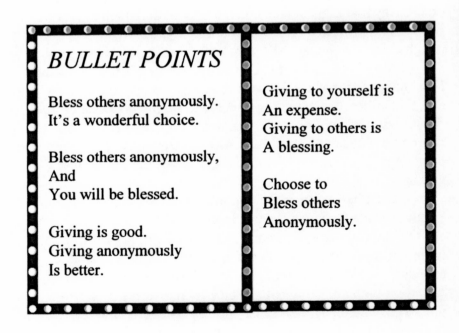

BULLET POINTS

Bless others anonymously.
It's a wonderful choice.

Bless others anonymously,
And
You will be blessed.

Giving is good.
Giving anonymously
Is better.

Giving to yourself is
An expense.
Giving to others is
A blessing.

Choose to
Bless others
Anonymously.

SCRIPTURE ANALYSIS

Matthew 6: 1 - 4

1. TAKE <u>heed</u>
   - From the Greek word *prosecho*, Strong's #4337: <u>be cautious about</u>.
   - Take <u>caution</u>
1. That <u>ye</u>
   - That <u>you</u>
1. Do <u>not</u>
   - Do <u>not [do]</u>
1. Your <u>alms</u>
   - From the Greek word *eleemosune*, Strong's #1654: <u>compassionateness (as exercised towards the poor)</u>.
   - Your <u>compassionate giving to poor [people]</u>
1. <u>Before</u>
   - From the Greek word *emprosthen*, Strong's #1715: <u>in front of</u>.
   - <u>In front of</u>
1. <u>Men, to be seen</u>
   - <u>[Other] men, [in order]</u> to be seen
1. <u>Of</u> them:
   - <u>By</u> them:
1. Otherwise <u>ye</u> have
   - Otherwise <u>you</u> have
1. No reward <u>of</u>
   - No reward <u>from</u>
1. Your <u>Father</u>
   - Your <u>Father (God)</u>
1. <u>Which</u> is in heaven.
   - <u>Who</u> is in heaven.
2. Therefore when <u>thou doest thine</u>
   - Therefore when <u>you do your</u>
2. <u>Alms,</u>
   <u>Compassionate giving to poor [people]</u>,
2. Do not sound a trumpet before <u>thee,</u>

- Do not sound a trumpet before <u>yourself [to announce your compassionate giving]</u>,

2. <u>As</u> the hypocrites do
- <u>Like</u> the hypocrites do

2. <u>In</u> the synagogues and in the streets,
- <u>[While they are] in</u> the synagogues and in the streets,

2. <u>That</u> they
- <u>[So] that</u> they

2. <u>May have</u>
- <u>Will receive</u>

2. <u>Glory</u>
- From the Greek word *doxazo*, Strong's #1392: <u>honour</u>.
- <u>Honor</u>

2. <u>Of</u> men.
- <u>From [other]</u> men.

2. <u>Verily</u> I say unto you,
- From the Greek word *amen*, Strong's #281: <u>surely</u>.
- <u>Surely</u> I say unto you,

2. <u>They have</u> their reward.
- <u>The hypocrites [who announce their compassionate giving to poor people] have [received all of]</u> their reward.

3. But when <u>thou doest alms,</u>
- But when <u>you do compassionate giving to poor [people]</u>,

3. Let <u>not</u>
- <u>[Do] not</u> let

3. <u>Thy</u> left hand know
- <u>Your</u> left hand know

3. What <u>thy</u> right hand
- What <u>your</u> right hand

3. <u>Doeth;</u>
- <u>[Is] doing;</u>

4. <u>That thine alms</u>
- <u>[So] that your compassionate giving to poor [people]</u>

4. May <u>be</u> in
- May <u>be [done]</u> in

4. <u>Secret:</u>
- From the Greek word *kruptos*, Strong's #2927: <u>private</u>.

- Private:
4. And thy Father
 - And [therefore] your Father (God)
4. Which seeth
 - Who sees [what happens]
4. In secret himself
 - In private himself
4. Shall reward thee openly.
 - Shall reward you openly.

CHOICE EXAMINATION

1. Why did Amy place the money in her sister's mailbox when nobody was around?

2. Why was the anonymous donation especially meaningful, coming from Amy?

3. What was Amy's motivation for giving the anonymous donation to her sister?

4. In the scripture, why did Jesus caution us to not give compassionately to poor people in front of other men?

5. How shall God reward people who give privately to poor people?

6. What choices do you need to make in order to *bless others anonymously*?

GIVE GOD OPPORTUNITIES TO BLESS YOU

≈ 33 ≈

And again he entered into Capernaum after some days; and it was noised that he was in the house. And straightway many were gathered together, insomuch that there was no room to receive them, no, not so much as about the door: and he preached the word unto them. And they come unto him, bringing one sick of the palsy, which was borne of four. And when they could not come nigh unto him for the press, they uncovered the roof where he was: and when they had broken it up, they let down the bed wherein the sick of the palsy lay.

When Jesus saw their faith, he said unto the sick of the palsy, Son, thy sins be forgiven thee.

And immediately he arose, took up the bed, and went forth before them all; insomuch that they were all amazed, and glorified God, saying, We never saw it on this fashion.

Mark 2: 1-5, 12

He stood up, squared his shoulders, looked me straight in the eyes and said, "It's a progressive disease, there is no cure. All we can do is control its symptoms through medication. We'll make your quality of life as good as we can for as long as we can." Those words were spoken to me by the neurologist, Dr. Andrews. He had just confirmed the diagnosis of the medical doctor, Dr. Barnes, who said he thought I had a disease called essential tremors.

My first noticeable symptoms occurred after doing some yard work. I had finished trimming the yard with a Weed Eater and walked into the house to get a drink of water. When I picked up the glass, my hand shook at the wrist. Barbie was alarmed, I was amused. "Surely this has been caused by the vibration of the Weed Eater" I said. "I'm certain it will go away soon." It didn't.

My symptoms progressed fairly rapidly. I lost coordination on the right side of my body, especially in my right arm. I had to use my left hand, which was unaffected, to hold cups and glasses.

It took me about five attempts to put the car keys into the ignition switch. I often cut myself while shaving, usually catching one of my ears with the razor. I frequently missed my mouth with a fork or spoon and got food on my face. One time a band instructor quickly stepped away from a parade to ask me to cut a tangled string from a student's hat. She stretched the string out tight between her hands. I awkwardly tried to help her but I was unable to control the knife. I almost cut her hand. She realized my predicament and took the knife from me to cut the string herself.

I couldn't keep my balance. Climbing a ladder was out of the question. Walking upstairs required either a hand rail or another person's hand for balance. Collecting the tithes and offerings at church was a difficult task. I had to strategically place one foot ahead of the other and open my eyes during prayer. The combination of bowing my head, closing my eyes, and standing still without something to hold onto was more than I was able to accomplish.

Motion made me dizzy. When I walked I had to change directions slowly. When I drove a car I had to move my head slowly to look for traffic at intersections. I remember walking into a restaurant that had a pair of off-set doors at the entrance. I walked through the first set of doors, turned to walk through the second set of doors, and then staggered sideways, bumping into the nearby table.

Despite my problems, I tried to act normally. I continued to work. I kept my management job at Wal-Mart. I baled hay on the farm. I cut and sold firewood. My work ability was definitely hindered, but I was determined to continue to do normal things as well as I could, for as long as I could.

I kept fighting. A concept which I often taught students who attended my Sunday School class was this: *you have to give God opportunities to bless you.* If your need is small, do whatever is appropriate in seeking God's help for your need. However, if your need is major, resort to extreme measures in seeking God's help. I knew I had to resort to extreme measures. I asked local ministers to have their congregations pray for my healing. I told the regular customers who shopped in my store about my affliction and asked them to pray for my healing. I prayed daily at home to be healed. I read and memorized healing scriptures in the Bible. Three times I tried to act on my faith and believe God to heal me by not taking my medication. (The medication treated symptoms only and was not designed for life sustaining or healing qualities.) One time I threw a full bottle of prescription medicine into the trash. All three times I ended up refilling my prescription and taking the medicine again.

Two years later I was still suffering with the disease, essential tremors. My symptoms grew steadily worse. The medication I was taking affected my mind as well as my body. I always felt tired and dull. I started dwelling on the things in life I was becoming unable to do. "Galen, you're depressed!" my mother said. "You need to snap out of it!"

She was right. I had allowed my frustration to turn into depression. I had a choice to make. I could live a diminished life because of the disease, or I could live a quality life despite the disease. I chose the quality life. I chose to muster my willpower and force myself to overcome the depression.

One evening at the close of a church service, we had prayer time around the altar. We were each given an opportunity to share our prayer requests with the congregation. When my turn came, I told the congregation that I knew I could live a quality life with my affliction, but I wanted to make myself available to God as an opportunity for a testimony of his greatness. "If God would heal my body," I said, "my life would serve as a witness of his greatness and his faithfulness to the promises in his Word, the Bible."

A few weeks later our church song leader, Lorna, gave a short testimony of how God had blessed her with a minor healing. Lorna said that when she prayed she knew God was going to heal her, because God had said he would heal her in his Word, the Bible. She had simply believed what God had said in his Word, and God had blessed her with the healing she needed.

When I woke up the next morning, Lorna's words were on my mind. God had healed her because God had said he would heal her in his Word, the Bible. I felt confident that God's promise for healing also included me, even in my present condition. I quit taking my medicine again. This time my symptoms diminished and gradually went away. Today, thankfully, I can testify that God has blessed me with complete healing from the disease, essential tremors. I no longer have any symptoms of the disease. I have been miraculously healed!

Why did God choose to heal me - this time? Why were my previous attempts to receive healing unsuccessful? Why have some people prayed and not received their healing? I believe one of the reasons that I received this blessing was that I gave God opportunities to bless me.

1. *I chose to act normally.* I kept doing normal things. I kept working. I tried to not act like I was sick. (Some of the store associates never realized how sick I was.) I tried to stay optimistic. When I became depressed, I chose to muster my willpower and force myself to overcome the depression.

2. *I chose to fight.* I asked no one to pray for me to have strength to endure my affliction. I asked everyone to pray for me to be healed .

3. *I took extreme measures.* I got as many people as possible to pray for my healing. I forced myself, against my normal tendencies, to stop people I didn't know well and ask them to pray for my healing.

4. *I stepped out in faith.* Remember that I quit taking my medicine three times and it didn't work. But the fourth time, after being inspired by Lorna's testimony, it did work.

5. *I gave my healing to God, for his glory.* I wanted my healing to serve as an opportunity for a testimony of God's greatness and his faithfulness to the promises in his Word, the Bible.

6. *I believed God would heal me* because God said he would heal me in his Word, the Bible.
And God is always true to his Word.

Surely he hath borne our griefs, and carried our sorrows: yet we did esteem him stricken, smitten of God, and afflicted. But he was wounded for our transgressions, he was bruised for our iniquities: the chastisement of our peace was upon him; and with his stripes we are healed.
Isaiah 53: 4, 5

Bless the LORD, O my soul, and forget not all his benefits:
Who forgiveth all thine iniquities; who healeth all thy diseases;
Psalm 103: 2, 3

And these signs shall follow them that believe; In my name
shall they cast out devils; they shall speak with new tongues;
They shall take up serpents; and if they drink any deadly
thing, it shall not hurt them; they shall lay hands on the sick,
and they shall recover.
Mark 16: 17, 18

Is any sick among you? let him call for the elders of the
church; and let them pray over him, anointing him with oil in
the name of the Lord: And the prayer of faith shall save the
sick, and the Lord shall raise him up; and if he have committed
sins, they shall be forgiven him.
James 5: 14, 15

SCRIPTURE ANALYSIS

Mark 2: 1 - 5, 12

1. And again <u>he</u> entered into
> - And again, <u>Jesus</u> entered into

1. <u>Capernaum</u>
> - Unger's Bible Dictionary states: "Capernaum was the residence of Jesus and his apostles, and the scene of many miracles and discourses. At Nazareth he was 'brought up,' but Capernaum was emphatically his 'own city;' it was when he returned thither that he is said to have been 'at home'."
> - [His home in] Capernaum

1. After some <u>days</u>;
> - After some <u>days [had passed]</u>;

1. And it was <u>noised</u> that
> - From the Greek word *akouo*, Strong's #191: <u>be reported</u>.

- And it was <u>reported</u> that
1. <u>He</u> was
    - <u>Jesus</u> was
1. In <u>the</u> house.
    - In <u>his</u> house.
2. And <u>straightway</u>
    - From the Greek word *eutheos*, Strong's #2112:
<u>immediately</u>.
    - And <u>immediately</u>
2. <u>Many</u> were gathered together,
    - <u>Many [people]</u> were gathered together,
2. Insomuch that there was no room to receive <u>them</u>,
    - Insomuch that there was no room to receive <u>the people</u>,
2. No, not <u>so</u> much as
    - No, not [even] <u>so</u> much as
2. <u>About</u> the door:
    - From the Greek word *pros*, Strong's #4314: <u>by</u>.
    - <u>By</u> the door:
2. And <u>he</u> preached
    - And <u>Jesus</u> preached
2. The <u>word</u>
    - The [holy] <u>word</u> [of God]
2. Unto <u>them</u>.
    - Unto <u>the [crowd of] people</u>.
2. <u>And</u>
    - <u>And</u> [then]
3. <u>They come</u>
    - <u>Four people came</u>
3. Unto <u>him</u>,
    - Unto <u>Jesus</u>,
3. Bringing <u>one</u> sick
    - Bringing <u>one [man who was]</u> sick
3. <u>Of the</u>
    - <u>From the [disease of]</u>
3. <u>Palsy</u>,
    - Unger's Bible Dictionary states: "Paralysis comes from several causes: (1) Inflammation of the brain or spinal cord. This in

the East is specially common in infancy, and in many cases leads to partial paralysis, as of the shoulder, arm, one or both legs, and sometimes the nerve of speech or hearing, or both. (2) Injuries to the spinal column. These are more apt to occur in adult life. (3) Pressure from curvature of the spine, or from tumors or other cause. (4) Apoplexy. The paralysis from the latter cause is sometimes cured. The cases brought to our Savior were undoubtedly of the incurable sort, and probably involved at least the lower limbs."

    - Paralysis.

3. Which was
    - And [he] was

3. Borne
    - From the Greek word *airo*, Strong's #142: carry.
    - Carried

3. Of
    - By [the]

3. Four.
    - Four [people].

4. And when they
    - And when the four people [carrying the paralyzed man]

4. Could not come nigh
    - Could not come near

4. Unto him
    - Unto Jesus

4. For the
    - Because [of] the

4. Press,
    - From the Greek word *ochlos*, Strong's #3793: number of people.
    - Number of people [in the house],

4. They
    - The four people

4. Uncovered the roof
    - Uncovered the roof [above]

4. Where he was:
    - Where Jesus was [located]:

4. And when they
> - And when the four men

4. Had broken it up,
> - Had broken the roof up,

4. They let down the bed
> - The four people let down the bed

4. Wherein the
> - Wherein the [man who was]

4. Sick of
> - Sick from

4. The palsy lay.
> - The [disease,] paralysis [was] lying.

5. When Jesus saw their faith,
> - When Jesus saw the four people's and the paralyzed man's faith,

5. He said
> - Jesus said

5. Unto the sick of the palsy,
> - Unto the [man who was] sick from the [disease] paralysis,

5. Son, thy sins
> - Son, your sins

5. Be
> - [Shall now] be

6. Forgiven thee.
> - Forgiven you.

12. And immediately he arose,
> - And immediately the paralyzed man arose,

12. Took up
> - From the Greek word *airo*, Strong's #142: lift up.
> - Lifted up

12. The bed,
> - The bed [he had been lying on],

12. And went forth
> - From the Greek word *exerchomai*, Strong's #1831: out.
> - And went out [of the house]

12. Before
> - From the Greek word *enantion*, Strong's #1726: in the

263

presence of.
- In the presence of

12. Them all;
- All the crowd of people;

12. Insomuch that they were all amazed,
- Insomuch that the crowd of people were all amazed,

12. And glorified God, saying,
- And [the crowd of people] glorified God, saying,

12. We never saw it
- We [have] never seen a miracle

12. On this fashion.
- The NIV says: "Like this!"

Isaiah 53: 4, 5

4. Surely he hath
- Surely Jesus has

4. Borne
- From the Hebrew word *nasa*, Strong's #5375: carry.
- Carried [the burden of]

4. Our griefs,
- From the Hebrew *choliy*, Strong's #2483: malady, anxiety, calamity, disease, grief, or sickness.
- Our maladies, anxieties, calamities, diseases, grief and sicknesses,

4. And carried our sorrows:
- And [Jesus has] carried [the burden of all] our sorrows:

4. Yet we did esteem
- From the Hebrew word *chashab*, Strong's #2803: regard.
- Yet we did regard

4. Him
- Jesus [to be]

4. Stricken,
- From the Hebrew word *naga*, Strong's #5060: defeat.
- Defeated,

4. Smitten
- From the Hebrew word *nakah*, Strong's #5221: Kill,

<u>punish,</u>

    - <u>Punished and killed</u>

4. Of God,

    - <u>By</u> God,

4. And afflicted.

    - From the Hebrew word *anah*, Strong's #6031: <u>humble</u>.

    - And <u>humiliated</u>.

5. But he was wounded

    - But <u>Jesus</u> was wounded

5. For our transgressions,

    - From the Hebrew word *pesha*, Strong's #6588: <u>a revolt</u> <u>(national, moral or religious)</u>.

    - For our <u>moral and religious revolt</u>.

5. He

    - <u>Jesus</u>

5. Was bruised

    - From the Hebrew word *daka*, Strong's #1792: <u>beat to</u> <u>pieces</u>.

    - Was <u>beat to pieces</u>

5. For our iniquities:

    - From the Hebrew word *avon*, Strong's #5771: <u>sin</u>.

    - For our <u>sins</u>:

5. The chastisement

    - From the Hebrew word *mowcerah*, Strong's #4149: <u>correction</u>

    - <u>The correction</u>

5. Of our peace

    - <u>[That provided] for</u> our peace

5. Was upon him;

    - Was upon <u>Jesus</u>;

5. And with his

    - And with <u>Jesus'</u>

5. Stripes we are healed.

    - From the Hebrew word *chabbuwrah*, Strong's #2250: <u>[a]</u> <u>black and blue mark, [or] wound</u>.

    - <u>Black and blue wounds</u> we are healed.

Psalm 103: 2,3

2: <u>Bless</u> the LORD,
  - From the Hebrew word *barak*, Strong's #1288: <u>praise</u>.
  - [I will] <u>praise</u> the Lord,
2. <u>O</u> my
  - [With all] <u>of</u> my
2. <u>Soul</u>,
  - From the Hebrew word *nephesh*, Strong's #5315: <u>breath</u> [and] vitality.
  - <u>Breath and vitality</u>,
2. And <u>forget not</u>
  - And [<u>I'll</u>] <u>not forget</u> [about]
2. All <u>his benefits</u>:
  - All [<u>of</u>] <u>the Lord's benefits</u> [when I praise him]:
3. <u>Who</u>
  - [It is the Lord] <u>who</u>
3. <u>Forgiveth</u>
  - <u>Forgives</u>
3. All <u>thine Iniquities</u>;
  - All [<u>of</u>] <u>your sins</u>;
3. <u>Who</u>
  - [<u>And</u>] <u>who</u>
3. <u>Healeth</u>
  - <u>Heals</u>
3. All <u>thy</u> diseases;
  - All [<u>of</u>] <u>your</u> diseases.

Mark 16: 17, 18

17. And these <u>signs</u>
  - From the Greek word *semeion,* Strong's #4592: <u>an indication</u>,
  - And these <u>indicators</u>
17. Shall follow <u>them</u>
  - Shall follow [<u>after</u>] <u>the people</u>
17. <u>That</u>

- <u>Who</u>
17. <u>Believe</u>;
    - From the Greek word *pisteuo*, Strong's #4100: <u>to have faith in</u>.
    - <u>Have faith in [Jesus]</u>;
17. In <u>my</u> name
    - In <u>my (Jesus')</u> name
17. Shall <u>they</u>
    - <u>They [who have faith in me]</u> shall
17. <u>Cast</u> out devils;
    - From the Greek word *ekballo*, Strong's #1544: <u>drive</u>.
    - <u>Drive</u> out devils;
17. <u>They</u>
    - <u>They [who have faith in me]</u>
17. Shall speak <u>with</u>
    - Shall speak <u>with [the gift of]</u>
17. New <u>tongues</u>;
    - From the Greek word *glossa*, Strong's #1100: <u>a language</u>.
    - New <u>languages</u>;
18. They <u>shall</u>
    - They <u>[who have faith in me]</u> shall <u>[be protected if they]</u>
18. Take up <u>serpents</u>;
    - From the Greek word *ophis*, Strong's #3789: <u>a snake</u>.
    - Take up <u>snakes</u>;
18. And if <u>they</u>
    - And if <u>they [who have faith in me (Jesus)]</u>
18. <u>Drink</u> any deadly thing,
    - <u>[Accidentally] drink</u> any deadly thing,
18. <u>It</u>
    - <u>The deadly thing</u>
18. Shall not hurt <u>them</u>;
    - Shall not hurt <u>the people [who have faith in me]</u>;
18. <u>They</u>
    - <u>They [who have faith in me (Jesus)]</u>
18. Shall lay <u>hands</u>
    - Shall lay <u>[their] hands</u>
18. On the <u>sick</u>,

- On the [people who are] sick,

18. And they

     - And the people [who are sick]

18. Shall recover.

     - Shall recover [from their sickness].

James 5: 14, 15

14. Is any sick among you?

     - Is [there] any [person who is] sick among you?

14. Let him

     - [If so,] let the person [who is sick]

14. Call for the elders of the church;

     - Defined by Webster's Dictionary as: One having authority by virtue of age and experience.

     - Call for the older and more experienced people of the church;

14. And let them

     - And let the older and more experienced people [of the church];

14. Pray over him,

     - Pray over the person [who is sick],

14. Anointing

     - Defined by Webster's Dictionary as: To smear or rub with oil or an oily substance.

     - Rubbing

14. Him

     - The person [who is sick]

14. With oil

     - Unger's Bible Dictionary states: "Oil was a fitting symbol of the Spirit, or spiritual principle of life, by virtue of it's power to sustain and fortify the vital energy; and the anointing oil, which was prepared according to divine instructions, was therefore a symbol of the Spirit of God."

     - With [anointing] oil

14. In the name of the Lord:

     - In the name of Jesus:

15. And the prayer of faith

- And the prayer [which is offered] in faith

15. Shall <u>save</u>

- From the Greek word *sozo*, Strong's #4982: <u>heal</u>.
- Shall <u>heal</u>

15. The <u>sick,</u>

- The <u>sick [person]</u>,

15. And the Lord shall raise <u>him up;</u>

- And the Lord shall raise <u>the sick person [back] up [to good health]</u>;

15. And if <u>he have</u> committed

- And if <u>the sick person has</u> committed

15. <u>Sins,</u>

- <u>[Any] sins [that may have caused the sickness]</u>,

15. <u>They</u>

- <u>The sins [which were committed]</u>

15. Shall be forgiven <u>him.</u>

- Shall be forgiven <u>[for] the sick person [too]</u>.

CHOICE EXAMINATION

1. What were some of the reasons that Galen received miraculous healing from God?

2. In the scripture, what did Jesus see that let him know the paralyzed man being carried by the four people had faith to be healed?

3. Why was Jesus beat to pieces with black and blue wounds?

4. What are some of the benefits for which we are supposed to praise the Lord?

5. Why is any person who is sick told to call for the older and more experienced people in the church to pray over him?

6. What choices do you need to make in order to *give God opportunities to bless you*?

LIVE EVERY DAY FOR GOD

≈ 34 ≈

Go to now, ye that say, Today or to morrow we will go into such a city, and continue there a year, and buy and sell, and get gain: Whereas ye know not what shall be on the morrow. For what is your life? It is even a vapour, that appeareth for a little time, and then vanisheth away. For that ye ought to say, If the Lord will, we shall live, and do this, or that.

James 4: 13 - 15

Today my father had a doctor's appointment at the veteran's hospital in Fayetteville, Arkansas. He was scheduled to receive his fifth chemotherapy treatment. It's part of an effort intended to lengthen his life. His birthday is tomorrow. He will be eighty-seven years old.

At the same moment my father was receiving his treatment, I was almost involved in a major automobile accident. I was hauling hay from a field near the highway. The brakes failed on the truck I was driving. I found myself in the middle of the highway with a loaded semi-truck speeding toward my driver's side door at fifty-five miles per hour. The truck driver locked up his brakes, skidded his tires, and missed me by only a few inches. If there had been one-half second difference in the times that we arrived, the truck would have hit me directly, and I would have been killed.

Life and time are connected. Conception to birth takes nine months. Infancy to adulthood takes twenty-one years. Adult life lasts perhaps a few decades. But death takes only an *instant*. It's only one heartbeat, one breath of air, or one final signal of a brain wave away.

We should choose to live every day for God. We don't know which one will be our last!

Honour thy father and thy mother: that thy days may be long
upon the land which the LORD thy God giveth thee.
Exodus 20: 12

Is there not an appointed time to man upon earth? are not his
days also like the days of an hireling? As a servant earnestly
desireth the shadow, and as an hireling looketh for the reward
of his work.
Job 7: 1, 2

For all our days are passed away in thy wrath: we spend our
years as a tale that is told. The days of our years are three
score years and ten; and if by reason of strength they be
fourscore years, yet is their strength labour and sorrow; for it
is soon cut off, and we fly away.
Psalm 90: 9, 10

CHILDREN, obey your parents in the Lord: for this is right.
Honour thy father and mother; which is the first
commandment with promise; That it may be well with thee,
and thou mayest live long on the earth.
Ephesians 6: 1 - 3

For I am now ready to be offered, and the time of my
departure is at hand. I have fought a good fight, I have finished
my course, I have kept the faith: Henceforth there is laid up
for me a crown of righteousness, which the Lord, the righteous
judge, shall give me at that day: and not to me only, but unto
all them also that love his appearing.
II Timothy 4: 6 - 8

SCRIPTURE ANALYSIS

James 4: 13 - 15

13. Go to now,
    - The NIV says: "Now listen,"

13. Ye that say,
    - You [people] who say,

13. Today or to morrow we will go into such a city,
    - From the Greek word *hode*, Strong's #3592: this or that one.
    - Today or tomorrow we will go into a city [like] this or that one,

13. And continue there a year,
    - From the Greek word *poieo*, Strong's #4160: abide.
    - And abide there a year,

13. And buy and sell, and get gain:
    - And buy and sell and get [the money we've] gained [from our efforts]:

14. Whereas ye know not
    - Whereas you [do] not know

14. What shall be on
    - What shall be [happening] on

14. The morrow.
    - From the Greek word *aurion*, Strong's #839: next day.
    - The next day.

14. For what is your life?
    - For what is your life's [purpose]?

14. It is
    - Your life is

14. Even a
    - From the Greek word *gar*, Strong's #1063: as.
    - [Much the same] as a

14. Vapour,
    - From the Greek word *atmis*, Strong's #822: mist.
    - Mist,

14. That appeareth

- That <u>appears</u>
14. For a little time, and then <u>vanisheth</u> away.
- For a little time, and then <u>vanishes</u> away.
15. For <u>that ye</u> ought
- For <u>what you</u> ought
15. To <u>say,</u>
- To <u>say [is this]</u>,
15. If the Lord <u>will,</u>
- If the Lord <u>will [approve of it]</u>,
15. We shall <u>live,</u>
- We shall <u>live [in this or that city]</u>,
15. And do this, or <u>that.</u>
- And do this, or <u>that [buying and selling]</u>.

Exodus 20: 12

12. Honour <u>thy</u> father
- Honor <u>your</u> father
12. And <u>thy</u> mother:
- And <u>your</u> mother:
12. <u>That thy days</u>
- <u>[So] that [the] days [of]</u> your <u>[life]</u>
12. May <u>be</u>
- May <u>be [extended for]</u>
12. <u>Long</u> upon the land
- <u>[A] long [time]</u> upon the land
12. Which the LORD <u>thy</u> God
- Which the Lord <u>your</u> God
12. <u>Giveth thee.</u>
- <u>[Has] given [to] you.</u>

Job 7: 1, 2

1. Is there not an <u>appointed</u> time
- From the Hebrew word t*saba*, Strong's #6635: <u>a mass of persons or soldiers, waiting upon warfare.</u>

- Is there not an <u>appointed</u> time [<u>as with soldiers waiting</u> <u>upon warfare</u>]

1. <u>To</u> man
> - For [each] man

1. Upon <u>earth</u>?
> - Upon [the] earth?

1. Are not <u>his</u> days
> - Are not [each] man's days

1. Also like the days of <u>an</u>
> - Also like the days of <u>a</u>

1. <u>Hireling</u>?
> - From the Hebrew word *sakiyr*, Strong's #7916: <u>hired</u> <u>servant</u>.
> - <u>Hired servant</u>?

2. <u>As</u>
> - [Such] as [when]

2. A servant earnestly <u>desireth</u>
> - A servant earnestly <u>desires</u>

2. <u>The shadow,</u>
> - [For] the [evening] shadow [to arrive],

2. And <u>as</u>
> - And [such] as [when]

2. <u>An hireling looketh</u> for
> - <u>A hired servant looks</u> for

2. The reward <u>of</u> his work:
> - The reward <u>for</u> his work:

Psalm 90: 9, 10

9. For all <u>our days</u>
> - For all [<u>of the remaining</u>] days [<u>of</u>] our [<u>lives</u>]

9. <u>Are passed</u> away
> - <u>Can pass</u> away

9. <u>In thy</u> wrath:
> - [Due] to God's wrath:

9. We spend our <u>years</u>

- We spend our <u>years [consumed with our own lives]</u>

9. <u>As</u> a tale that is told.

- [<u>Only to be remembered</u>] <u>as</u> a tale that is told.

10. The <u>days of</u> our

- The [<u>total number</u>] of days [<u>in</u>] our

10. <u>Years</u> are

- <u>Years [of life]</u> are

10. <u>Threescore years and ten</u>;

- <u>Seventy</u>;

10. And <u>if</u> by reason

- And <u>if [we live longer]</u> by reason

10. Of <u>strength</u>

- Of [<u>good</u>] strength [<u>in our bodies and</u>]

10. <u>They</u>

-<u>The total number of days [that we live]</u>

10. Be <u>fourscore</u> years,

- Be [<u>increased to</u>] eighty years,

10. Yet is <u>their strength</u>

- Yet is <u>our strength [expended by the]</u>

10. Labour and <u>sorrow</u>;

- Labor and <u>sorrow [that remains ahead of us]</u>;

10. For <u>it</u>

- For <u>our [remaining] days of life</u>

10. <u>Is</u> soon cut off,

- <u>Are</u> soon cut off,

10. And we fly <u>away</u>.

- And we fly <u>away [to our eternal home]</u>.

Ephesians 6: 1 - 3

1. CHILDREN, obey your parents <u>in</u> the Lord:

- Children, obey your parents [<u>which is a requirement</u>] for [<u>obeying</u>] the Lord:

1. For <u>this</u>

- For <u>obedience [to your parents]</u>

1. Is <u>right</u>.

- From the Greek word *dikaios*, Strong's #1342: <u>innocent, holy, [or] righteous</u>.
    - Is <u>innocent, holy and righteous</u>.
2. Honour <u>thy</u> father and mother;
    - Honor <u>your</u> father and mother;
2. Which is the first <u>commandment</u>
    - Which is the first [of the ten] commandments
2. With <u>promise</u>;
    - With <u>promises [attached to it. (See Deuteronomy 5:16) And those promises are</u>]:
3. That <u>it</u>
    - That <u>your life</u>
3. May <u>be</u> well
    - May <u>go</u> well
3. With <u>thee</u>,
    - With <u>you</u>,
3. And <u>thou</u>
    - And [that] <u>you</u>
3. <u>Mayest</u>
    - <u>May</u>
3. Live <u>long</u> on the earth.
    - Live [a] <u>long</u> [life] on the earth.

II Timothy 4: 6 - 8

6. For <u>I</u>
    - For <u>I</u> (Paul)
6. Am now <u>ready</u>
    - Am now <u>ready</u> [for my life]
6. To be <u>offered</u>,
    - To be <u>offered</u> [to God],
6. And the time of my <u>departure</u> is at hand.
    - And the time of my <u>departure</u> [from this life] is at hand.
7. I have fought a good <u>fight</u>,
    - I have fought a good [spiritual] <u>fight</u>
7. I have finished my <u>course</u>,
    - From the Greek word *dromos*, Strong's #1408: <u>a race</u>.

- I have finished my [portion of life's] race,

7. I have <u>kept</u>
- From the Greek word *tereo*, Strong's #5083: <u>to guard</u>.
- I have <u>guarded</u>

7. The <u>faith</u>:
- The <u>faith [I have in God]</u>:

8. Henceforth there is laid up for <u>me</u>
- Henceforth there is laid up for <u>me [in heaven]</u>

8. A crown <u>of</u> righteousness,
- A crown [representative] of [God's] righteousness,

8. Which the Lord, <u>the</u> righteous judge,
- Which the Lord, [who is] the righteous judge,

8. Shall give <u>me</u>
- Shall give [to] me

8. At <u>that day</u>:
- At <u>the day</u> [of Christ's second coming (see verse #1)]

8. And not <u>to</u> me only,
- And not [just] <u>to</u> me only,

8. But unto all <u>them</u>
- But unto all <u>other people [who are judged as righteous and]</u>

8. Also who love <u>his appearing</u>.
- Who also love [Jesus and are anxious for] <u>him [to] appear</u>.

CHOICE EXAMINATION

1. How much time would there have been to prepare for death if the semi-truck would have collided with the hay hauling truck?

2. How might his perspective have been affected if he knew previously that he could die on that day?

3. In the scripture, why is seeking the Lord's approval to live in this or that city and to do this or that buying and selling an important attitude for life?

4. Why did God attach the promise of long life to honoring your mother and your father?

5. Why did Paul think he was ready to be offered to God?

6. What choices do you need to make in order to *live every day for God?*

CHOOSE TO BE WISE

KEEP YOUR PRIORITIES IN THE RIGHT ORDER

≈ 35 ≈

And when he had called the people unto him with his disciples also, he said unto them, Whosoever will come after me, let him deny himself, and take up his cross, and follow me. For whosoever will save his life shall lose it; but whosoever will lose his life for my sake and the gospel's, the same shall save it. For what will it profit a man, if he shall gain the whole world, and lose his own soul? Or what shall a man give in exchange for his soul? Whosoever therefore shall be ashamed of me and of my words in this adulterous and sinful generation; of him also shall the Son of man be ashamed, when he cometh in the glory of his Father with the holy angels.

Mark 8: 34 - 38

"You have to keep your priorities in the right order.
Your number one priority is God.
Your number two priority is your spouse.
Your number three priority is your children.
Your number four priority is your work."

December 31, 1976. It was our wedding day. Our pastor, Brother Dean, had given us advice about priorities that was still fresh on our minds. We didn't have a clue of what spiritual, family, or career opportunities were ahead of us - but we knew our priorities and we were excited about starting this new chapter in our lives.

It's been thirty years since Brother Dean gave us that good advice. Despite our good intentions, here's what I've noticed about our lives:

We've spent more time with our co-workers than with our children.
We've spent more time taking care of our children than taking care of each other.
We've spent more time talking with each other than talking with God.

Even with all of our faults, we've learned three things:

Being a good employee is part of being a responsible parent.
Being an involved parent is part of being a loving spouse.
Being an attentive spouse is part of being a dedicated Christian.

We've come to the following conclusions about applying Brother Dean's advice:

You have keep your priorities in the right order, and
You have to allow your priorities to influence the choices you make each day.

Always remember:

Your number one priority is God.
Your number two priority is you spouse.
Your number three priority is your children.
Your number four priority is your work.

BULLET POINTS

Keep your priorities in the right order.
Your number one priority is God.
Your number two priority is your spouse.
Your number three priority is your children.
Your number four priority is your work.

Keep your priorities in the right order.
Allow your priorities to influence the
Choices you make each day.

The highest priority may take the least time,
But it's still the highest priority.

The lowest priority may take the most time,
But it's still the lowest priority.

Choose to
Keep your priorities
In the right order.

SCRIPTURE ANALYSIS

Mark 8: 34 - 38

34. And when <u>he</u> had called the people
   - And when <u>Jesus</u> had called the people
34. <u>Unto</u> him
   - [To come] <u>unto</u> him
34. <u>With</u> his disciples also,
   - [Along] <u>with</u> his disciples also,
34. <u>He</u> said
   - <u>Jesus</u> said

34. Unto <u>them</u>,
- Unto <u>the people</u>,

34. <u>Whosoever</u> will come after me,
- <u>Whoever</u> will come after me,

34. Let him <u>deny</u> himself,
- From the Greek word *aparneomai*, Strong's #533: <u>disown</u>.
- Let him <u>disown</u> himself,

34. And <u>take</u> up his cross,
- From the Greek word *airo*, Strong's #142: <u>lift up</u>.
- And <u>lift</u> up his cross,

34. And <u>follow</u> me.
- From the Greek word *akoloutheo*, Strong's #190: <u>to be in the same way with</u>.
- And <u>be in the same way as</u> me.

35. For <u>whosoever</u>
- For <u>whoever</u>

35. Will <u>save</u>
- Will <u>[prioritize] saving</u>

35. His <u>life</u>
- His <u>life [on earth]</u>

35. Shall lose <u>it</u>;
- Shall lose <u>his life [in heaven]</u>;

35. But <u>whosoever</u>
- But <u>whoever</u>

35. Shall <u>lose</u>
- Shall <u>[prioritize] losing</u>

35. His <u>life</u>
- His <u>life [on earth]</u>

35. For my sake and <u>the gospel's</u>,
- For my sake and <u>[for] the gospel's [sake]</u>,

35. <u>The same</u>
- <u>That same [person]</u>

35. Shall save <u>it</u>.
- Shall save <u>his life [in heaven]</u>.

36. For <u>what</u> shall it profit a man,
- For <u>how</u> shall it profit a man,

36. If he shall <u>gain</u> the whole world,
>- If he shall gain [the value of] the whole world,

36. <u>And</u> lose his own soul?
>- And [yet] lose his own soul?

37. <u>Or</u>
>- Or [in other words]

37. <u>What shall</u> a man give in exchange for his soul?
>- What [things which can be gained from the world] can a
man give in exchange for his soul?

38. <u>Whosoever</u> therefore
>- Whoever therefore

38. Shall be ashamed <u>of</u> me
>- Shall be ashamed [to be associated] with me

38. And <u>of</u>
>- And [shall be ashamed to be associated] with

38. My <u>words</u>
>- From the Greek word *logos*, Strong's #3056: doctrine.
>- My doctrine

38. <u>In</u> this adulterous
>- [While living] in this adulterous

38. And sinful <u>generation</u>;
>- From the Greek word *genea*, Strong's #1074: time.
>- And sinful time;

38. Of <u>him</u>
>- Of the person who is ashamed of me and of my doctrine

38. <u>Also</u>
>- Likewise

38. Shall the Son of <u>man</u> be ashamed,
>- Shall the Son of man (Jesus) be ashamed,

38. When he <u>cometh</u>
>- When he comes [back]

38. In the glory <u>of</u>
>- In the glory [that comes] from

38. His <u>Father</u>
>- His Father (God)

38. <u>With</u> the holy angels.
>- [Along] with the holy angels.

CHOICE EXAMINATION

1. Why did Brother Dean place the four priorities in the order of God, spouse, children, work?

2. How can you be placing your priorities in the order of God, spouse, children and work when you:
- spend more time talking with each other than talking with God
- spend more time taking care of your children than taking care of your spouse.
- spend more time with co-workers than with your children

3. How do being a good employee, an involved parent, an attentive spouse, and a dedicated Christian relate to each other?

4. In the scripture, why did Jesus say his followers must disown themselves?

5. Why would a person who prioritizes saving his life on earth lose his life in heaven?

6. What choices do you need to make in order to *keep your priorities in the right order*?

LIVE WITHIN YOUR MEANS
≈ 36 ≈

For which of you, intending to build a tower, sitteth not down first, and counteth the cost, whether he have sufficient to finish it? Lest haply, after he hath laid the foundation, and is not able to finish it, all that behold it begin to mock him, saying, This man began to build, and was not able to finish.

Or what king, going to make war with another king, sitteth not down first, and consulteth whether he be able with ten thousand to meet him which cometh against him with twenty thousand?

Luke 14: 28 - 31

It was a beautiful pickup. It was brand new! It had four-wheel drive. It was bright and shiny. It had all the extras that any young man could ever want. He loved his new truck. Unfortunately, he didn't have much time to drive it. He was trying to work three jobs to pay for it!

I was the store's co-manager. I visited with the young man about his work schedule. "Let me explain this. You're a sales clerk. You've only worked at this store for two months. You can't expect me to continue to schedule you for forty hours of work if you're suddenly not available evenings or weekends. Your job requires you to be here when the customers are here. I will accommodate all reasonable requests you have for specific days and times off. I will only make a schedule which matches your availability. However, I will not create a forty hour schedule for you which does not match the needs of our customers."

"But, I've got this opportunity to work two other jobs, one in the evenings, another one over the weekends."

"Why would you choose to work all the time like that?"

"Because I just bought this new truck, and..."

I spent several minutes visiting with the young man. I

conceded to him that it's exciting for a young man to have an impressive new pickup. I also suggested that he might want to consider the value of having a new truck at this stage of his life if he has to work seven days a week in order to afford the truck payment.

I visited with the manager about the young man's situation. They got together later and worked out a compromise. The young man would work forty hours a week in a job which we had available overnights. That way he would be free to work at his other two jobs if he chose to keep them.

I admired his ambition. He hadn't done anything bad. He just wasn't living within his means. He wanted a fancy new pickup, and one entry level job was not sufficient to pay for it. I was proud of him for attempting to pay for the truck himself instead of relying on someone else to meet the payments. I was pleased for him to have the new truck. I was pleased that his Wal-Mart job was helping him to purchase the new truck. I just didn't want the burden of his truck payments to significantly affect his responsibilities to the customers of the store.

I was thinking about the young man's situation as I walked across the parking lot to go home that evening. I could have easily afforded his truck payment. I would have enjoyed driving a new pickup home. I was pleased, however, to go home in my eleven year old Buick instead, because... it was paid for.

BULLET POINTS

Live within your means.
If you want it,
You need it, and
You can afford it,
Buy it.

Live within your means.
If you want it,
You need it, and
You can't afford it,
Rent it.

If you want it,
You don't need it, and
You can't afford it,
Admire it.

If you don't want it,
You don't need it, and
You can't afford it,
Ignore it,
Even if it's a good deal.

The seller sells,
The buyer buys,
The winner grins,
The loser cries.

Never buy then
Wonder why.

Major purchases require
Thorough consideration.

Avoid credit whenever
Possible.

Pay as little interest as
Possible.

If possible, save the money
First, then
Make the purchase
Later.

Choose to
Live within
Your means.

SCRIPTURE ANALYSIS

Luke 14: 28 - 30

28. For <u>which</u> of you,
　　- For <u>which [person]</u> of you,

28. Intending
- [Who is] intending
28. To build a tower,
- The Unger's Bible Dictionary states that a tower is: "A fortified structure rising to a considerable height, to repel a hostile attack, or to enable a watchman to see in every direction. Besides these military structures, we read in scripture of towers built in vineyards as an almost necessary appendage to them. Such towers are still in use in Palestine in vineyards, especially near Hebron, and are used as lodges for the keepers of the vineyards."
- To build a tower,
28. Sitteth not down first,
- [Does] not sit down first,
28. And counteth
- To count
28. The cost,
- The cost [of construction],
28. Whether he
- [To find out] whether he
28. Have sufficient
- Has sufficient [resources]
28. To finish it?
- To finish [building] the tower?
29. Lest
- Unless
29. Haply,
- Webster's Dictionary defines *haply*, as: by chance.
- By chance,
29. After he hath
- After the person [who intended to build the tower] has
29. Laid the foundation,
- Laid the foundation [of the tower],
29. And is not able to finish it,
- And is not able to finish [building] the tower,
29. All
- [Then] all [the people]
29. That behold

- From the Greek word *theoreo*, Strong's #2334: <u>see</u>.
- That <u>see</u>

29. <u>It</u>
- The <u>[unfinished] tower</u>

29. <u>Begin</u> to
- <u>[Will]</u> <u>begin</u> to

29. <u>Mock him,</u>
- Webster's Dictionary defines mock as: <u>ridicule</u>.
- <u>Ridicule the man [who was intending to build the tower]</u>,

30. Saying, This man began to <u>build</u>,
- Saying, This man began to <u>build</u> [a tower],

30. And was not able to <u>finish</u>.
- And was not able to <u>finish [it]</u>.

31. Or what king, going to make war against another king, <u>sitteth not</u> down first,
- Or what king, going to make war against another king, <u>[does] not sit</u> down first,

31. <u>And consulteth</u>
- <u>To consult [with his advisors to see]</u>

31. Whether he <u>be</u> able
- Whether he <u>is</u> able

31. With ten <u>thousand</u>
- With ten <u>thousand [soldiers]</u>

31. To meet <u>him</u>
- To meet <u>[in battle] he</u>

31. <u>That cometh</u> against him
- <u>Who comes</u> against him

31. With twenty <u>thousand?</u>
- With twenty <u>thousand [soldiers]</u>?

CHOICE EXAMINATION

1. Why did the young man buy such an expensive new pickup?

2. How did the young man's purchase affect other areas of his life?

3. How did the young man's purchase affect other people's lives?

4. In the scripture, what options should have been considered by the person who intended to build a tower?

5. What options should have been considered by the king who had ten thousand soldiers, when consulting with his advisors about going to battle against twenty thousand soldiers?

6. What choices do you need to make in order to *live within your means*?

SPEND MONEY WISELY

≈ 37 ≈

And he said, A certain man had two sons: And the younger of them said to his father, Father, give me the portion of goods that falleth to me. And he divided unto him his living.

And not many days after the younger son gathered all together, and took his journey into a far country, and there wasted his substance with riotous living. And when he had spent all, there arose a mighty famine in that land; and he began to be in want. And he went and joined himself to a citizen of that country; and he sent him into his fields to feed swine. And he would fain have filled his belly with the husks that the swine did eat: and no man gave unto him.

And when he came to himself, he said, How many hired servants of my father's have bread enough and to spare, and I perish with hunger!

Luke 15: 11 - 17

He was the richest man in America! He was on the phone, and he needed help from *me*!!

All of us at Wal-Mart were tremendously proud when the October 1985 edition of Forbes magazine proclaimed Sam Walton, founder and chairman of Wal-Mart stores Inc., to be the "Richest Man in America." I believe that we associates, Wal-Mart's word for employees, were more excited about this distinction than he was. Mr. Sam, as he was affectionately called, would rather be known as a *frugal* man than as a *rich* man, and his lifestyle proved it.

The telephone rang at the store. The caller had asked to speak to the manager. I answered with my usual, "This is Galen Manning. May I help you please?"

"Hello, Galen, this is Sam Walton." (I thought it was a joke, another store manager playing a trick on me.)

"Yeah, I'll bet it's Sam Walton," I said.

"How are your sales this week, Galen?"

"Oh! Is it really you sir? Uh, oh yeah, uh sales! They're up 8 ½ % this week, uh, sir! (I was really nervous.)

"Good, Galen, now listen up. I need your help. I'm staying at my cabin near your store. I hit a culvert with my pickup and now the engine won't start. I think maybe I broke a gas line or something. Do you have someone at the store who is pretty good at mechanical work, that can take a look at my truck?"

"Yes sir, Mr. Sam. I'll send a couple of people down there right away!"

When John and Cecil returned from inspecting the truck they were laughing out loud. "Broken gas line!! Well… he rammed the whole engine back and bent the frame on the truck! We told him it's totaled. It's not worth fixing. He needs to buy a new truck!"

Two days later I was standing at the front of the building with the store's associates conducting the morning meeting. I was going over the sales report and discussing the day's agenda when someone interrupted me. "Isn't that Sam Walton's pickup being pulled down the highway behind that wrecker truck?"

Yes, it was. It was heading toward Bentonville, Arkansas, Mr. Sam's home. It was being pulled to the repair shop. Somehow, some mechanic was going to figure out how to replace and straighten the various mangled parts on the old truck well enough to get it running again.

Mr. Sam liked the old truck. It took him to all the places a new truck would have taken him, and it got him there just as quickly. He never did choose to replace it with a new one. But, had he wanted to purchase a new truck, he certainly could have afforded it. He was the "Richest Man in America".

BULLET POINTS

Spend money wisely.
Money wasted is not
Easily replaced.

Spend money wisely.
Choose frugality when
It makes sense.

Earning money requires
Time and effort.
Saving money requires
Only a choice.

Make spending choices in the order of
Need,
Affordability, and then
Value.

Disregard spending choices made only
Because of appeal.

Being able to afford it is
Not sufficient reason,
To buy it.

Choose to
Spend money
Wisely.

SCRIPTURE ANALYSIS

Luke 15: 11 - 17

11. And <u>he</u> said, A certain man had two sons:
 - And <u>Jesus</u> said, A certain man had two sons:
12. And the younger of <u>them</u> said to his father,
 - The Unger's Bible dictionary states: "According to an old-standing custom, the father's property went to his sons, the *first born* receiving a double portion, the other sons [receiving] single and equal portions - i.e., of five sons the firstborn got two sixths, and each of the others a sixth of the father's entire property. In consideration of this division, the firstborn, as head of the family, had to provide food, clothing, and other necessities in his house, not only for his mother, but also for his sisters until their marriage."
 - And the younger of <u>the two sons</u> said to his father,
12. Father, give <u>me</u>
 - Father, give me [<u>now</u>]
12. The portion of <u>goods</u>
 - From the Greek word *ousia*, Strong's #3776: <u>possessions</u>.
 - The portion of [<u>your</u>] <u>possessions</u>
12. That <u>falleth</u>
 - That [<u>will</u>] <u>fall</u>
12. To <u>me</u>.
 - To <u>me [for my inheritance]</u>.
12. And <u>he</u>
 - And [<u>so</u>] <u>his father</u>
12. <u>Divided</u>
 - <u>Divided [up]</u>
12. Unto <u>him</u>
 - Unto <u>the younger son</u>
12. His <u>living</u>.
 - From the Greek word *bios*, Strong's #979: <u>the means of livelihood</u>.
 - <u>The means of</u> his [<u>own</u>] <u>livelihood</u>.
13. And not many days <u>after</u>

- And not many days <u>after [the younger son had received his portion of his father's possessions]</u>

13. The younger son gathered <u>all</u> together,
- The younger son gathered <u>all [of his newly acquired possessions]</u> together,

13. And took <u>his</u> journey
- And took <u>a</u> journey

13. Into a <u>far</u> country,
- Into a <u>far [away]</u> country,

13. And <u>there</u>
- And <u>there [in the far away country, the younger son]</u>

13. <u>Wasted</u>
- <u>Wasted [the inheritance money that he had acquired from receiving]</u>

13. His <u>substance</u>
- Also from the Greek word *ousia*, Strong's #3776: <u>possessions</u>. The same word was translated as *goods* in verse # 12.
- His <u>[father's] possessions</u>

13. With <u>riotous</u>
- Webster's dictionary defines *riotous* as: <u>exuberant</u>.
- With <u>[an] exuberant</u>

13. <u>Living</u>.
- <u>Lifestyle</u>.

14. And when <u>he</u>
- And when <u>the younger son</u>

14. Had spent <u>all</u>,
- Had spent <u>all [of his inheritance money]</u>,

14. There arose a mighty famine in <u>that land</u>;
- There arose a mighty famine in <u>the land [where the younger son was living]</u>;

14. And <u>he</u>
- And <u>the younger son</u>

14. Began to be in <u>want</u>.
- From the Greek word *hustereo*, Strong's #5302: <u>suffer need</u>.
- Began to be in <u>need</u>.

15. And <u>he</u> went

- And the <u>younger son</u> went

15. <u>And joined</u> himself
- <u>To join</u> himself

15. To a citizen of that <u>country</u>;
- To a citizen of that [<u>far away</u>] <u>country</u>;

15. And <u>he</u>
- And <u>the citizen [of the far away country]</u>

15. Sent <u>him</u> into his fields
- Sent <u>the younger son</u> into his fields

15. To feed <u>swine</u>.
- From the Greek word *choiros*, Strong's #5519: <u>a hog</u>.
- To feed [<u>his</u>] <u>hogs</u>.

16. And <u>he</u>
- And the <u>younger son</u>

16. Would <u>fain</u> have filled his belly
- Defined by Webster's dictionary as: <u>willing</u>.
- Would [<u>have been</u>] <u>willing</u> [<u>to</u>] have filled his belly

16. With the <u>husks</u>
- From the Greek word *keration*, Strong's #2769: <u>something horned, i.e. the pod of the carob tree</u>.
- With the <u>carob tree pods</u>

16. That the <u>swine did eat</u>:
- That the <u>hogs were eating</u>:

16. And no <u>man</u>
- And no <u>man [in the far away country where the younger son was living]</u>

16. <u>Gave</u>
- <u>Gave [anything]</u>

16. Unto <u>him</u>.
- Unto <u>the younger son</u>.

17. And when he came to <u>himself</u>,
- The NIV says: "And when he came to <u>his senses</u>,"

17. <u>He said</u>,
- <u>The younger son said [to himself]</u>,

17. How many hired servants of my father's have <u>bread enough</u>
- How many hired servants of my father's have [<u>plenty of</u>]

bread, enough [to eat]
17. And to spare,
  - And [more] to spare,
17. And I perish with hunger!
  - And I [am about to] perish with hunger!

CHOICE EXAMINATION

1. Why did Sam Walton call the store for help instead of calling a mechanic?

2. Why did Sam Walton repair the truck instead of purchasing a new one?

3. What impact did Sam Walton's personal frugalness have on spending habits throughout the company?

4. In the scripture, how was the son's sense of responsibility affected by the fact that he was younger?

5. How did the younger son's attitude change after he had spent all of his inheritance?

6. What choices do you need to make in order to *spend money wisely*?

SEEK SIMPLE SOLUTIONS TO SIMPLE PROBLEMS

≈ 38 ≈

And Jesus entered and passed through Jericho. And, behold, there was a man named Zaccheus, which was the chief among the publicans, and he was rich. And he sought to see Jesus who he was; and could not for the press, because he was little of stature. And he ran before, and climbed up into a sycomore tree to see him: for he was to pass that way. And when Jesus came to the place, he looked up, and saw him, and said unto him, Zaccheus, make haste, and come down; for to day I must abide at thy house.

Luke 19: 1 - 5

I was shoveling as fast as I could and I couldn't keep up! The auger wagon was hitched to the tractor's PTO (power take-off) shaft and the engine was revved up to a high rate of speed. The grain auger was shooting the oat seeds into one of the seed cribs in the barn. I was sitting on the tractor seat watching the operation, when the oat seeds started spilling over the wall of the crib and onto the ground. "Oh no!" I panicked. "The crib's getting full!"

I quickly grabbed a shovel, scaled the wall of the crib and started scooping the oat seed away from the outer wall. As long as I worked at a furious pace, I was able to stay ahead of the growing pile of seeds. If I quit for one second, however, I fell behind the grain auger's progress and seed spilled onto the ground. The dust was terrible! I could scarcely see or breathe! I was at the point of exhaustion when I chose to stop shoveling and start *thinking*. Then, the simple solution occurred to me - - - GALEN, (YOU GOOFY IDIOT) STOP SHOVELING AND TURN THE TRACTOR OFF!

I disengaged the PTO, moved the auger wagon to another location, and finished unloading the seeds.

BULLET POINTS

Seek simple solutions to simple problems.
The simple solution is always
The best solution.

Seek simple solutions to simple problems.
If the simple solution wasn't
The best solution, then
It wasn't actually a solution.

If the easy way and the hard way
Produce the same result,
Choose the easy way.

If the quick way and the slow way
Produce the same result,
Choose the quick way.

If the inexpensive way and
The expensive way
Produce the same result,
Choose the inexpensive way.

To solve a problem,
Find out what caused the problem.
Then fix the cause of the problem.

If a solution doesn't have permanence,
Or at least longevity,
It isn't really a solution,
It's only a repair.

Don't repair a problem
When you can fix a problem
With a simple solution.

Choose to
Seek simple solutions
To simple problems.

SCRIPTURE ANALYSIS

Luke 19: 1 - 5

1. And Jesus <u>entered</u>
> - And Jesus <u>entered [the city of Jericho]</u>

1. And <u>passed</u> through
> - And <u>[was] passing</u> through

1. <u>Jericho</u>.
> - <u>[The city of]</u> Jericho.

2. And, behold, there was a man named Zaccheus, <u>which</u> was
> - And, behold, there was a man named Zaccheus, <u>who</u> was

2. The <u>chief</u>
> - From the Greek word *architelones*, Strong's #754: <u>a principal tax-gatherer</u>.
> - The <u>principal tax-gatherer [standing]</u>

2. Among the <u>publicans</u>,
> - Also from the Greek word *architelones,* Strong's #754: <u>a principal tax-gatherer</u>. The same word was translated as *chief* earlier in this verse.
> - Among the <u>[other] tax-gatherers,</u>

2. And <u>he</u> was rich.
> - And <u>Zaccheus</u> was rich.

3. And <u>he</u> sought to see Jesus
> - And <u>Zaccheus</u> sought to see Jesus

3. <u>Who he</u> was;
> - <u>[So he would know]</u> who Jesus was;

3. <u>And</u>
> - <u>But [Zaccheus]</u>

3. Could <u>not</u>
> - Could <u>not [see Jesus]</u>

3. <u>For</u>
> - <u>Because</u>

3. The <u>press</u>,
> - From the Greek word *ochlos*, Strong's #3793: <u>multitude</u>.
> - The <u>multitude [of people were blocking his view]</u>,

3. Because <u>he</u>

- Because <u>Zaccheus</u>

3. Was <u>little</u>
- Was [a] little [man]

3. <u>Of</u> stature.
- [Short] in stature.

4. And <u>he</u> ran
- And <u>Zaccheus</u> ran

4. <u>Before</u>, and climbed
- [On ahead] of [Jesus], and climbed

4. Up into a <u>sycomore</u> tree
- The Unger's Bible Dictionary states that the sycamore is: "A fig tree... often planted by roadsides, where it affords a favorable point of view for sightseers. It also grows wild and reaches a very large size. It's wood is light but durable, and much used for house carpentry and fuel. It was once abundant in the holy land and in Egypt."
- Up into a <u>fig</u> tree

4. To see <u>him:</u>
- To see <u>Jesus</u>:

4. For <u>he</u>
- For <u>Jesus</u>

4. Was to pass <u>that way</u>.
- Was to pass [by] that way [soon].

5. And when Jesus came to the <u>place,</u>
- And when Jesus came to the <u>place [where Zaccheus was located]</u>,

5. <u>He</u> looked up,
- <u>Jesus</u> looked up,

5. And saw <u>him,</u>
- And saw <u>Zaccheus,</u>

5. And <u>said</u>
- And [Jesus] said

5. Unto <u>him,</u>
- Unto <u>Zaccheus,</u>

5. Zaccheus, make haste, and come <u>down;</u>
- Zaccheus, make haste, and come <u>down [from that fig tree]</u>;

5. For <u>to day</u>
> - For <u>today</u>

5. I must <u>abide</u>
> - From the Greek word *meno*, Strong's #3306: <u>to stay</u>.
> - I must <u>stay</u>

5. At <u>thy</u> house.
> - At <u>your</u> house.

CHOICE EXAMINATION

1. Why did Galen not immediately identify the simple solution to his problem and turn the tractor off?

2. What potential damage could have occurred by initially overlooking the simple solution?

3. In the scripture, why did Jesus specifically notice Zaccheus among the multitude of people?

4. What did Zaccheus' willingness to climb up into a fig tree indicate about his desire to see Jesus?

5. What additional event took place because Zaccheus climbed up into a fig tree to see Jesus?

6. What choices do you need to make in order to *seek simple solutions to simple problems*?

UTILIZE YOUR AVAILABLE RESOURCES

≈ 39 ≈

And they said unto him, We are come down to bind thee, that we may deliver thee into the hand of the Philistines.

And Samson said unto them, Swear unto me, that ye will not fall upon me yourselves.

And they spake unto him, saying, No; but we will bind thee fast, and deliver thee into their hand: but surely we will not kill thee.

And they bound him with two new cords, and brought him up from the rock. And when he came unto Lehi, the Philistines shouted against him: and the Spirit of the LORD came mightily upon him, and the cords that were upon his arms became as flax that was burnt with fire, and his bands loosed from off his hands. And he found a new jawbone of an ass, and put forth his hand, and took it, and slew a thousand men therewith.

Judges 15: 12 - 15

Nobody noticed him. There were people everywhere, but nobody noticed *him*.

The elderly man brought his car to the Wal-Mart Tire & Lube Express (TLE) for an oil change. He stepped outside for a moment to look at the sky. A bad storm was rolling in. The wind caught his hat and blew it off his head. The hat came to rest against a weed growing high on the side of a nearby hill. The gentleman started walking up the hill to retrieve his hat when the storm hit. Hurrying down the hill, his foot slipped on the wet grass, and he fell down - hard.

Snap! His right leg broke just above the ankle. He cried for help but nobody heard him. His wife was inside the store waiting by the register. "Why was he taking so long?" she wondered. "Where did he go? Doesn't he realize I'm waiting for him?"

The noise of the rain pounding loudly on the metal roof of the service bay made a deafening roar. The mechanics, only ten to fifteen yards away, were unaware of the man's situation. We can only imagine his frustration. He was immobile, in pain, soaking wet, in eyesight of people who could help him, yet unable to yell loudly enough to catch their attention. Then he had a brilliant revelation! He did have another resource!

Can you imagine how incredibly loud that continuous car horn sound would be if you were the mechanic with your head underneath the hood when the gentleman on the hillside *set the alarm off*!

"Ma'am, do you have the control to your car alarm? Something must have set it off."

"No, my husband has it. I think he was going to step outside for just a moment and…"

The first alert I had to the situation was a frantic call over the intercom speaker. "We need management to the TLE immediately!!"

I ran to the TLE. By the time I got to the hill by the service bay there was a crowd of several associates on the scene. Someone had grabbed a plastic sack from the trash can. Two people were holding the corners of the sack above the man's head to keep the rain off his face. One of the clerks ran outside and yelled, "An ambulance is on the way!"

Some people give up too easily. Other people choose to not give up until they have utilized their available resources. No matter who you are, no matter where you are, no matter how grim the situation appears, never give up until you have utilized your available resources.

___

BULLET POINTS

Utilize your available
Resources.
Don't give up too easily.

Utilize your available
Resources.
Everyone needs help
Sometimes.

Much can be accomplished
By yourself, but
More can be accomplished if
You'll utilize your available
Resources.

If it needs done, do it.
If you need help, get it.

There are many resources
Available to you.

Doing it alone may feel
Noble,
Until you fail.
Asking for help may feel
Weak,
Until you succeed.

Doing it alone is a natural
Tendency.
Asking for help is a
Choice.

No matter who you are,
No matter where you are,
No matter how grim
The situation appears,
Never give up until
You have utilized
Your available resources.

Choose to
Utilize your
Available resources.

SCRIPTURE ANALYSIS

Judges 15: 12 - 15

12. And <u>they</u> said
  - And <u>the three thousand men [of Judah]</u> (see verse # 11) said
12. Unto <u>him</u>,
  - Unto <u>Samson,</u>

12. We are
- We have

12. Come down
- Come down [to the top of the rock Etam (see verse #8)]

12. To bind thee,
- To bind you [securely with two new ropes (see verse #13), so]

12. That we may deliver thee
- That we may deliver you

12. Into the hand of the Philistines.
- Into the hands of the Philistines.

12. And Samson said unto them,
- And Samson said unto the three thousand men [of Judah],

12. Swear unto me, that ye
- Swear unto me, that you

12. Will not fall upon me yourselves.
- The NIV says: "Won't kill me yourselves."

13. And they spake
- And the three thousand men [of Judah] spoke

13. Unto him, saying,
- Unto Samson, saying,

13. No;
- No [we will not kill you];

13. But we will bind thee fast
- But we will bind you fast [with two new ropes]

13. And deliver thee
- And deliver you

13. Into their hand:
- Into the hands [of the Philistines]:

13. But surely we will not kill thee.
- But surely we will not kill you.

13. And they
- And the three thousand men [of Judah]

13. Bound him
- Bound Samson

13. With two new cords,
- From the Hebrew word *aboth*, Strong's #5688: rope.

- With two new ropes,

13. And brought him up

    - And brought Samson up

13. From the rock.

    - From the [top of the] rock [Etam where Samson was living].

14. And when he came

    - And when Samson came

14. Unto Lehi,

    - From the Hebrew word *Lechiy*, Strong's #3896, a form of *lchiy*, Strongs #3895: jawbone.

    - Unger's Bible Dictionary identifies Lehi as: "The place in Judah where Samson slew the Philistines with a jawbone."

    - Unto [a place in Judah which became known as] Lehi,

14. The Philistines shouted

    - From the Hebrew word *ruwa*, Strong's #7321: shout for alarm or joy.

    - The Philistines shouted for alarm

14. Against him:

    - Against Samson:

14. And the Spirit of the LORD came mightily upon him,

    - And the Spirit of the Lord came mightily upon Samson,

14. And the cords

    - And the ropes

14. That were upon his arms

    - That were [tied] upon Samson's arms

14. Became as

    - Became as [weak as]

14. Flax

    - Unger's Bible Dictionary identifies flax as: "A well known plant, *Linum sativum.* The fibers of the bark, when separated, twisted, bleached, and woven, are *linen.*"

    - Linen

14. That was burnt with fire,

    - That has [been] burned with fire,

14. And his

    - And Samson's

14. Bands <u>loosed</u> from off his hands.
> - Bands [of rope] loosed [themselves] from off his hands.

15. And <u>he</u> found
> - And <u>Samson</u> found

15. A <u>new</u> jawbone
> - From the Hebrew word *tariy*, Strong's #2961: <u>fresh</u>.
> - A <u>fresh</u> jawbone

15. Of <u>an ass,</u>
> - The NIV says: "Of <u>a donkey,</u>"

15. And <u>put</u> forth his hand,
> - And [Samson] <u>put</u> forth his hand,

15. And took <u>it</u>,
> - And took <u>the jawbone,</u>

15. And slew a thousand men <u>therewith</u>.
> - And slew a thousand men <u>with [the jawbone]</u>.

CHOICE EXAMINATION

1. What things motivated the man to not give up until he had found a way to let people know that he needed help?

2. What resources were utilized in helping the man?

3. What prevented people from coming to the man's aid before he sounded the car alarm?

4.. In the scripture, why did Samson not try to escape before he was delivered to the Philistines?

5. Why did Samson utilize the jawbone of a donkey to slay a thousand men?

6. What choices do you need to make in order to *utilize your available resources*?

GET THE FACTS BEFORE GIVING THE ADVICE

≈ 40 ≈

So Haman came in. And the king said unto him, What shall be done unto the man whom the king delighteth to honour?

Now Haman thought in his heart, To whom would the king delight to do honour more than to myself? And Haman answered the king, For the man whom the king delighteth to honour, Let the royal apparel be brought which the king useth to wear, and the horse that the king rideth upon, and the crown royal which is set upon his head: And let this apparel and horse be delivered to the hand of one of the king's most noble princes, that they may array the man withal whom the king delighteth to honour, and bring him on horseback through the street of the city, and proclaim before him, Thus shall it be done to the man whom the king delighteth to honour.

Then the king said to Haman, Make haste, and take the apparel and the horse, as thou hast said, and do even so to Mordecai the Jew, that sitteth at the king's gate: let nothing fail of all that thou hast spoken.

Esther 6: 6 - 10

I told her to walk on it. "I've sprained my ankle a dozen times," I said. "Put some light pressure on it. That will help to loosen it up." She took one step and cried out in pain. I had obviously given her wrong advice. Her ankle was broken!

It was quitting time. We had one more project to finish up before we went home. Darlene was a sales clerk in a soft-lines department. Always an aggressive worker, Darlene volunteered to help some other associates build the candy display at the checkouts. Someone laid a stacking board onto the floor intending to place it on the next layer of product. Darlene stepped on the board, slipped, and fell to the floor. That's when she broke her ankle. I was standing right beside her when it happened. I made a quick assumption of what was probably wrong with her. My assumption was wrong. I chose to give her advice when I didn't know the facts.

People of authority are often sought out for advice for situations that are beyond their area of expertise. When I was a young assistant manager at Wal-Mart, I became surprised to find associates asking me for advice for personal issues in their lives. My job position did not magically enable me to advise people with their personal problems. I was, however, an available source for people to talk to and I could give them an unbiased, objective opinion. I soon learned the following three step process:

1. Ask defining questions.
2. Listen for specific information.
3. Analyze the facts.

If I was unable to advise someone, I learned to send that person to someone who was qualified to help them with their specific need.

Twenty years later, I'm still not enabled with an ability to fix everyone's personal problems. I did learn one thing recently though; you're not supposed to walk on a broken ankle.

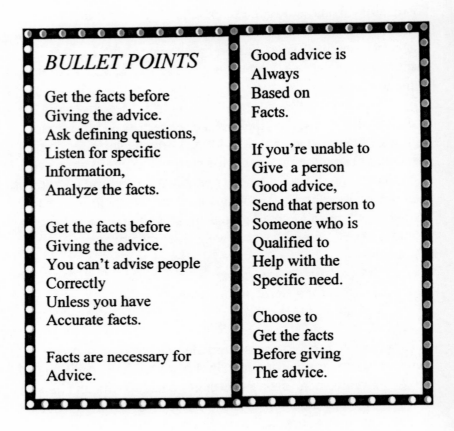

BULLET POINTS

Get the facts before
Giving the advice.
Ask defining questions,
Listen for specific
Information,
Analyze the facts.

Get the facts before
Giving the advice.
You can't advise people
Correctly
Unless you have
Accurate facts.

Facts are necessary for
Advice.

Good advice is
Always
Based on
Facts.

If you're unable to
Give a person
Good advice,
Send that person to
Someone who is
Qualified to
Help with the
Specific need.

Choose to
Get the facts
Before giving
The advice.

SCRIPTURE ANALYSIS

Esther 6: 6 - 10

6. So Haman came in.
    - So Haman came into [the king's palace].
6. And the king said unto him,
    - And the king said unto Haman,
6. What shall
    - What should
6. Be done unto
    - Be done for
6. The man whom
    - The man [of] whom [I]

6. The king <u>delighteth</u> to honour?

- The king [am] delighted [with and want] to honor?

6. Now Haman thought in his <u>heart</u>,

- Defined by Webster's Dictionary as: <u>One's innermost character, feelings, or inclinations.</u>

- Now Haman thought in [<u>the innermost feelings of</u>] his heart,

6. To whom would the king <u>delight</u>

- To whom would the king [<u>be</u>] delighted

6. To do <u>honour</u>

- To do [<u>something to show</u>] honor

6. More than to <u>myself</u>?

- More than to <u>me</u>?

7. And Haman <u>answered</u> the king,

- And Haman [<u>gave this</u>] answer [<u>to</u>] the king,

7. For the man whom the king <u>delighteth</u> to honour,

- For the man whom the king [<u>is</u>] delighted [<u>with and wants</u>] to honor,

8. Let the royal apparel be <u>brought</u>

- Let the royal apparel be <u>brought [to one of the king's most noble princes (see verse #9)]</u>

8. Which the king <u>useth</u> to wear,

- Which the king <u>uses</u> to wear,

8. And <u>the horse</u>

- And [<u>let</u>] the horse [<u>be brought</u>]

8. That the king <u>rideth</u> upon,

- That the king <u>rides</u> upon,

8. <u>And</u>

- <u>With</u>

8. The crown <u>royal</u>

- The crown [<u>that designates</u>] royalty

8. Which is set upon <u>his</u> head:

- Which is set upon [<u>the horse's</u>] head:

9. And let this apparel and horse be delivered <u>to</u>

- And let this apparel and horse be delivered <u>into</u>

9. The <u>hand</u> of one of the king's most noble princes,

- The <u>hands</u> of one of the king's most noble princes,

9. That they
 - [So] that the king's noble princes

9. May array
 - From the Hebrew word *labash*, Strong's #3847: to put on a garment or clothe oneself or another.
 - May clothe

9. The man withal
 - From the Hebrew word *kol*, Strong's #3605: in all manner
 - The man in all manner [as I have described for the man]

9. Whom the king delighteth to honour,
 -Whom the king [is] delighted [with and wants] to honor,

9. And bring him
 - And bring the man [whom the king wants to honor]

9. On horseback
 - On [the] back [of the] horse [that has the crown on his head]

9. Through the street
 - Through the streets

9. Of the city,
 - Of the city [of Shushan (see Esther 1: 2)],

9. And proclaim before him,
 - And proclaim before the man [whom the king wants to honor],

9. Thus shall it be done
 - This [is how] it shall be done

9. To
 - For

9. The man whom the king delighteth to honour.
 - The man whom the king [is] delighted [with and wants] to honor.

10. Then the king said to Haman, make haste, and take the apparel
 - Then the king said to Haman, make haste, and take the [royal] apparel

10. And the horse,
 - And the horse [that I ride upon],

10. As thou hast said,

- As <u>you have</u> said,
10. And do <u>even so</u>
- The NIV says: "And do <u>just as you have suggested</u>"
10. To Mordecai the Jew, <u>that sitteth</u> at the king's gate:
- To Mordecai the Jew, <u>who sits</u> at the king's gate:
10. Let nothing <u>fail</u>
- Let nothing <u>fail [to be done out]</u>
10. Of all that <u>thou hast</u> spoken.
- Of all that <u>you have</u> spoken.

CHOICE EXAMINATION

1. What influenced the manager to assume that Darlene had a sprained ankle?

2. What potential harm could have resulted from the manager giving the wrong advice?

3. Why is it important to ask defining questions (instead of general elaboration), listen for specific information (instead of unrelated information), and analyze the facts (instead of biased opinions)?

4. In the scripture, why did Haman assume the king was delighted to do something to show honor to him?

5. How might Haman's advice have been different if he would have asked defining questions, listened to specific information, and analyzed the facts - first?

6. What choices do you need to make in order to *get the facts before giving the advice*?

KEEP YOUR COMPOSURE DURING STRESSFUL SITUATIONS

≈ 41 ≈

Now he that betrayed him gave them a sign, saying, Whomsoever I shall kiss, that same is he: hold him fast. And forthwith he came to Jesus, and said, Hail, master; and kissed him.

And Jesus said unto him, Friend, wherefore art thou come? Then came they, and laid hands on Jesus, and took him.

And, behold, one of them which were with Jesus stretched out his hand, and drew his sword, and struck a servant of the high priest's, and smote off his ear. Then said Jesus unto him, Put up again thy sword into his place: for all they that take the sword shall perish with the sword. Thinkest thou that I cannot now pray to my Father, and he shall presently give me more than twelve legions of angels? But how then shall the scriptures be fulfilled, that thus it must be?

Matthew 26: 48 - 54

It was the top news item on our local television stations. The bus driver had overreacted! The kids had misbehaved, and she'd had enough. She stopped the bus and told them to climb off. Then she drove off and left them!

We see it happen all the time. Someone's reaction to a problem causes more harm than the original problem. Here are some more actual local news stories:

- A teenager being stopped for a minor traffic violation tries to outrun the police officer and dies in a crash.
- A man facing financial difficulties commits suicide.
- Two families argue about a dog. One man is shot and killed.

Reacting to stressful situations is normal. Overreacting is common. Keeping your composure during stressful situations is a choice.

```
BULLET POINTS

Keep your composure
During stressful situations.
Don't overreact.

Keep your composure
During stressful situations.
Think about the
consequences.

Overreaction brings
Temporary satisfaction,
And permanent regret.

Some things can't be
undone later.

Choose to
Keep your composure
During stressful situations.
```

SCRIPTURE ANALYSIS
Matthew 26: 48 - 54

48. Now he
- Now Judas Iscariot (see 26:14,15)
48. That
- [The person] who
48. Betrayed him
- Betrayed Jesus
48. Gave them a sign,
- Gave the multitude of people [who were sent by the chief

priests and the elders of the people (see verse #47)] a sign,
48. Saying, <u>Whomsoever</u> I shall kiss,
    - Saying, <u>Whoever [the person is that]</u> I shall kiss,
48. That <u>same</u>
    - That <u>same [person]</u>
48. Is <u>he</u>:
    - Is <u>Jesus</u>:
48. <u>Hold</u>
    - From the Greek word *krateo*, Strong's #2902: <u>seize</u>.
    - <u>Seize [and]</u>
48. Him <u>fast</u>.
    - The NIV says: "<u>Arrest</u> him."
49. And <u>forthwith</u>
    - From the Greek word *eutheos*, Strong's #2112: <u>soon</u>.
    - And <u>soon</u>
49. <u>He</u> came to Jesus, and said,
    - <u>Judas Iscariot</u> came to Jesus, and said,
49. <u>Hail</u>,
    - From the Greek word *chairo*, Strong's #5463: <u>greeting</u>.
    - <u>Greetings</u>,
49. <u>Master</u>;
    - From the Greek word *rhabbi*, Strong's #4461: <u>Rabbi</u>.
    - The Unger's Bible Dictionary states: "[Rabbi is] a respectful term applied by the Jews to their teachers and spiritual instructors. The terms rabbi and raboni both mean simply 'master'".
    - <u>Rabbi</u>;
49. And <u>kissed him</u>.
    - And <u>[then Judas Iscariot] kissed Jesus</u>.
50. And Jesus said unto <u>him</u>,
    - And Jesus said unto <u>Judas Iscariot</u>,
50. Friend, <u>wherefore</u>
    - From the Greek word *epi*, Strong's #1909: <u>with</u>. And from the Greek word *hos*, Strong's #3739: <u>what</u>.
    - Friend, <u>with what [purpose]</u>
50. <u>Art thou</u>
    - <u>Are you</u>

50. <u>Come</u>?
>   - From the Greek word *pareimi*, Strong's #3918: <u>be here</u>.
>   - <u>Here</u>?

50. Then <u>came</u> they, and
>   - Then [<u>the multitude of people sent by the chief priests and the elders of the people</u>] came, and they

50. <u>Laid hands on Jesus, and took</u> him.
>   - The NIV says: "<u>Seized Jesus and arrested</u> him."

51. And, behold, one of <u>them</u>
>   - And behold, one of <u>them (Peter, see John 18:10)</u>

51. <u>Which were</u> with Jesus stretched out his hand,
>   <u>Who was</u> with Jesus stretched out his hand,

51. And drew <u>his</u> sword,
>   - And drew <u>his (Peter's, see verse #52)</u> sword,

51. And struck a servant of the high <u>priest's</u>,
>   - And struck a servant of the high <u>priest [with his sword]</u>

51. And <u>smote</u> off
>   - From the Greek word *aphaireo*, Strong's #851: <u>cut</u>.
>   - And <u>cut</u> off

51. <u>His</u> ear.
>   - <u>The servant of the high priest's</u> ear.

52. Then said Jesus unto <u>him</u>,
>   - Then said Jesus unto <u>Peter</u>,

52. Put up again <u>thy</u> sword
>   - Put <u>your</u> sword up again

52. Into <u>his</u> place:
>   - Into <u>its</u> place:

52. For all <u>they that</u>
>   - For all <u>the people who</u>

52. Take the <u>sword</u>
>   - Take the <u>sword [to fight with]</u>

52. Shall perish <u>with</u> the sword.
>   - Shall perish <u>by [means of]</u> the sword.

53. <u>Thinkest thou</u> that I cannot now pray
>   - [<u>Do</u>] <u>you think</u> that I cannot now pray

53. To my <u>Father</u>,
>   - To my <u>Father (God)</u>

53. And <u>he</u> shall

- And [my] Father (God) shall

53. Presently
- From the Greek word *paristemi*, Strong's #3936: assist.
- Assist [me by]

53. Give me
- Giving me

53. More than twelve legions
- More than 72,000

53. Of Angels?
- Angels to [fight for me]?

54. But how then shall the scriptures be fulfilled,
- But how then would the scriptures be fulfilled,

54. That thus it
- That [say] this [is how] it

54. Must be?
- Must be [done]?

CHOICE EXAMINATION

1. Why were each of the reactions to the problems more harmful than the original problems?

2. Why is overreacting common?

3. In the scripture, why did Judas Iscariot identify Jesus with a kiss?

4. Why did Jesus tell Peter to put his sword up again unto its place?

5. Why did Jesus not ask his Father for 72,000 angels to assist him?

6. What choices do you need to make in order to *keep your composure during stressful situations*?

TELL THE TRUTH
EVEN IF IT HURTS

≈ 42 ≈

And it came to pass, when he was come near to enter into Egypt, that he said unto Sarai his wife, Behold now, I know that thou art a fair woman to look upon: Therefore it shall come to pass, when the Egyptians shall see thee, that they shall say, This is his wife: and they will kill me, but they will save thee alive. Say, I pray thee, thou art my sister: that it may be well with me for thy sake; and my soul shall live because of thee.

And it came to pass, that, when Abram was come unto Egypt, the Egyptians beheld the woman that she was very fair. The princes also of Pharaoh saw her, and commended her before Pharaoh: and the woman was taken into Pharaoh's house. And he entreated Abram well for her sake: and he had sheep, and oxen, and he asses, and menservants and maidservants, and she asses, and camels.

And the LORD plagued Pharaoh and his house with great plagues because of Sarai Abram's wife. And Pharaoh called Abram, and said, What is this that thou hast done unto me? why didst thou not tell me that she was thy wife? Why saidst thou, She is my sister? so I might have taken her to me to wife: now therefore behold thy wife, take her, and go thy way. Genesis 12: 11 - 19

He was a good young man. He hadn't done anything wrong on purpose. He was just scared! He had just wrecked his boss's pickup!

I handed him my keys and said, "Use my pickup to move those cases of paper towels from the storage trailer to the stockroom. As soon as you finish, bring the keys right back to me. I need to hurry down to the bank to verify the store's deposits."

Thirty minutes later the young man met me at the front door. He handed me the keys and said, "Thanks for letting me use your truck." I walked to the pickup, stopped, stared, turned around, and then walked back inside the store. I found the *very nervous* young man sitting in the lounge.

"Did you have any problems when you hauled the paper towels around the building?"

"No, why?"

"Well, I can't open the driver's side door. It's dented in so badly that it's almost rubbing against the steering wheel."

He stopped and thought for a moment before speaking. "Oh yeah, I think that I may have scraped the side of the building a little bit when I was driving to the stockroom."

He was barely sixteen years old. He had received his driver's license only two weeks prior to this event. Perhaps he had never driven a standard transmission before and he wasn't used to operating a clutch. In reality, it wasn't his fault the accident occurred. It was my fault. I had placed him in that situation and I hadn't ask him if he was able to do it. He felt insecure about telling me that he wasn't an experienced driver. After the accident occurred, he just wanted it to go away. That's why he chose to not tell me about it. It didn't go away, of course. I tried to reassure him.

"Don't worry about the door. We can fix it. Next time, though, if you have a problem like this, don't be afraid to tell the truth, even if it hurts."

A local repair shop fixed the damaged door.

It was only a month later that I had a flat tire on my pickup while driving to work. I pulled into a friend's driveway. The husband came out and volunteered to take me the rest of the way into work so that I wouldn't be late. I rode in his vehicle and left my pickup in his driveway, directly behind his wife's car. A few minutes later, the wife backed her car out of the driveway…and stopped abruptly…very abruptly…immediately after she slammed the rear bumper of her car into my *new driver's side door*.

She immediately called me and told me what had happened. She said that her car had not received any damage, but unfortunately, the door on my pickup was crushed in against the steering wheel.

I told her to not worry about it. It was my fault. I shouldn't have left the pickup behind her car. Besides, I knew of a local repair shop that could fix it.

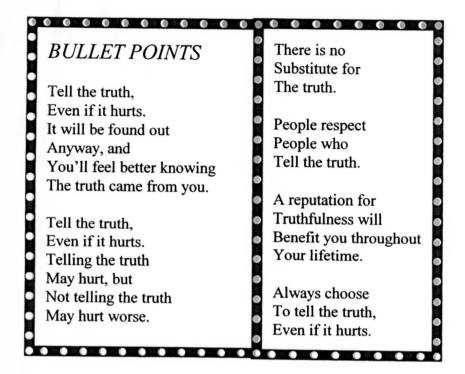

BULLET POINTS

Tell the truth,
Even if it hurts.
It will be found out
Anyway, and
You'll feel better knowing
The truth came from you.

Tell the truth,
Even if it hurts.
Telling the truth
May hurt, but
Not telling the truth
May hurt worse.

There is no
Substitute for
The truth.

People respect
People who
Tell the truth.

A reputation for
Truthfulness will
Benefit you throughout
Your lifetime.

Always choose
To tell the truth,
Even if it hurts.

SCRIPTURE ANALYSIS

Genesis 12: 11 - 19

11. And it came to pass, when <u>he</u>
    - And it came to pass, when <u>Abram (see 12:10)</u>
11. Was <u>come</u> near
    - Was <u>coming</u> near
11. To <u>enter</u> into Egypt,
    - To <u>entering</u> into Egypt,
11. That <u>he</u> said to Sarai his wife,
    - That <u>Abram</u> said to Sarai his wife,
11. <u>Behold</u> now,
    - From the Hebrew word *hinneh*, Strong's #2009: <u>see</u>.
    - <u>See</u> now,
11. I know that <u>thou art</u>
    - I know that <u>you are</u>

11. A <u>fair</u> woman to look upon:
- From the Hebrew word *yapheh*, Strong's #3303: <u>beautiful</u>.
- A <u>beautiful</u> woman to look upon:

12. Therefore it shall come to pass, <u>when</u> the Egyptians
- Therefore it shall come to pass, [that] <u>when</u> the Egyptians

12. Shall see <u>thee</u>,
- Shall see <u>you</u>,

12. That <u>they</u> shall say,
- That <u>the Egyptians</u> shall say,

12. <u>This</u> is
- <u>Sarai</u> is

12. <u>His</u> wife:
- <u>Abram's</u> wife:

12. And <u>they</u> will kill me,
- And <u>[in order to take you for themselves]</u> <u>the Egyptians</u> will kill me,

12. But <u>they</u>
- But <u>the Egyptians</u>

12. Will save <u>thee alive</u>.
- Will save <u>your life</u>.

13. <u>Say</u>,
- <u>Say [to the Egyptians]</u>,

13. I <u>pray</u>
- From the Hebrew word *na*, Strong's #4994: <u>beseech</u>.
- I <u>beseech</u>

13. <u>Thee, thou art</u> my sister:
- <u>You, [instead that] you are</u> my sister:

13. <u>That it</u>
- <u>[So] that living in Egypt</u>

13. May <u>be</u> well with me
- May <u>go</u> well with me

13. For <u>thy</u> sake;
- For <u>your</u> sake;

13. And my <u>soul</u>
- From the Hebrew word *nephesh*, Strong's #5315: <u>life</u>.
- And my <u>life</u>

13. Shall <u>live</u>

- From the Hebrew word *chayah*, Strong's #2421: <u>save</u>.
- Shall [be] <u>saved</u>

13. Because of <u>thee</u>.
- Because of <u>you</u>.

14. And it came to pass, that, when Abram <u>was</u> come into Egypt,
- And it came to pass, that, when Abram <u>had</u> come into Egypt,

14. The Egyptians <u>beheld</u>
- From the Hebrew word *raah*, Strong's #7200: <u>to see</u>.
- The Egyptians <u>saw</u>

14. <u>The woman</u> that
- <u>Sarai [and the Egyptians noticed]</u> that

14. <u>She</u> was
- <u>Sarai</u> was

14. Very <u>fair</u>.
- Very <u>beautiful</u>.

15. The princes also of Pharaoh saw <u>her</u>,
- The princes of Pharaoh also saw <u>Sarai</u>,

15. And <u>commended</u>
- From the Hebrew word *halal*, Strong's #1984: <u>to boast [or to] give in marriage</u>.
- And <u>boasted [about]</u>

15. <u>Her before</u> Pharaoh:
- <u>Sarai [recommending that she be given in marriage]</u> to Pharaoh:

15. And <u>the woman</u> was taken into Pharaoh's house.
- And <u>Sarai</u> was taken into Pharaoh's house.

16. And <u>he entreated</u> Abram well
- And <u>Pharaoh treated</u> Abram well

16. For <u>her</u> sake:
- For <u>Sarai's</u> sake:

16. And <u>he</u> had sheep, and oxen,
- And <u>Abram</u> had sheep, and oxen,

16. And <u>he asses</u>,
- And <u>male donkeys</u>,

16. And menservants and maidservants, and <u>she asses</u>

- And menservants and maidservants, and <u>female donkeys</u>
16. And <u>camels</u>.
   - And <u>camels [given to him from Pharaoh]</u>.
17. <u>And</u>
   - <u>But</u>
17. The LORD <u>plagued</u> Pharaoh
   - From the Hebrew word *naga*, Strong's #5060: <u>punish</u>.
   - The Lord <u>punished</u> Pharaoh
17. And <u>his house</u>
   - And <u>Pharaoh's household</u>
17. With great <u>plagues</u>
   - From the Hebrew word *nega*, Strong's #5061: <u>sore [or]
infliction, a leprous person</u>.
   - The NIV says: "<u>serious diseases</u>"
   - With great [and] <u>serious diseases [such as] leprosy</u>
17. Because of <u>Sarai</u> Abram's wife.
   - Because of [Pharaoh taking] Sarai [into his house when
she was] Abram's wife.
18. And Pharaoh <u>called</u> Abram,
   - And Pharaoh <u>called [for]</u> Abram,
18. And <u>said</u>,
   - And [Pharaoh] said [to Abram],
18. What is this that <u>thou hast</u> done unto me?
   - What is this that <u>you have</u> done unto me?
18. Why <u>didst thou</u> not tell me
   - Why <u>did you</u> not tell me
18. That <u>she was thy</u> wife?
   - That <u>Sarai is your</u> wife?
19. Why <u>saidst thou</u>,
   - Why <u>[did] you say</u>,
19. <u>She</u> is my sister?
   - <u>Sarai</u> is my sister?
19. <u>So</u> I might
   - <u>So [that]</u> I might
19. Have <u>taken her</u>
   - Have [mistakenly] taken Sarai
19. To me <u>to</u> wife:

- To me <u>to [be my]</u> wife:
19. Now therefore <u>behold thy</u> wife,
    - Now therefore <u>see [here is] your</u> wife,
19. Take <u>her</u>,
    - Take <u>Sarai</u>,
19. And go <u>thy</u> way.
    - And go <u>your</u> way.

CHOICE EXAMINATION

1. Why was the young man hesitant to tell his boss about the damaged door?

2. How did the young man's decision to not tell his boss about the damaged door make him feel while he was sitting in the lounge?

3. Why did the friend's wife immediately notify the boss about the re-damaged door?

4. In the scripture, why did Abram ask Sarai to tell the Egyptians that she was his sister?

5. How many people were affected by the false claim that Sarai was Abram's sister?

6. What choices do you need to make in order to *tell the truth, even if it hurts*?

ANALYZE YOUR ACTIONS

≈ 43 ≈

Now therefore thus saith the LORD of hosts; Consider your ways. Ye have sown much, and bring in little; ye eat, but ye have not enough; ye drink, but ye are not filled with drink; ye clothe you, but there is none warm; and he that earneth wages earneth wages to put it into a bag with holes. Thus saith the LORD of hosts; Consider your ways.

Haggai 1: 5 - 7

He stole a padlock. I was struck by the irony of the situation. I suppose he wanted to protect some of his possessions from thieves. He had money in his pocket. He could have easily paid for the item, but he chose to steal it instead. Why did he do it? Perhaps he thought it was only a small item and Wal-Mart was a big company, therefore it wasn't that big of a deal. Perhaps he thought that life for him had been difficult, and therefore he deserved a free padlock from Wal-Mart. Perhaps he thought that lots of people have stolen small items, so he should have the privilege of stealing small items too. But, no matter what logic he used to rationalize his actions, the fact is that he knew it was wrong, or he would not have hidden it underneath his shirt before he walked out the door.

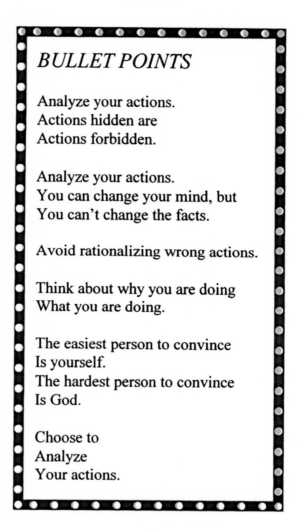

BULLET POINTS

Analyze your actions.
Actions hidden are
Actions forbidden.

Analyze your actions.
You can change your mind, but
You can't change the facts.

Avoid rationalizing wrong actions.

Think about why you are doing
What you are doing.

The easiest person to convince
Is yourself.
The hardest person to convince
Is God.

Choose to
Analyze
Your actions.

SCRIPTURE ANALYSIS

Haggai 1: 5 - 7

5: Now therefore <u>thus saith</u> the LORD
- Now, therefore <u>this says</u> the Lord
5. Of <u>hosts</u>;
- From the Hebrew word *tsaba*, Strongs #6635: <u>a mass of</u>
<u>persons</u>.

- Of the masses of people;

5. Consider
- The NIV says: "Give careful thought to"

5. Your ways.
- From the Hebrew word *Derek*, Strongs #1870: a course of life or mode of action.
- Your modes of action [for they direct] the course [your] life [is taking].

6. Ye have
- You have

6. Sown much,
- Sown much [seed],

6. And bring
- But [you have] brought

6. In little;
- In little [harvest];

6. Ye eat,
- You [have plenty to] eat,

6. But ye
- But you

6. Have not
- [Do] not have

6. Enough;
- Enough [to quench your hunger];

6. Ye drink,
- You [have plenty to] drink,

6. But ye
- But you

6. Are not filled with drink;
- Are not filled with [enough of what you] drink [to quench your thirst];

6. Ye clothe you, but
- You [put your] clothes [on] your [body], but

6. There is none warm;
- There is no [feeling of being] warm;

6. And he that earneth wages
- And he that earns wages

6. Earneth wages

- <u>Earns</u> wages
6. To put <u>it</u>
　　- To put <u>the [money from his] wages</u>
6. Into a bag with <u>holes.</u>
　　- Into a bag with <u>holes [in it]</u>.
7. <u>Thus saith</u>
　　- <u>This says</u>
7. The LORD of <u>hosts;</u>
　　- The Lord of <u>the masses of people;</u>
7. <u>Consider</u>
　　- The NIV says: "<u>Give careful thought to</u>"
7. Your <u>ways.</u>
　　- Your <u>modes of action</u>.

CHOICE EXAMINATION

1. Why was stealing a padlock an ironic situation?

2. What logic did he perhaps use to rationalize his actions?

3. Why was hiding the padlock under his shirt an indication that he knew his actions were wrong?

4. In the scripture, why are we told to give careful thought to our modes of action?

5. Why was the wage earner putting money into a bag with holes in it?

6. What choices do you need to make in order to *analyze your actions*?

TAKE RESPONSIBILITY FOR YOUR ACTIONS

≈ 44 ≈

Then said he unto him, A certain man made a great supper, and bade many: And sent his servant at supper time to say to them that were bidden, Come; for all things are now ready.

And they all with one consent began to make excuse. The first said unto him, I have bought a piece of ground, and I must needs go and see it: I pray thee have me excused.

And another said, I have bought five yoke of oxen, and I go to prove them: I pray thee have me excused.

And another said, I have married a wife, and therefore I cannot come.

So that servant came, and shewed his lord these things. Then the master of the house being angry said to his servant, Go out quickly into the streets and lanes of the city, and bring in hither the poor, and the maimed, and the halt, and the blind.

And the servant said, Lord, it is done as thou hast commanded, and yet there is room.

And the lord said unto the servant, Go out into the highways and hedges, and compel them to come in, that my house may be filled. For I say unto you, That none of those men which were bidden shall taste of my supper.

Luke 14: 16 - 24

"If excuses were acceptable," he said, "everybody would have one."

We thought if we could come up with some good excuses, we wouldn't be held accountable for our actions.

"We didn't have time!" we complained.

"We were too busy!" we explained.

"There were too many other things which had to be done!"

We reassured him, though, with a "We'll be sure to get it done later!" statement. "Surely the district manager will understand" we thought.... He didn't.

I was a young sales clerk. This was my first direct experience with Wal-Mart's *sense of urgency* attitude. At Wal-Mart, when a customer needs help, when a safety issue arises, or when direction is given to do a certain task, all involved personnel are supposed to consider it urgent that the work gets accomplished in its proper time frame. When an emphasis is placed on getting work completed on time, it normally does get completed on time. Excuses are not acceptable.

Once the district manager finished his tour of our area we stopped searching for excuses and we started finding solutions. It didn't take long to get it done. It became a priority to us the very moment we chose to take responsibility for our actions.

BULLET POINTS

Take responsibility
For your actions.
If excuses were acceptable,
Everybody would have one.

Take responsibility
For your actions.
Stop looking for an excuse, and
Start finding a solution.

When an emphasis is placed on
Getting work completed on time,
It normally does get completed on time.

Develop a sense of urgency attitude.

Choose to
Take responsibility for
Your actions.

SCRIPTURE ANALYSIS

Luke 14: 16 - 24

16. Then said <u>he</u>
- Then <u>Jesus</u> said
16. Unto <u>him</u>, A certain man made a great supper,
- Unto <u>one of the people [who was eating with him (see verse #15)]</u>, a certain man made a great supper,
16. And <u>bade</u>
- From the Greek word *kaleo*, Strong's #2564: <u>to call</u>.
- The NIV says, "<u>Invited</u>"
- And [the man] <u>invited</u>
16. <u>Many</u>:
- <u>Many [people to come]</u>:
17. And <u>sent</u> his servant at supper time
- And <u>[the man]</u> <u>sent</u> his servant at supper time
17. To say to <u>them that were bidden</u>,
- To say to <u>those who had [been] invited,</u>
17. <u>Come</u>;
- <u>[It's time for you to]</u> <u>come</u>;
17. For all <u>things</u> are now ready.
- For all <u>things [related to the great supper]</u> are now ready.
18. And <u>they</u> all
- And <u>the people [who had been invited]</u> all
18. With one <u>consent</u>
- Defined by Webster's Dictionary as: <u>agreement as to action or opinion</u>.
- With one <u>agreed upon action</u>
18. Began to make <u>excuse</u>.
- Began to make <u>excuses</u>.
18. The <u>first</u> said
- The <u>first [person invited]</u> said
18. Unto <u>him</u>,
- Unto <u>the servant [of the man who made the great supper]</u>,
18. I have bought a piece of <u>ground</u>,
- From the Greek word *agros*, Strong's #68: <u>land</u>.

- I have bought a piece of <u>land,</u>
18. And I must <u>needs</u> go
 - And I must [be allowed my] need [to] go
18. And see <u>it</u>:
 - And see <u>the piece of land</u>:
18. I <u>pray</u>
 - From the Greek word *erotao*, Strong's #2065: <u>to request</u>.
 - I <u>request</u>
18. <u>Thee</u>
 - <u>[For] you [to]</u>
18. Have me <u>excused</u>.
 - Have me <u>excused [from attending the great supper]</u>.
19. And <u>another</u> said,
 - And <u>another [person who was invited]</u> said,
19. I have bought five yoke of oxen, and I <u>go</u>
 - I have bought five yoke of oxen, and I [must] <u>go</u>
19. To <u>prove</u>
 - From the Greek word *dokimazo*, Strong's #1381: <u>try</u>.
 - To <u>try [out]</u>
19. <u>Them</u>:
 - <u>The five yoke of oxen</u>:
19. I <u>pray thee</u>
 - I <u>request [for] you [to]</u>
19. Have me <u>excused</u>.
 - Have me <u>excused [from attending the great supper]</u>.
20. And <u>another</u> said, I have married a wife, and therefore I cannot come.
 - And <u>another [person who was invited]</u> said, I have married a wife, and therefore I cannot come.
21. So that <u>servant</u>
 - So that <u>servant [who had been sent to tell the people who had been invited to the great supper that it was time to come]</u>
21. <u>Came</u>,
 - <u>Came [back to his master's house]</u>,
21. And <u>shewed</u>
 - From the Greek word *apaggello*, Strong's #518: <u>tell</u>.
 - And <u>told</u>

21. His <u>lord</u>
   - From the Greek word *kurios*, Strong's #2962: <u>master</u>.
   - His <u>master [about]</u>
21. <u>These things</u>.
   - <u>[All] these things [which the people had told him in order to get themselves excused]</u>.
21. Then the master of the <u>house</u>
   - Then the master of the <u>house [who had invited the people to his great supper]</u>,
21. Being <u>angry</u> said to his servant,
   - Being <u>angry [about the people's excuses]</u> said to his servant,
21. Go out quickly into the streets and lanes of the city, and bring in <u>hither</u>
   Go out quickly into the streets and lanes of the city, and bring in <u>here</u>
21. The <u>poor</u>,
   - The <u>[people who are] poor</u>,
21. And the <u>maimed</u>,
   - From the Greek word *anaperos*, Strong's #376: <u>crippled [or] maimed</u>.
   - Defined by Webster's Dictionary as: <u>loss of a member of the body</u>.
   - And the <u>[people who are] crippled [or have] lost of a member of the body</u>,
21. And the <u>halt</u>,
   - From the Greek word *cholos*, Strong's #5560: <u>lame</u>.
   - And the <u>[people who are] lame</u>,
21. And the <u>blind</u>.
   - And the <u>[people who are] blind</u>.
22. And the servant said, <u>Lord</u>,
   - And the servant said, <u>Master</u>,
22. <u>It is</u> done
   - <u>The bringing in of the poor, crippled, lame, and blind people has [been] done</u>
22. As <u>thou hast</u> commanded,
   - As <u>you have</u> commanded,
22. And yet there is <u>room</u>.

- And yet there is [still more] room [in your house for people to attend the great supper].

23. And the <u>lord</u> said

- And the <u>master</u> said

23. Unto <u>the</u> servant,

- Unto <u>his</u> servant,

23. Go out into the <u>highways</u>

- From the Greek word *hodos*, Strong's #3598: <u>a road</u>.
- Go out into the <u>roads</u>

23. And <u>hedges</u>,

- From the Greek word *phragmos*, Strong's #5418: <u>fence, or inclosing barrier</u>.
- And [into the] fences or [other] barriers [along the roads],

23. And compel <u>them</u>

- And compel <u>the people in the roads and along the fences and other barriers</u>

23. To come <u>in</u>,

- To come <u>into [my house for the great supper]</u>,

23. <u>That</u> my house

- [So] <u>that</u> my house

23. <u>May</u> be

- <u>Will</u> be

23. <u>Filled</u>.

- <u>Filled [with people to eat the great supper]</u>.

24. For I say unto you, That none of those men <u>which</u> were

- For I say unto you, That none of those men <u>who</u> were

24. <u>Bidden</u> shall

- <u>[Originally] invited</u> shall

24. <u>Taste</u> of my supper.

- [Even] <u>taste</u> of my supper.

CHOICE EXAMINATION

1. Why were excuses not acceptable to the district manager?

2. When did the work assignment become a priority to the sales clerks?

3. In the scripture, why were the three people's excuses made with one agreed upon action?

4. Why did the three people make up excuses instead of telling the servant that they didn't want to go to the great supper?

5. What did the master do in response to the three people's excuses?

6. What choices do you need to make in order to *take responsibility for your actions*?

CHOOSE TO SUCCEED

SET ACHIEVEABLE GOALS AND PURSUE THEM AGGRESSIVELY

≈ 45 ≈

Brethren, I count not myself to have apprehended: but this one thing I do, forgetting those things which are behind, and reaching forth unto those things which are before, I press toward the mark for the prize of the high calling of God in Christ Jesus.

Philippians 3: 13, 14

"Dad, I want a purple vest! I'm not going to stop trying until I get one. I'm going to get me a purple vest!"

It was Joshua's first job. He was as a cashier at Wal-Mart. He had found out that whoever was chosen to be the store's best cashier for the month was awarded a purple vest. That cashier was celebrated as the store's *star cashier*.

I wasn't sure how serious he was about this goal. Josh has a good sense of humor and this sounded like something he would have fun teasing about. Then one day I walked into his store and I saw him working.

"Hello ma'am. How are you? Are you having a good day? Here, let me lift that for you." Beep, beep, swish, swish. He was scanning and bagging the items quickly and efficiently, working so hard that he had sweat beading on his forehead. "Goodbye ma'am. Have a nice day! Hello sir! How are you today? Can I help you with that?" Beep, beep, swish, swish. He was working just as hard for the next customer. "Thank you. We appreciate you! Have a good day! Well, hi there Ms. Smith! How are you doing today? Can I help you with that?"

He soon got his purple vest.

"Dad, I want to be the best cart pusher in all of Wal-Mart!" The store was needing some responsible influence among some of the cart pushers. Joshua was engaged to be married. As an ulterior motive, he wanted to get more exercise so he could lose some weight. Technically it was a less demanding, lower paying job, but Joshua wanted to do it.

Once again he was in constant motion. If he wasn't pushing carts, he was helping customers load their groceries into their cars or helping elderly people and mothers with small children walk through the traffic to get to their vehicles. Wal-Mart doesn't award purple vests for cart pushers, but if they did I think Josh might have received one.

"Dad, I want to be a CSM (Customer Service Manager, the person in charge of the checkouts)! By this time, Joshua and Lauren had married and moved to another city. He transferred to his new home's local Wal-Mart and became a cashier. He got another purple vest. Three months later he became a CSM.

"Dad, Mom, I've decided, actually Lauren and I have decided, that I would like to pursue a management career at Wal-Mart. Lauren and I would like for you to come and visit us. We will take you out to dinner so we can talk about it."

There's another part to this story. Joshua had studied to be a school teacher like his mother, his sisters and his wife. He has a bachelor's degree in elementary education. While Joshua was doing his practice teaching one day, some of the students got totally unruly and he became very frustrated. It caught the attention of his administrator. His confidence was shaken. Barbie and I were worried that he would let a one time experience affect his entire future plans for a career. I gave him some advice:

"If that's what you want to do (teach), don't let anyone or anything stand in the way of you accomplishing your goals! Just keep working at it. Learn from your mistakes. You can do anything you choose to do!"

My advice wasn't received well. It appeared that he hadn't listened to me. It caused some hard feelings.

Josh and Lauren took us to dinner at a restaurant near their new home. They asked if we would approve of him entering the management program for Wal-Mart. "Of course we approve!" we said. "Absolutely we approve! We just want you to be sure that you're not giving up on your teaching career because of one bad experience. Don't you remember the advice we gave you?"

Then it hit me hard, real hard. Of course he had remembered my advice. "Don't let anyone or anything stand in the way of you accomplishing your goals. Just keep working at it. Learn from your mistakes. You can do *anything* you choose to do!" "Anything," I had said, *"anything"*. He could do *anything* he chose to do!

"Dad, I want a purple vest! I'm not going to stop trying until I get one. I'm going to get me a purple vest!"

"Dad, I want to be the best cart pusher in all of Wal-Mart!"

"Dad, I want to be a CSM!"

"Dad, I've decided, that I would like to pursue a management career at Wal-Mart."

I'm proud to say that at the time of this writing, Joshua Manning is currently an assistant manager at the Wal-Mart Super Center in Miami, Oklahoma.

Barbie and I kept one of his purple vests hanging in the closet for a very long time.

BULLET POINTS

Set achievable goals and
Pursue them aggressively.
Don't let anyone or
Anything
Stand in the way of you
Accomplishing your
Goals.

Set achievable goals and
Pursue them aggressively.
You can do anything
You choose to do, and
That means *anything*.

Don't let one bad
Experience
Destroy your potential for
Success.

Don't let one bad
Experience
Destroy your
Confidence.

Keep working at it and
Learn from your mistakes.

Choose to
Set achievable goals and
Pursue them aggressively.

SCRIPTURE ANALYSIS

Philippians 3: 13, 14

13. Brethren,
- From the Greek word *adelphos*, Strongs #80: brother.
- [Christian] brothers,

13. I
- I (Paul, see 1:1)

13. Count not myself
- The NIV says: "Do not consider myself"

13. To have apprehended:
- From the Greek word *katalambano*, Strong's #2638: obtain.
- To have obtained [all of the excellency of the knowledge of Christ. (See verse # 8)]:

13. But this one thing I do,
- But this one thing I do [understand],

13. Forgetting those things
- Forgetting those things [that have happened in the past and]

13. Which are behind,
- Which are behind [me now],

13. And reaching forth
- Both words are from the Greek word *epekteinomai*, Strong's #1901: stretch oneself forward upon.
- And stretching [myself] forward [reaching]

13. Unto
- For

13. Those things which are before,
- Those things which are [still] before [me in the future],

14. I press
- I press [forward]

14. Toward the mark
- From the Greek word *skopos*, Strong's #4649: a goal.
- Toward the goal

343

14. For the <u>prize</u>
    - For the [<u>purpose of obtaining the</u>] <u>prize</u>
14. <u>Of the high calling of God</u>
    - The NIV says: <u>For which God has called me heavenward</u>
14. <u>In</u> Christ Jesus.
    - <u>By [following the example of</u>] Christ Jesus.

CHOICE EXAMINATION

1. Why did Joshua have confidence to continue setting new goals to achieve?

2. Why was Joshua successful in each Wal-Mart career move?

3. How did Joshua's dad figure out that Joshua had listened to his advice after all?

4. In the scripture, why did Paul say to forget those things that have happened in the past?

5. Why did Paul say to stretch yourself forward to reach for those things that are still in the future?

6. What choices do you need to make in order to *set achievable goals and pursue them aggressively*?

WORK HARD AND BE DEPENDABLE AT YOUR LEVEL OF RESPONSIBILITY

≈ 46 ≈

If thou hast run with the footmen, and they have wearied thee, then how canst thou contend with horses? and if in the land of peace, wherein thou trustedst, they wearied thee, then how wilt thou do in the swelling of Jordan?

Jeremiah 12: 5

"I've never had a strategy for developing a management career at Wal-Mart. I just worked hard every day and kept showing up. My career advancements came as a natural result of people noticing that I was working hard and being dependable at my level of responsibility. It will work that way for you too." Those were comments to my son-in-law Jon. He was a sales clerk at an O'Reilly Auto Parts store. He was asking me how to develop a management career with his company.

I've worked with many people who have had a desire to turn their jobs into management careers. Some have accomplished this goal and some have not. No matter what their individual abilities were, the people who learned to work hard and be dependable at their level of responsibility were the ones who became successful managers.

One young man I worked with had the responsibility of stocking the shelves which hold the bathroom tissue on the sales floor. Each time I saw him he would stop me to tell me how much he wanted to develop a management career at Wal-Mart. I always told him the same thing, "Work hard and be dependable. That's what brings opportunities your way." He chose to not listen to my advice. He kept trying to get involved in all the noticeable things that were happening around the store while neglecting his basic job of stocking the bathroom tissue. One day, after stopping me to tell

me again how much he wanted to develop a management career at
Wal-Mart, I told him; "Listen, if I can't trust you to stock the
bathroom tissue, what makes you think I can trust you to supervise
the entire store?"

Another young man I worked with was tremendously
capable. He worked incredibly fast. He was highly intelligent and
he had experience in several areas of the store. He also wanted to
develop a management career at Wal-Mart. He could have been a
real asset to the company as a management associate, but his
attendance was absolutely terrible. When I did a performance
coaching with him to address his poor attendance, I told him,
"When you're here, you are the best worker in the store. But when
you're not here, you're the worst worker in the store. You don't get
anything accomplished at the store when you don't come to work."

Jon listened to my advice. Last winter, when a major
snowstorm was coming, he rented a motel room in town so he
wouldn't miss work the next day. When staffing difficulties
occurred at his store, Jon worked extra days without complaining.
When the manager developed personal problems which affected
his work at the store, Jon stepped in and performed extra duties as
needed. When Jon's manager at O'Reilly Auto Parts stepped down,
the district manager interviewed management candidates from
several surrounding stores before choosing someone to promote to
store manager. He didn't have to go very far to find his eventual
selection. He found Jon, right there in the very same store, working
hard and being dependable at his level of responsibility.

Jon didn't need a complicated strategy for pursuing a
management career at O'Reilly Auto Parts. His career opportunity
came to him. He just worked hard every day and he kept showing
up.

BULLET POINTS

Work hard and be dependable at
Your level of responsibility.
Career advancements will be a
Natural result.

Work hard and be dependable at
Your level of responsibility.
That's what brings opportunities
Your way.

What you say will get you noticed.
What you do will get you promoted.

No one was hired to
Not work hard.
No one was hired to
Not be dependable.

Work is a requirement of the job.
Attendance is a requirement of the work.

To build a career,
Build a history of
Hard work and dependability at
Your level of responsibility.

Choose to
Work hard and
Be dependable
At your level of responsibility.

SCRIPTURE ANALYSIS

Jeremiah 12: 5

5. If <u>thou hast</u> run
> - If <u>you have</u> run

5. With the <u>footmen</u>,
> - From the Hebrew word *ragliy*, Strong's #7273: <u>a soldier on foot</u>.
> - With the <u>soldiers on foot</u>,

5. And <u>they have</u>
> - And [<u>running with</u>] the <u>soldiers on foot</u> has

5. <u>Wearied thee</u>,
> - [<u>Made</u>] <u>you weary</u>,

5. Then how <u>canst thou</u>
> - Then how <u>can you</u>

5. <u>Contend</u>
> - From the Hebrew word *tacharah*, Strong's #8474: <u>the idea of the heat of jealousy; to vie with a rival</u>.
> - <u>Jealously vie with your rivals</u>

5. <u>With horses</u>?
> - [<u>To gain the opportunity to fight</u>] on horse[<u>back</u>]?

5. And if in the land of <u>peace</u>,
> - From the Hebrew word *shalowm*, Strong's #7965: <u>safety</u>.
> - And if in the land of <u>safety</u>,

5. Wherein <u>thou trustedst</u>,
> - Wherein <u>you</u> [<u>have placed your</u>] <u>trust</u>,

5. <u>They have</u>
> - [<u>Running with</u>] the <u>soldiers on foot</u> has

5. <u>Wearied thee</u>,
> - [<u>Made</u>] <u>you weary</u>,

5. Then how <u>wilt thou</u> do
> - Then how <u>will you</u> do

5. In the <u>swelling</u>
> - From the Hebrew word *ga'own*, Strong's #1347: <u>excellency</u>.
> - In the [<u>time when</u>] <u>excellency</u> [<u>is required</u>]

5. Of Jordan?
  - [In the land] of [the] Jordan?

CHOICE EXAMINATION

1. Why did Jon not need a strategy for developing a management career at O'Reilly Auto Parts?

2. What was wrong with the career advancement strategy for the young man who stocked bathroom tissue?

3. What was wrong with the career advancement strategy for the tremendously capable young man?

4. In the scripture, why was the soldier on foot unable to vie with his rivals for the opportunity to fight on horseback?

5. Why was it important for the soldiers on foot to do well in the land of safety before excellency would be required in the land of the Jordan?

6. What choices do you need to make in order to *work hard and be dependable at your level of responsibility?*

TAKE CHARGE WHEN RESPONSIBILITY IS GIVEN TO YOU

≈ 47 ≈

And the LORD looked upon him, and said, Go in this thy might, and thou shalt save Israel from the hand of the Midianites: have not I sent thee?

And he said unto him, Oh my Lord, wherewith shall I save Israel? behold, my family is poor in Manasseh, and I am the least in my father's house.

And the LORD said unto him, Surely I will be with thee, and thou shalt smite the Midianites as one man.

Judges 6: 14 - 16

"Act like you're the manager of the store," he said. "Don't be afraid to do anything." He was the store manager, I was a department manager. It was the Christmas season. The district manager had given approval for him to choose a couple of responsible hourly associates to help with management duties over the busy weekends. It was my first opportunity to involve in supervisory responsibilities for the entire store. I had asked how much authority I was to have before I was expected to ask for permission. His answer surprised me. He used the word manager. He didn't say, "Act like you're an assistant manager." He didn't say, "Act like you're a department manager with slightly more authority." He said, "manager." He said, "Act like you're the manager of the store." He didn't want me to be afraid to do anything.

I could have chosen to decline the opportunity to help with management duties that Christmas season. I could have chosen to take the job, and then not take charge of my responsibilities. I don't remember anything significant that happened. I assume there were times when I didn't know the best way to take care of situations and I assume I made some mistakes. I am certain, though, of two things:

I challenged my capacity to make decisions, and

I gained confidence in my ability to supervise people.

I took my responsibility seriously. I acted like I was the manager of the store.

Take charge when responsibility is given to you. Consider yourself the manager of your responsibility.

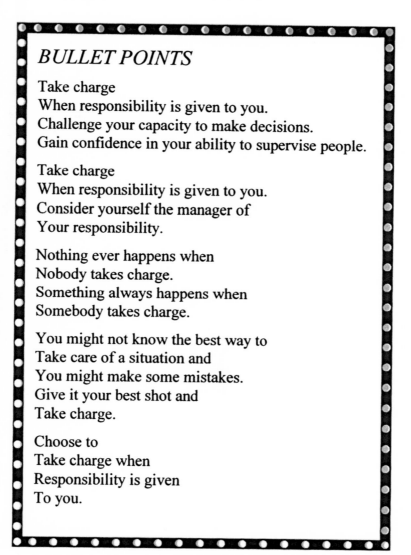

BULLET POINTS

Take charge
When responsibility is given to you.
Challenge your capacity to make decisions.
Gain confidence in your ability to supervise people.

Take charge
When responsibility is given to you.
Consider yourself the manager of
Your responsibility.

Nothing ever happens when
Nobody takes charge.
Something always happens when
Somebody takes charge.

You might not know the best way to
Take care of a situation and
You might make some mistakes.
Give it your best shot and
Take charge.

Choose to
Take charge when
Responsibility is given
To you.

SCRIPTURE ANALYSIS

Judges 6: 14 - 16

14. And the <u>LORD</u>
    - And the <u>Lord, (God)</u>

14. Looked upon <u>him</u>, and said,
    - Looked upon <u>Gideon (see verse #13)</u>, and said,

14. Go <u>in this</u>
    - Go <u>with this [confidence in]</u>

14. <u>Thy</u>
    - <u>Your</u>

14. <u>Might,</u>
    - From the Hebrew word *koach*, Strong's #3581: <u>capacity</u>.
    - <u>Capacity,</u>

14. And <u>thou shalt</u>
    - And [know this,] you shall

14. Save <u>Israel</u>
    - Save [the people of] Israel

14. From the <u>hand</u>
    - From the Hebrew word *kaph*, Strong's #3709: <u>power</u>.
    - From the <u>power</u>

14. Of the <u>Midianites</u>:
    - Unger's Bible Dictionary states: "When Midian appears again, it is not as an organized army of warriors, nor as a nation powerful enough to bring the Israelites under its despotic sway. Israel by idolatry lost the divine protection and the national cohesion which would have protected the nation against such marauders. They oppressed Israel, not by a strong military despotism, ... but by coming up when the harvest was ripe, 'like grasshoppers,' and destroying 'the increase of the earth.'"
    - Of the <u>Midianites [because of this knowledge]</u>:

14. Have not <u>I</u>
    - Have not <u>I[the Lord (God)]</u>

14. Sent <u>thee</u>?
    - Sent <u>you</u>?

15. And <u>he</u> said

- And <u>Gideon</u> said

15. Unto <u>him</u>,

    - Unto <u>the angel (see verse #12)</u>

15. Oh <u>my</u> Lord,

    - Oh [angel of] <u>my</u> Lord,

15. <u>Wherewith</u>

    - From the Hebrew word *mah*, Strong's #4100: <u>how</u>.

    - <u>How</u>

15. Shall I save <u>Israel</u>?

    - Shall I save <u>[the people of] Israel</u>?

15. Behold, my family is poor in <u>Manasseh</u>,

    - Behold, my family is <u>[a] poor [family] in [the tribe of]</u> <u>Manasseh</u>,

15. And I am the <u>least</u>

    - And I am the <u>least [notable]</u>

15. In my father's <u>house</u>.

    - From the Hebrew word *bayith*, Strong's #1004: <u>family</u>.

    - In my father's <u>family</u>.

16. And the <u>LORD</u>

    - And the <u>Lord (God)</u>

16. Said unto <u>him</u>,

    - Said unto <u>Gideon</u>,

16. Surely I will be with <u>thee</u>,

    - Surely I will be with <u>you</u>,

16. And <u>thou shalt</u>

    - And <u>you shall</u>

16. <u>Smite</u> the Midianites

    - From the Hebrew word *nakah*, Strong's #5221: <u>slaughter</u>.

    - <u>Slaughter</u> the Midianites

16. <u>As</u> one man.

    - <u>As [if they were only]</u> one man.

CHOICE EXAMINATION

1. Why did he say to "act like you're the manager of the store," instead of "act like you're an assistant manager," or "act like you're a department manager with slightly more authority?"

2. How did the store manager's instruction affect the department manager's confidence?

3. How was the department manager able to gain confidence in his ability to supervise people while assuming that he made some mistakes?

4. In the scripture, why did Gideon feel insecure about his ability to save the people of Israel?

5. What gave Gideon confidence in his capacity to save the people of Israel from the power of the Midianites?

6. What choices do you need to make in order to *take charge, when responsibility is given to you*?

STAND UP TO CONFRONTATION
≈ **48** ≈

And there went out a champion out of the camp of the Philistines, named Goliath, of Gath, whose height was six cubits and a span. And he had an helmet of brass upon his head, and he was armed with a coat of mail; and the weight of the coat was five thousand shekels of brass. And he had greaves of brass upon his legs, and a target of brass between his shoulders. And the staff of his spear was like a weaver's beam; and his spear's head weighed six hundred shekels of iron: and one bearing a shield went before him. And he stood and cried unto the armies of Israel, and said unto them, Why are ye come out to set your battle in array? am not I a Philistine, and ye servants to Saul? choose you a man for you, and let him come down to me. If he be able to fight with me, and to kill me, then will we be your servants: but if I prevail against him, and kill him, then shall ye be our servants, and serve us.

And David said to Saul, Let no man's heart fail because of him; thy servant will go and fight with this Philistine.

And he took his staff in his hand, and chose him five smooth stones out of the brook, and put them in a shepherd's bag which he had, even in a scrip; and his sling was in his hand: And he drew near to the Philistine. Then said David to the Philistine, Thou comest to me with a sword, and with a spear, and with a shield: but I come to thee in the name of the LORD of hosts, the God of the armies of Israel, whom thou hast defied.

And it came to pass, when the Philistine arose, and came and drew nigh to meet David, that David hasted, and ran toward the army to meet the Philistine. And David put his hand in his bag, and took thence a stone, and slang it, and smote the Philistine in his forehead, that the stone sunk into his forehead; and he fell upon his face to the earth.

I Samuel 17: 4 - 9, 32, 40, 45, 48, 49

He said he needed to talk to me. His wife had been caught shoplifting in the store the night before. I had called the police department to have her arrested. I had told her that she could no longer shop at this store. I took him to a back office. He sat down, pulled his chair close to mine, looked me square in the eyes and threatened to kill me. I stared back into his eyes and said, " If you kill me, I guess I'll be dead, but your wife still will not be allowed to shop at this store."

We talked for several minutes. When he got ready to leave, he shook my hand and thanked me for my time. I saw him almost daily after that occasion. (He had to do all of his wife's shopping.) I was deliberately cautious for a period of time. I always made a special effort to acknowledge him, in a respectful manner, when I saw him in the store. He was always courteous when he spoke back.

I suppose he realized that he couldn't intimidate me. I had chosen to stand up to his confrontation.

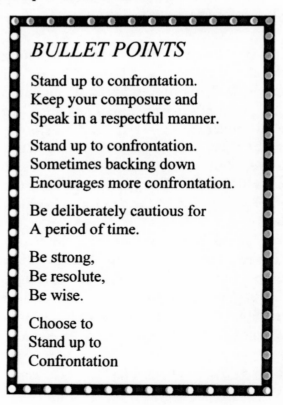

BULLET POINTS

Stand up to confrontation.
Keep your composure and
Speak in a respectful manner.

Stand up to confrontation.
Sometimes backing down
Encourages more confrontation.

Be deliberately cautious for
A period of time.

Be strong,
Be resolute,
Be wise.

Choose to
Stand up to
Confrontation

SCRIPTURE ANALYSIS

I Samuel 17: 4 - 9, 32, 40, 45, 49

4. And there went out a champion <u>out</u> of
- And there went out a champion [from] out of

4. The <u>camp</u> of the Philistines,
- From the Hebrew word *machaneh*, Strong's #4264: <u>army</u>.
- The <u>army</u> of the Philistines,

4. Named Goliath, <u>of</u>
- Named Goliath, [from the city] of

4. <u>Gath</u>,
- The Unger's Bible Dictionary states: "Gath [was] one of the cities of the Philistine pentapolis. It was the nearest of the large Philistine towns to Hebrew territory. It had a reputation for huge men like Goliath."
- <u>Gath</u>,

4. Whose height was <u>six cubits and a span</u>.
- Whose height was <u>nine feet, nine inches</u>.

5. And <u>he</u> had
- And <u>Goliath</u> had

5. <u>An</u> helmet
- <u>A</u> helmet

5. Of <u>brass</u> upon his head,
- Unger's Bible Dictionary states that: "Brass should in the scriptures be generally rendered bronze, or sometimes copper. Brass, the alloy of copper and zinc, is largely a modern material, while bronze (copper and tin) was used to an enormous extent in ancient times."
- [Made] of <u>bronze</u> upon his head,

5. And <u>was</u>
- And [Goliath] <u>was</u>

5. <u>Armed</u>
- From the Hebrew word *labash*, Strong's #3847: <u>clothe oneself or another</u>.
- <u>Clothed</u>

5. With a <u>coat of mail</u>;

- The Unger's Bible Dictionary states: "The breastplate, or cuirass [was] enumerated in the description of the arms of Goliath [as] a coat of mail, literally, a breastplate of scales. The cuirass of the Egyptians [for example] consisted of about eleven horizontal rows of metal plates, well secured by brass pins, with narrower rows forming a protection for the throat and neck. Each plate or scale was about an inch in width. In length the cuirass may have been little less than two and one half feet, covering the thigh nearly to the knee."
- With a breastplate of metal scales;

5. And the weight of the coat
- And the weight of the breastplate of metal scales

5. Was five thousand shekels
- Was [about] one hundred twenty five pounds

5. Of brass.
- [And it was made] of bronze.

6. And he
- And Goliath

6. Had greaves of
- The Unger's Bible Dictionary states: "Greaves [are] a facing for covering the leg, made of brass."
- Had facings of

6. Brass upon his legs,
- Bronze upon his legs,

6. And a target of
- From the Hebrew word *kiydown*, Strong's #3591: something to strike with, spear.
- And a spear of

6. Brass
- Bronze

6. Between his shoulders.
- [Slung] between his shoulders.

7. And the staff
- From the Hebrew word *chets*, Strong's #2671: the shaft of a spear.
- And the shaft

7. Of his spear
- Of Goliath's spear

7. Was <u>like</u>
- Was like [the size of]

7. A weaver's <u>beam</u>;
- From the Hebrew word *manowr*, Strong's #4500: <u>the frame of a loom.</u>
- <u>The frame of a loom [which is used by]</u> a weaver;

7. And <u>his</u>
- And <u>Goliath's</u>

7. Spear's head weighed <u>six hundred shekels</u>
- Spear's head weighed <u>[about] fifteen pounds</u>

7. <u>Of</u> iron:
- <u>[And was made] of</u> iron:

7. And <u>one</u> bearing a shield
- And <u>someone</u> bearing a shield

7. Went before <u>him</u>.
- Went before <u>Goliath</u>.

8. And <u>he stood</u>
- And <u>Goliath stood [at the front of the Philistine army]</u>

8. And <u>cried</u> unto the armies of Israel,
- And <u>[cried [out]</u> unto the armies of Israel,

8. And said unto <u>them</u>,
- And said unto <u>the people [of the armies of Israel]</u>,

8. Why <u>are ye</u> come out to
- Why <u>have you</u> come out to

8. <u>Set your battle in array?</u>
- The NIV says: "<u>Line up for battle?</u>"

8. Am not I a Philistine, and <u>ye</u> servants
- Am not I a Philistine, and <u>[are] you [not]</u> servants

8. To <u>Saul?</u>
- To <u>[king] Saul?</u>

8. <u>Choose you</u>
- <u>You choose</u>

8. A man <u>for</u> you,
- A man <u>to [represent]</u> you,

8. And let <u>him</u> come down
- And let <u>the man [you choose to represent you]</u> come down

8. <u>To</u> me.

- To [fight with] me.

9. If he be able to fight with me, and to kill me,

- If the man [you've chosen to represent you] is able to fight with me, and to kill me,

9. Then will we be your servants:

- Then we (Philistines) will be your servants:

9. But if I prevail against him,

- But if I prevail against the man [you've chosen to represent you],

9. And kill him,

- And [I] kill the man [you've chosen to represent you],

9. Then shall ye be our servants,

- Then shall you (Israelites) be our servants,

9. And serve us. And

- And [you (Israelites) shall be required to] serve us. And

32. David said to Saul, Let no man's heart fail

- The NIV says: "David said to Saul, let no one lose heart"

32. Because of him;

- Because of Goliath;

32. Thy servant

- [I,] your servant [David]

32. Will go and fight with this Philistine.

- Will go and fight with Goliath.

40. And he

- And David

40. Took his staff in his hand,

- From the Hebrew word *maqqel*, Strong's #4731: stick for walking, striking [or] guiding.

- Unger's Bible Dictionary states: "The staff of the shepherd was used to aid in climbing hills, beating bushes and low brush in which the flock strayed, and where snakes and reptiles abounded."

- Took his [shepherds] staff in his hand,

40. And chose him five smooth stones out of the brook, and put them

- And chose him five smooth stones out or the brook, and put the five smooth stones

40. In <u>a shepherd's bag which he had, even in a scrip</u>;
     - <u>Scrip</u> is from the Hebrew word *yalquwt*, Strong's #3219: <u>a traveling pouch</u>.
     - The NIV says: "In <u>the pouch of his shepherd's bag</u>"

40. And <u>his</u>
     - And <u>David's</u>

40. <u>Sling</u> was in his hand:
     - The Unger's Bible Dictionary states: "The sling may be justly reckoned as among the most ancient instruments of warfare. The weapon was very simple, being made of a couple of strings of sinew, leather, or rope, with a leathern receptacle in the middle to receive the stone. After being swung once or twice around the head it was discharged by letting go [of] one of the strings.
     - <u>Sling</u> was in his hand:

40. And <u>he</u> drew near
     - And <u>David</u> drew near

40. To <u>the Philistine</u>.
     - To <u>Goliath</u>.

45. Then said David to <u>the Philistine</u>,
     - Then David said to <u>Goliath</u>,

45. <u>Thou comest</u> to me with a sword, and with a spear, and with a shield:
     - <u>You come</u> to me with a sword, and with a spear, and with a shield:

45. But I come to <u>thee</u>
     - But I come to <u>you</u>

45. In the name of the LORD of <u>hosts</u>,
     - From the Hebrew word *tsaba*, Strong's #6635: <u>army</u>.
     - In the name of the Lord of <u>[the] armies</u>,

45. The God of the armies of Israel, <u>whom thou hast</u>
     - The God of the armies of Israel, <u>[of] whom you have</u>

45. <u>Defied</u>.
     - Defined by Webster's Dictionary as: <u>to challenge to combat</u>.
     - <u>Challenged to combat</u>.

48. And it came to pass, when <u>the Philistine</u> arose,
     - And it came to pass, when <u>Goliath</u> arose,

48. And <u>came</u> and

- And <u>came [toward David]</u> and

48. <u>Drew nigh to meet David,</u>

- The NIV says: "<u>Moved closer to attack him</u>"

48. That David <u>hasted,</u>

- From the Hebrew word *mahar*, Stong's #4116: <u>to hurry</u>.
- That David <u>hurried,</u>

48. And ran toward the <u>army</u>

- And ran toward the <u>army [of the Philistines]</u>

48. To meet <u>the Philistine.</u>

- To meet <u>Goliath</u>.

49. And David put his hand in his bag, and took <u>thence</u> a stone,

- From the Hebrew word *sham*, Strong's #8033: <u>there</u>.
- And David put his hand in his bag, and took <u>[from] there</u>

a stone,

49. And <u>slang it,</u>

- And <u>slung the stone,</u>

49. And <u>smote</u>

- And <u>struck</u>

49. <u>The Philistine</u> in his forehead,

- <u>Goliath</u> in his forehead,

49. <u>That</u>

- <u>[So] that</u>

49. The stone sunk into <u>his</u> forehead;

- The stone sunk into <u>Goliath's</u> forehead;

49. And <u>he</u> fell upon his face to the earth.

- And <u>Goliath</u> fell upon his face to the earth.

CHOICE EXAMINATION

1. What did the man hope to accomplish by threatening the store manager?

2. Why did the manager always make a special effort to acknowledge the man in a respectful manner?

3. In the scripture, why did the Philistine army send Goliath to challenge a representative of the armies of Israel to combat?

4. Who did David say that Goliath had actually challenged to combat?

5. Why did David hurry and run toward the army of the Philistines to meet Goliath?

6. What choices do you need to make in order to *stand up to confrontation*?

RESPOND WITH ACTION!

≈ 49 ≈

And there were four leprous men at the entering in of the gate: and they said one to another, Why sit we here until we die? If we say, We will enter into the city, then the famine is in the city, and we shall die there: and if we sit still here, we die also. Now therefore come, and let us fall unto the host of the Syrians: if they save us alive, we shall live; and if they kill us, we shall but die.

And they rose up in the twilight, to go unto the camp of the Syrians: and when they were come to the uttermost part of the camp of Syria, behold, there was no man there. For the lord had made the host of the Syrians to hear a noise of chariots, and a noise of horses, even the noise of a great host: II Kings 7: 3 - 6

Smoke was quickly filling the upstairs bedrooms where our children were sleeping. Charity responded first, "EEEEIIIIKKKK!!! THE HOUSE IS ON FIRE!!" The smoke alarms were screaming. Charity was screaming. The rest of us were jumping out of bed in an amazing flurry of *action*! I grabbed the fire extinguisher from the closet and quickly used up its contents. Barbie and Charity started filling pans and bowls with water to throw on the flames. Joshua and Amy ran out the door to hook up the garden hose. I scrambled outside to grab the step ladder so I could climb high enough to reach the location where the fire was burning. Joshua and Amy ran the garden hose through the front door. It wasn't quite long enough. I found that if I stood up high on the ladder and put my thumb over the end of the hose, the water would barely reach to the wall above the fireplace where the flames were still burning.

Barbie shouted out instructions. "Charity!" (who was currently engaged to be married), "Get your wedding dress! Carry it outside now! Joshua! Drive the cars away from the house! Amy! Grab us some clothing! (It was winter. We were all in our pajamas.) Throw them in a vehicle! Go stand by the tree in the front yard!" Ten minutes into our frenzy-filled fight with the fire I was able to break away long enough to call the fire department.

We built our house with a seventeen foot tall ceiling in the living room. The rock fireplace is there. Halfway up the ceiling in the center of the rock-work is a cedar, wooden structure. An error in construction allowed heat from the fireplace to escape to the wooden structure. After five years of building fires in our fireplace, this was the night the cedar boards chose to ignite.

I called my brother David. "Our house is on fire! Come quickly!" He called my nephew, Marc, who was staying at my parent's house that night. They were there within minutes.

"I heard your call over the scanner! I came to help!" It was the local police officer from Southwest City, eight miles away. We didn't know the man. We were grateful for his help. He was the first person to arrive on the scene.

I heard Joshua yell out, "Dad, I'm going down to the road to catch the fire truck and show them where our house is!" (Our house is located at the edge of the woods at the end of a long driveway.)

People were running everywhere. The upstairs portion of the house was so smoke-filled that we couldn't see. David and Marc grabbed wet handkerchiefs, held them over their mouths and climbed the stairs to see how far the fire had traveled. David opened the trap door to the attic. The wall was glowing red but there were no visible flames. "The fire's burning inside the wall! It's almost to the roof-line!"

The police officer scurried up to the top rung of the stepladder and started beating the wall with a crowbar. He was trying to break the wall open so he could get the garden hose to where the fire was burning. The ladder teetered and fell over sideways. As we all gasped or screamed and lunged toward him, the ladder slung him several feet across the house to the center of the room, directly onto our living room couch. He was fine. It was a perfect, soft landing.

The fire truck arrived. "Oh Galen! When I heard the call I hoped it wasn't your house! We got here as quickly as we could!" It was Shane Clark, the fire chief, and a friend of ours from church.

The volunteer fire crew quickly scaled the outside wall of

the house. One man took a hatchet and started chipping away at the siding in order to break through to the inner wall to where the fire was still burning. The flames were working their way through the wall between the rock fireplace and the siding, only six inches from the shingled roof.

"We're going too slow. It'll get away from us!" I shouted. "I'll get my chainsaw!"

The barn is only 50 yards from the house. I quickly retrieved the saw, ran inside my smoke-filled living room and started the engine. (A chainsaw is really loud inside of a house.) Climbing to the top of the ladder, as two people held it steady, I proceeded to cut a large hole in the wall of our house. The fire truck had been spraying water onto the outside wall during this time. Two firemen brought the hose inside our house, stuck the nozzle into the newly manufactured hole and turned the water back on. Finally, the fire extinguished.

We expressed our appreciation to all of these people who had graciously come to our rescue in the middle of the night. We thanked and bragged on our children for their quick responses. Then we looked at our house, smoke filled, nasty, and wet. The garden hose was still running, full force, onto the wooden floor of our living room. I stepped outside and shut the water off.

"We've got to save our hardwood floor," Barbie said. "Let's get towels and dry it off." Barbie and I worked another couple of hours trying to dry off the floor. At 5:00 A.M., we took a short nap. At 8:00 A.M. we called our insurance providers.

Several things happened which worked together to save our house. Two weeks prior to the fire Barbie had routinely changed out the batteries in all our smoke alarms. One week prior to the fire I had visited with my friend, Bill, a volunteer fireman. He had told me of a family who *thought* they could get a house fire put out themselves, so they did not call the fire department. They ended up losing everything. The morning of the fire I *almost* put the ladder in the barn. I had actually picked it up before I changed my mind and put it back by the house. The afternoon of the fire, after I had finished cutting the last piece of firewood, the chainsaw ran out of gas. I put gas and oil in the saw so it would be ready to operate the next time I needed it. The evening of the fire, Joshua had picked up children in the church van for the Wednesday night service. He was suddenly overcome with an urge to pray for protection. He pulled the van off the road and prayed.

I'm totally convinced that the saving of our house from the fire was a miracle. We're thankful for God's protection on our house and family. But I also wonder, what would have happened if we had not chosen to respond to each corresponding event with *action*? What if Barbie hadn't changed the smoke alarm batteries? What if I hadn't followed Bill's advice and called the fire department? What if I hadn't followed my instinct to leave the ladder by the house? What if I hadn't taken time to gas and oil the chainsaw? What if Joshua hadn't pulled the van off the side of the road to pray for protection? What if Charity hadn't responded so quickly and screamed for help? What if Barbie and Charity hadn't filled pans and bowls with water to throw on the fire? What if Joshua and Amy hadn't hooked up the garden hose and ran it through the front door? What if the police officer had stayed in town? What if David and Marc had not come so quickly? What if the firemen didn't come?

I know what would have happened if any one of us hadn't done what we did. The house would have been lost. But the house, including the hardwood floor, was saved because *everyone* responded. Everyone responded with *action!*

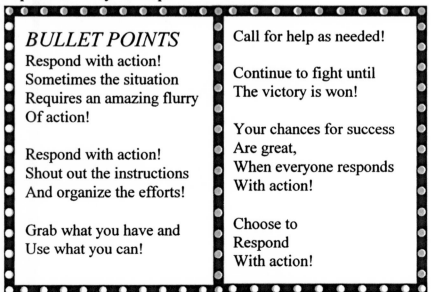

BULLET POINTS
Respond with action!
Sometimes the situation
Requires an amazing flurry
Of action!

Respond with action!
Shout out the instructions
And organize the efforts!

Grab what you have and
Use what you can!

Call for help as needed!

Continue to fight until
The victory is won!

Your chances for success
Are great,
When everyone responds
With action!

Choose to
Respond
With action!

SCRIPTURE ANALYSIS

II Kings 7: 3 - 6

3. And there were four <u>leprous</u> men
　　- Unger's Bible Dictionary states: "Biblical leprosy is a whiteness which disfigured its victim, but did not disable him. A victim of this superficial scaly disease was unclean [morally and spiritually impure] only as long as the affection was partial. Once the whole body was covered he was clean, and could enter the temple. Instructions were given for the removal of the lepers from the society of men. While thus excluded the leper was to wear mourning costume, rend his clothes, leave the hair of his head disordered, keep the beard covered, and cry 'Unclean! Unclean!' that everyone might avoid him for fear of being defiled, and as long as the disease lasted he was to dwell apart without [outside of] the camp."
　　- And there were four <u>leprous</u> men

3. <u>At</u>
　　- [Sitting] at

3. The <u>entering</u>
　　- The <u>entrance</u>

3. <u>In of</u>
　　- [Leading] in to

3. The <u>Gate</u>:
　　- The [city] gate:

3. And <u>they</u> said one to another,
　　- And <u>the four leprous men</u> said one to another,

3. Why <u>sit we</u> here
　　- Why [are] we sitting here

3. <u>Until</u> we die?
　　- [Waiting] until we die?

4. <u>If</u>
　　- [For] If

4. We <u>say</u>,
　　- We <u>say</u> [to each other],

4. We will enter into the <u>city</u>,

    - We will enter into the <u>city [of Samaria (see verse #1)</u>],

4. Then

    - <u>Then [we will not go in because of</u>]

4. The famine <u>is</u> in

    - The famine <u>[that] is</u> in

4. The <u>city</u>,

    - The <u>city [of Samaria</u>],

4. <u>And we</u> shall

    - <u>For [we know that] we</u> shall

4. Die <u>there</u>:

    - Die <u>[of starvation if we go into] the city of Samaria</u>:

4. And if we <u>sit</u> still

    - And if we <u>[continue to] sit</u> still

4. <u>Here</u>,

    - <u>Here [at the entrance of the city gate</u>],

4. We <u>die</u> also.

    - We <u>[will] die [here</u>] also.

4. Now therefore <u>Come</u>, and let us

    - From the Hebrew word *yalak*, Strong's #3212: <u>go</u>.

    - Now therefore let us <u>go</u>, and

4. <u>Fall unto</u> the

    - <u>[Give ourselves a chance by] falling into</u> the

4. <u>Host</u> of the Syrians:

    - From the Hebrew word *machaneh*, Strong's #4264: <u>army</u>.

    - <u>[Hands of the] army</u> of the Syrians:

4. If <u>they</u>

    - If <u>the army of the Syrians</u>

4. <u>Save us alive</u>, we shall live;

    - <u>Saves our lives</u>, we shall live;

4. And if <u>they</u> <u>kill</u> us,

    - And if <u>the army of the Syrians kills</u> us,

4. We shall <u>but die</u>.

    - We shall <u>[have been destined] to die [anyway</u>].

5. <u>And they</u> rose up in the twilight,

    - <u>So the [four leprous] men</u> rose up in the twilight,

5. To go <u>unto</u>

    - To go <u>[fall] into [the hands of</u>]

5. The <u>camp</u> of the Syrians:
    - Also from the Hebrew word *machaneh,* Strong's #4264: <u>army</u>. This is the same word which was translated as *host* in verse # 4.
    - The <u>army</u> of the Syrians:
5. And when <u>they</u>
    - And when <u>the [four leprous] men</u>
5. Were come to the <u>uttermost</u> part
    - From the Hebrew word *qatseh,* Strong's #7097: <u>outside</u>.
    - Were come to the <u>outside</u> part
5. Of the <u>camp</u> of Syria,
    - Of the <u>army</u> of Syria,
5. Behold, there was <u>no man</u> there.
    - Behold, there was <u>not [a] man [from the Syrian army]</u> there.
6. For the Lord had made the <u>host</u> of the Syrians
    - For the Lord had made the <u>army</u> of the Syrians
6. To hear a noise <u>of</u> chariots,
    - To hear a noise <u>[which sounded] like</u> chariots,
6. And a noise <u>of</u> horses,
    - And a noise <u>[which sounded] like</u> horses,
6. <u>Even the noise of</u>
    - <u>[And] even a noise [which sounded] like</u>
6. A great <u>host</u>:
    - A great <u>army</u>:

CHOICE EXAMINATION

1. What things did people do that helped save the house from total destruction?

2. Why did the people work together so well in their efforts to save the house?

3. What would have happened if any one of the people had not responded with action?

4. In the scripture, why were the four leprous men willing to fall into the hands of the army of the Syrians?

5. How did the four leprous men's actions affect the people inside the city of Samaria?

6. What choices do you need to make in order to *respond with action*?

LEARN FROM YOUR MISTAKES
≈ 50 ≈

NOW Naaman, captain of the host of the king of Syria, was a great man with his master, and honourable, because by him the LORD had given deliverance unto Syria: he was also a mighty man in valour, but he was a leper.

And the Syrians had gone out by companies, and had brought away captive out of the land of Israel a little maid; and she waited on Naaman's wife. And she said unto her mistress, Would God my lord were with the prophet that is in Samaria! for he would recover him of his leprosy.

And one went in, and told his lord, saying, Thus and thus said the maid that is of the land of Israel.

So Naaman came with his horses and with his chariot, and stood at the door of the house of Elisha. And Elisha sent a messenger unto him, saying, Go and wash in Jordan seven times, and thy flesh will come again to thee, and thou shalt be clean.

But Naaman was wroth, and went away, and said, Behold, I thought, He will surely come out to me, and stand, and call on the name of the LORD his God, and strike his hand over the place, and recover the leper. Are not Abana and Pharpar, rivers of Damascus, better than all the waters of Israel? may I not wash in them, and be clean? So he turned and went away in a rage.

And his servants came near, and spake unto him, and said, My father, if the prophet had bid thee do some great thing, wouldst thou not have done it? how much rather then, when he saith to thee, Wash, and be clean?

Then went he down, and dipped himself seven times in Jordan, according to the saying of the man of God: and his flesh came again like unto the flesh of a little child, and he was clean.

II Kings: 5: 1 - 4, 9 - 14

Mr. Browning stared at me for a couple of seconds. A big grin came across his face and he laughed out loud!

"Man, you are so scared," he said. "Your face is as white as a ghost! Listen to me. The only person who never makes a mistake is the person who doesn't do anything. Don't worry about it! Just choose to learn from it and you'll never make the same mistake again."

It was my first real job. I was a sales clerk at a convenience store. I had been on the job for less than a month when a gentleman paid for ten dollars worth of gasoline with his credit card. I ran the credit card through the imprinter and handed it back to him with the hard copy of the credit card receipt. The hard copy was the store's copy, not the customer's copy. The net effect was, I lost the store *ten whole dollars*, and it was totally my fault! No sooner had I realized my mistake than I looked up and saw Mr. Browning, the owner, walking into the store.

"Oh no!" I thought. "Mr. Browning will probably yell at me! I'll probably be fired!" Mr. Browning, however, was a gentle Christian man. His comments put me at ease and laid my fears to rest.

I've made a lot of mistakes. Everyone who does anything makes mistakes. Some of my mistakes have cost my employers a lot more money than ten dollars. But I think that none of my mistakes on the job have bothered me as much as that initial ten dollar mistake at the convenience store. Thank goodness for Mr. Browning. I've never forgotten this kind man's comments to me: "The only person who doesn't make a mistake is the person who doesn't do anything. Don't worry about it! Just choose to learn from it and you'll never make the same mistake again."

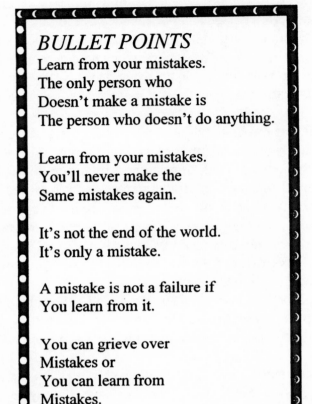

BULLET POINTS

Learn from your mistakes.
The only person who
Doesn't make a mistake is
The person who doesn't do anything.

Learn from your mistakes.
You'll never make the
Same mistakes again.

It's not the end of the world.
It's only a mistake.

A mistake is not a failure if
You learn from it.

You can grieve over
Mistakes or
You can learn from
Mistakes.

Choose to
Learn from
Your mistakes.

SCRIPTURE ANALYSIS
II Kings 5: 1 - 4, 9 - 14

1. NOW Naaman, captain of the <u>host</u> of the king of Syria,

    - From the Hebrew word *tsaba*, Strong's #6635: <u>a mass of persons [or] an army</u>.

    - Now Naaman, captain of the <u>army</u> of the king of Syria,

1. Was a great man <u>with</u>

    - Was a great man <u>with [regards to the opinion of]</u>

1. His <u>master</u>,
   - His <u>master (the king of Syria)</u>,

1. And <u>honourable</u>,
   - And [Naaman was known as an] honorable [man],

1. Because <u>by him</u>
   - Because <u>through Naaman's [efforts]</u>

1. The LORD had given <u>deliverance</u> unto Syria:
   - From the Hebrew word *tshuwah*, Strong's #8668: <u>victory</u>.
   - The Lord had given [a military] <u>victory</u> unto Syria:

1. <u>He</u> was also a mighty man
   - <u>Naaman</u> was also a mighty man

1. <u>In</u>
   - [Who showed qualities] of

1. <u>Valour</u>,
   - Defined by Webster's Dictionary as: <u>personal bravery</u>.
   - <u>Personal bravery</u>,

1. But <u>he was</u>
   - But <u>Naaman was [infected with]</u>

1. A <u>leper</u>.
   - Unger's Bible Dictionary states: "Biblical leprosy is a whiteness which disfigured it's victim, but did not disable him. A victim of this superficial scaly disease was unclean [morally and spiritually impure] only as long as the affection was partial."
   - A [disease called] leprosy.

2. And the Syrians had gone out by <u>companies</u>,
   - And the Syrians had gone out by <u>companies [of soldiers]</u>,

2. And had brought away <u>captive</u>
   - And had brought away <u>captive [to them]</u>

2. Out of the land of Israel a little <u>maid</u>;
   - From the Hebrew word *naarah*, Strong's #5291: <u>a girl</u>.
   - Out of the land of Israel a little <u>girl;</u>

2. And <u>she</u>
   - And <u>the little girl</u>

2. <u>Waited</u>
   - From the Hebrew words *hayah*, Strong's #1961: <u>require</u>; and *paniym*, Strong's #6440: <u>serve</u>.
   - [Was] required [to be a] servant

2. On Naaman's wife.
- To Naaman's wife.

3. And she said unto
- And the servant girl said unto

3. Her mistress,
- Her mistress (Naaman's wife),

3. Would God
- [It] would [be a blessing from] God

3. My lord were
- [If] Naaman were

3. With the prophet that is in Samaria!
- [To meet] with the prophet that is in Samaria!

3. For he
- For the prophet [Elisha (see verse #9)]

3. Would recover him of his leprosy.
- Would [cause] Naaman [to] recover from his leprosy.

4. And one
- And Naaman

4. Went in,
- Went with [this information to the king of Syria (see verse #5)],

4. And told his lord,
- And told the king of Syria [about what he had heard],

4. Saying, Thus and thus said the maid that is of the land of Israel.
- Saying, Thus and thus said the little girl who came from the land of Israel.

9. So Naaman came with
- So Naaman went with

9. His horses and with his chariot, and stood at the door of the house of Elisha.
- His horses and his chariot, and stood [himself] at the door of the house of Elisha.

10. And Elisha sent a messenger unto him, saying,
- And Elisha sent a messenger unto Naaman, saying,

10. Go and wash in Jordan
- Go and wash in [the] Jordan [river]

10. Seven times,
- Unger's Bible Dictionary states: "The ceremony
prescribed for the purification of persons cured of leprosy is based
upon the idea that this malady is the bodily symbol, not so much of
sin merely as of death. The officiating priest caused two clean and
living birds, along with some cedar wood, scarlet wool, and hyssop
to be brought. One of the birds was killed over running water, i. e.,
water from a spring or stream, in such a way that the blood would
flow into the water. He then dipped into this the living bird, the
cedar, the scarlet wool, and the hyssop - the symbol of duration of
life, vigor of life, and purity. He then sprinkled it seven times upon
the leper, after which the living bird was set free, thus symbolizing
that the leper was at liberty to return to society. The sprinkling was
repeated seven times."
- Seven times [in accordance to the ceremony prescribed
for the purification of persons cured of leprosy],

10. And thy flesh
- And your flesh

10. Shall come again
- Shall become [clean] again

10. To thee,
- To you,

10. And thou shalt
- And you shall

10. Be clean.
- Be cleansed [from leprosy].

11. But Naaman was wroth,
- But Naaman was wroth [at Elisha],

11. And went away, and said,
- And [Naaman] went away, and said,

11. Behold, I thought, He will surely come out
- Behold, I thought, Elisha would surely come out

11. To me,
- To [see] me,

11. And stand, and call on the name of the LORD his God,
- And stand [by me], and call on the name of the Lord his
God,

11. And strike his hand

- From the Hebrew word *nuwph*, Strong's #5130: <u>wave</u>.
- And <u>wave</u> his hand

11. Over the <u>place</u>,
- Over the <u>place [where the leprosy's located]</u>,

11. And <u>recover</u>
- And [cause me to] <u>recover [from]</u>

11. The <u>leper</u>.
- The <u>leprosy</u>.

12. Are not Abana and Pharpar, <u>rivers of</u> Damascus,
- Are not Abana and Pharpar, [which are] <u>rivers in</u> Damascus,

12. <u>Better</u> than all the waters
- <u>Better [rivers]</u> than all the waters

12. <u>Of</u> Israel?
- [Located] <u>in</u> Israel?

12. May I not wash in <u>them</u>,
- May I not wash in [<u>the rivers of</u>] Abana and Pharpar [instead of the Jordan river],

12. And be <u>clean</u>?
- And be <u>cleansed [from leprosy]</u>?

12. So <u>he turned</u>
- So <u>Naaman</u> turned [around to leave]

12. And went <u>away</u> in a rage.
- And Naaman went <u>away [from Elisha's house]</u> in a rage.

13. And <u>his</u> servants
- And <u>Naaman's</u> servants

13. Came <u>near</u>,
- Came <u>near [to Naaman]</u>,

13. And <u>spake</u>
- And <u>spoke</u>

13. Unto <u>him</u>, and said,
- Unto <u>Naaman</u>, and said,

13. My <u>father</u>,
- The Unger's Bible Dictionary states: "This word, besides it's natural sense of progenitor, has a number of other meanings, as: (1) Any ancestor near or remote, (2) Founder, i. e., the first ancestor of a tribe or nation, (3) Benefactor, as doing good and

providing for others as a father.

    - My <u>benefactor</u>,

13. If the prophet had <u>bid</u>

    - From the Hebrew word *dabar*, Strong's #1696: <u>tell</u>.

    - If the prophet had <u>told</u>

13. <u>Thee</u> do some great thing,

    - <u>You [to]</u> do some great thing,

13. <u>Wouldest thou</u> not have done it?

    - <u>Would you</u> not have done it?

13. How much <u>rather</u> then,

    - How much <u>rather [to be preferred]</u> then,

13. When <u>he saith</u>

    - When <u>Elisha says</u>

13. To <u>thee</u>,

    - To <u>you</u>,

13. Wash, and be <u>clean</u>?

    - Wash and be <u>cleansed [from leprosy]</u>?

14. Then went <u>he down</u>,

    - Then <u>Naaman</u> went <u>down [to the Jordan river]</u>,

14. And dipped himself seven times in <u>Jordan</u>,

    - And dipped himself seven times in <u>[the] Jordan [river]</u>,

14. According to the <u>saying</u>

    - From the Hebrew word *dabar*, Strong's #1697: <u>message</u>.

    - According to the <u>message [given to him]</u>

14. <u>Of the man of God</u>:

    - <u>By Elisha</u>:

14. And <u>his</u> flesh

    - And <u>Naaman's [diseased]</u> flesh

14. <u>Came</u> again

    - <u>Became [cleansed from leprosy]</u> again

14. <u>Like</u> unto the flesh of a little child,

    - <u>Like [flesh that could be compared]</u> unto the flesh of a little child,

14. And <u>he</u>

    - And <u>Naaman</u>

14. Was <u>clean</u>.

    - Was <u>cleansed [from Leprosy]</u>.

CHOICE EXAMINATION

1. Why was the sales clerk scared after he lost the store ten dollars?

2. What logic did Mr. Browning use to put the sales clerk at ease?

3. In the scripture, why was Naaman wroth at Elisha?

4. Why did Naaman think that the prophet should have told him to do some great thing?

5. Why did Naaman want to wash in the rivers of Abana and Pharpar instead of the Jordan river?

6. What choices do you need to make in order to *learn from your mistakes*?

LEARN FROM FAILURE AND TRY AGAIN

≈ 51 ≈

And the Lord said, Simon, Simon, behold, Satan hath desired to have you, that he may sift you as wheat: But I have prayed for thee, that thy faith fail not: and when thou art converted, strengthen thy brethren.

And he said unto him, Lord, I am ready to go with thee, both into prison, and to death.

And he said, I tell thee, Peter, the cock shall not crow this day, before that thou shalt thrice deny that thou knowest me.

Then took they him, and led him, and brought him into the high priest's house. And Peter followed afar off. And when they had kindled a fire in the midst of the hall, and were set down together, Peter sat down among them. But a certain maid beheld him as he sat by the fire, and earnestly looked upon him, and said, This man was also with him.

And he denied him, saying, Woman, I know him not.

And after a little while another saw him, and said, Thou art also of them.

And Peter said, Man, I am not.

And about the space of one hour after another confidently affirmed, saying, Of a truth this fellow also was with him: for he is a Galilean.

And Peter said, Man, I know not what thou sayest. And immediately, while he yet spake, the cock crew. And the Lord turned, and looked upon Peter. And Peter remembered the word of the Lord, how he had said unto him, Before the cock crow, thou shalt deny me thrice.

And Peter went out, and wept bitterly.

Luke 22: 31 - 34, 54 - 62

I heard a message over the intercom system telling me to go to one of the back offices. When I arrived, the management team was seated in a neatly arranged circle with one empty chair. Nobody was smiling. I took my seat. The store manager spoke to me in an uncharacteristically gentle voice. "Galen, we've decided to take you out of the department manager position. We are going to put your friend Steve in your place. We'd like you to be his sales clerk."

I was twenty-four years old. I had worked at Wal-Mart for three years. I had been a department manager for only one year. I was devastated.

Sometimes life isn't fair. When the department manager job for sporting goods and automotives became available, I campaigned for the job. I told the manager that I could handle it. He told me that I was inexperienced and needed more time to learn the required duties. He was right. Nevertheless, I got my opportunity. After some brief instructions on how to order the merchandise and a description of the expectations, I was officially placed in charge of my departments. No one ever told me that I was doing a good job, or a bad job, until the day that I was called into the office to be told that I was being demoted to sales clerk.

I was angry and embarrassed. I wanted to quit my job at Wal-Mart and start a new career with another company. I applied for a job at the local Farmer's Co-op. (I have a college degree in farm management.) They didn't hire me. I applied for a job at the MFA (Missouri Farmer's Association) store. They didn't hire me either.

I ended up staying right where I was. I became Steve's sales clerk. More importantly, I chose to do exactly what the store manager had told me I needed to do a year earlier. I observed how Steve ran his departments. I took time to learn the required duties. I gained the experience I needed.

One year later the store was remodeled and expanded. Additional department managers were needed. Steve took a job as the Electronics department manager. I was asked to be the new Sporting Goods department manager. This time I was ready. Four years later, my sales clerks and I were proudly honored for having the number one Sporting Goods department in the entire company.

All of the company's top department managers, including me, got to sit on the stage directly behind the executive leaders at the annual Wal-Mart shareholder's meeting. The following year, I was promoted to assistant manager.

I'm thankful that I work for Wal-Mart. Not every company would allow you to fail and then give you another chance. I even appreciate the fact that I failed in my first attempt at being a department manager. I've shared my story of failure to struggling store associates numerous times. I made a commitment to myself, after I was promoted into management, that I would never allow anyone to fail in their job without someone talking to them about their inadequacies first. There should never be a surprise demotion. We should all have opportunities to change and succeed. However, if we do fail, we should also remember that the person who overcomes a failure has probably learned more about what it takes to succeed than the person who has never had to struggle through the same situation. Second chances are a good thing for people who don't quit trying.

BULLET POINTS

Learn from failure and
Try again.
The person who overcomes a failure
Has probably learned more about
Struggling for success than
The person who has never suffered
Through a failure.

Learn from failure and
Try again.
Second chances are a
Good thing for
People who don't quit trying.

People don't choose to fail, but
Sometimes people choose to
Quit trying.

If someone fails,
Give them another chance if
They still want to try.

You haven't failed if
You haven't quit trying.

Observe and learn the
Required duties.

Gain the experience
You need.

Choose to
Learn
From failure and
Try again.

SCRIPTURE ANALYSIS

Luke 22: 33 - 34, 54 - 61

31. And <u>the Lord</u> said,
- And <u>Jesus</u> said,

31. <u>Simon, Simon,</u> behold
- <u>Peter, Peter (see Mark 3: 16)</u>, behold

31. Satan <u>hath</u> desired
- Satan <u>has</u> desired

31. To <u>have</u> you,
- To have <u>[control of]</u> you,

31. <u>That</u>
- <u>[So]</u> that

31. He <u>may</u>
- He <u>may</u> [be allowed to]

31. Sift you <u>as</u> wheat:
- Sift you <u>as [if you were grains of]</u> wheat:

32. But I have prayed for <u>thee,</u>
- But I have prayed for <u>you,</u>

32. <u>That thy</u> faith
- <u>[So] that your</u> faith

32. <u>Fail not:</u>
- <u>[Will] not fail [to sustain you]</u>:

32. And <u>when thou art</u>
- And <u>after you have</u>

32. <u>Converted,</u>
- From the Greek word *epistrepho*, Strong's #1994: <u>to revert</u>.
- <u>[Recuperated and] reverted [back to your faith]</u>,

32. <u>Strengthen thy</u>
- <u>[I want you to] strengthen your</u>

32. <u>Brethren.</u>
- From the Greek word *adelphos*, Strong's #80: <u>brother</u>.
- <u>[Spiritual] brothers</u>.

33. And <u>he</u> said
- And <u>Peter</u> said

33. Unto <u>him, Lord,</u>

    - Unto <u>Jesus</u>, Lord,

33. I am ready to go with <u>thee,</u> both into prison, and to death.

    - I am ready to go with <u>you</u>, both into prison, and to death.

34. And <u>he</u> said,

    - And <u>Jesus</u> said,

34. I tell <u>thee,</u> Peter,

    - I tell <u>you [the truth]</u>, Peter,

34. The cock shall not crow <u>this</u> day,

    - The cock shall not crow <u>[on] this</u> day,

34. Before that <u>thou shalt thrice</u>

    - Before that <u>you shall three</u> [times]

34. Deny that <u>thou knowest</u> me.

    - Deny that <u>you [even] know</u> me.

54. Then took <u>they</u>

    - Then <u>a multitude [of people (see 22:47)]</u> took

54. <u>Him,</u>

    - <u>Jesus</u>,

54. And led <u>him,</u>

    - And led <u>Jesus [away]</u>,

54. And <u>brought him</u>

    - And <u>[they] brought Jesus</u>

54. Into the <u>high priest's</u> house.

    - The Unger's Bible dictionary states: "The high priest had the supervision of the rest of the priests and of the entire worship, and was at liberty to exercise all the other sacerdotal [priestly] functions as well. In addition to his strictly religious duties, the high priest was the supreme civil head of the people, the supreme head of the state, in so far, that is, as the state was not under the sway of foreign rulers.

    - Into the <u>high priest's</u> house.

54. And Peter <u>followed</u> afar off.

    - And Peter <u>followed [Jesus and the multitude from]</u> afar off.

55. And when <u>they</u>

    - And when <u>some people [from the multitude]</u>

55. Had kindled a fire in the midst of the <u>hall,</u>

- From the Greek word *aule*, Strong's #833: <u>a yard (as open to the wind) [or] court</u>.
- Had kindled a fire in the midst of the <u>open courtyard,</u>

55. And <u>were</u>
- And <u>[after they] had</u>

55. <u>Set</u> down together,
- From the Greek word *sugkathizo*, Strong's #4776: <u>sit down together</u>.
- <u>Sat</u> down together,

55. Peter sat down among <u>them</u>.
- Peter sat down among <u>the multitude [of people]</u>.

56. But a certain <u>maid</u>
- From the Greek word *paidiske*, Strong's #3814: <u>a girl</u>
- But a certain <u>girl</u>

56. <u>Beheld</u>
- From the Greek word *eido*, Strong's #1492: <u>be aware</u>.
- <u>Became aware</u>

56. <u>Him</u>
- <u>[Of] Peter</u>

56. As <u>he</u> sat by the fire,
- As <u>Peter</u> sat by the fire,

56. <u>And</u>
- <u>And [the girl]</u>

56. Earnestly looked upon <u>him</u>,
- Earnestly looked upon <u>Peter</u>,

56. And said, This man was also with <u>him</u>.
- And said, This man was also with <u>Jesus</u>.

57. And <u>he</u>
- And <u>Peter</u>

57. Denied <u>him</u>, saying,
- Denied <u>[knowing] Jesus</u>, saying,

57. Woman, I know <u>him not</u>.
- Woman, I <u>[do] not</u> know <u>Jesus</u>.

58. And after a little while <u>another</u>
- And after a little while <u>another [person]</u>

58. Saw <u>him</u>, and said,
- Saw <u>Peter</u>, and said,

58. Thou art also
- You are also [one]

58. Of them.
- Of the people who was with Jesus.

58. And Peter said, Man, I am not.
- And Peter said, Man, I am not [one of the people who was with Jesus].

59. And about the space
- And [after] about the space

59. Of one hour
- Of one hour's [time]

59. After another
- After another [person]

59. Confidently affirmed, saying,
- Confidently affirmed [the other two people's accusation about Peter], saying,

59. Of a truth
- [It] is a truthful [statement]

59. This fellow also was with him: for he is a Galilean.
- This fellow also was with Jesus: for he is a Galilean.

60. And Peter said,
- Then Peter said,

60. Man, I know not
- Man, I [do] not know

60. What thou sayest.
- What you [are] saying.

60. And immediately, while he yet spake,
- And immediately, while Peter [was] still speaking,

60. The cock crew.
- The cock crowed.

61. And the Lord turned,
- And Jesus turned [his head],

61. And looked upon Peter.
- And looked at Peter.

61. And Peter remembered the word
- And Peter remembered the words

61. Of the Lord,

- Of <u>Jesus,</u>
61. How <u>he</u> had said unto him,
   - How <u>Jesus</u> had said unto him,
61. Before the cock <u>crow, thou shalt</u>
   - Before the cock <u>crows, you shall</u>
61. Deny me <u>thrice.</u>
   - Deny me <u>three [times]</u>.
62. And Peter went <u>out,</u> and wept bitterly.
   - And Peter went <u>out [from the open courtyard]</u>, and wept bitterly.

CHOICE EXAMINATION

1. Why did Galen lose his job as department manager for sporting goods and automotives?

2. Why did Galen become a successful department manager one year later?

3. Why does Galen appreciate the fact that he failed in his first attempt at being a department manager?

4. In the scripture, why was Peter confident that he would not fail Jesus?

5. Why did Jesus assign Peter the responsibility of strengthening his spiritual brothers after he had recuperated and reverted back to his faith?

6. What choices do you need to make in order to *learn from failure and try again*?

DEVELOP A PURPOSE FOR YOUR LIFE

≈ 52 ≈

And Jesus answered them, saying, The hour is come that the Son of man should be glorified. Verily, verily, I say unto you, Except a corn of wheat fall into the ground and die, it abideth alone: but if it die, it bringeth forth much fruit. He that loveth his life shall lose it; and he that hateth his life in this world shall keep it unto life eternal. If any man serve me, let him follow me; and where I am, there shall also my servant be: if any man serve me, him will my father honour. Now is my soul troubled; and what shall I say? Father, save me from this hour: but for this cause came I unto this hour. Father, glorify thy name.

John 12:23 - 28

I read the following parable in **Luke 12: 16 - 20**, during my personal Bible study time at home.

The ground of a certain rich man brought forth plentifully: And he thought within himself, saying, What shall I do, because I have no room where to bestow my fruits? And he said, This will I do: I will pull down my barns, and build greater; and there will I bestow all my fruits and my goods. And I will say to my soul, Soul, thou hast much goods laid up for many years; take thine ease, eat, drink, and be merry.

But God said unto him, Thou fool, this night thy soul shall be required of thee: then whose shall those things be, which thou hast provided.

I realized something about this story which got me excited. "Barbie," I said, "Let's think about this concept. If the rich man would have purposed in his heart to do something with his harvest *for God*, then God would have had a reason to extend his life. But since the rich man's only interest was keeping the extra harvest for himself, God had no reason to intervene and extend his life. One way for people to give God a reason to extend their lives is to develop purposes for their lives that honor God."

Further meditation on this scripture inspired me to develop a purposeful ministry for God. I chose to write a book about making *RIGHT CHOICES*. I had no idea that a few months later, that inspiration would directly affect my life.

I'm not a doctor. There were no indications that I was a candidate to have a stroke, so I won't claim that I had one. At the time, however, that's what I thought had happened. My body felt totally lifeless except for the tingling sensation in my face and arms. Seven people - my wife, my two daughters, and four emergency responders - were all crowded in or around my bathroom. I had been lying motionless on the floor for over an hour. The ambulance was backed up to the front porch preparing to take me to the hospital.

It was sometime after 1:00 A.M. when I got out of bed to go to the bathroom. I felt myself losing consciousness and collapsing to the floor. Barbie heard the fall and immediately rushed to my aid. She supported me as I tried to walk back to bed. I started to collapse again. Amy came downstairs. They began praying.

"We're taking you to the hospital," they said. Barbie put shoes on my feet while I was lying on the bed.

"I think I can walk," I groaned. I took one step toward the bathroom and collapsed again. Charity arrived. She called the ambulance. They prayed fervently while they waited for the ambulance to arrive.

They said I drifted in and out of consciousness. All I can remember, of course, are the times when I was awake. I remember thinking that I might die, or perhaps, become physically impaired for the rest of my life. I remember appreciating and loving my family, not wanting to die now and abandon them this early in our lives. I remember thinking that I didn't want to become physically impaired, unable to care for my family in the manner I was used to. I remember thinking about the things in life that I still wanted to do. Then, suddenly, I remembered something which let me know that I would surely recover from whatever was happening to me. I knew I wasn't going to die! God would surely deliver me from this affliction because, I still had a book to write - *this book*! God was giving me inspiration for this book and therefore, I couldn't die yet. I hadn't finished the book! There was a purpose for my life! There was a reason for God to intervene and extend my life!

They strapped me onto a flat board and cinched straps around my legs, arms, and head. I remember gaining enough awareness of the situation to weakly tell Shane, a first responder and a member of our church, thanks for coming. I felt so humble. I hated that I had disrupted the night's sleep for so many people. As the ambulance drove up the road, one of the attendants began speaking to me. I assume that he was gathering data about my condition in order to report the information to the emergency room personnel. A few miles up the road, the tingling sensation ceased and my mind totally cleared up. I realized that I was cinched down from head to toe with several straps, and I realized that I am a little bit CLAUSTROPHOBIC!

"Sir, I want you to take these straps off of my head and arms please," I said.

"I'm sorry sir. We're not allowed to transport you without the straps in place," he said. "You'll get them off when you arrive at the hospital."

"Sir, you don't understand. I need you to take these straps off of me NOW!" I said.

"I'm sorry sir but we are required to---"

"No, sir, you do not UNDERSTAND ME! YOU **ARE** GOING TO TAKE THESE STRAPS OFF OF ME **RIGHT NOW!!**"

"Yes, sir!! But you are going to have to sign this release form ..."

By the time we arrived at the hospital I was conversing freely. I still felt weak, but otherwise well. When they pulled me out of the ambulance on the stretcher, I looked to the side and saw my wife, my children, and my two brothers standing by the emergency room entrance door. They were all looking worried and frightened. I raised my head and motioned to them with my arms and hands, (my body was still strapped down) and told them I was all right.

It had to be three of the most boring days of my life. I was lying in a hospital bed, feeling well, and in between the various tests they ran on me, doing nothing. They never found anything wrong with me. There wasn't anything wrong with me. I was fine and I knew I was fine because sometime earlier I had chosen to develop a purpose for my life. I had chosen to write a book, this book, and God had a reason to extend my life.

Make right choices.

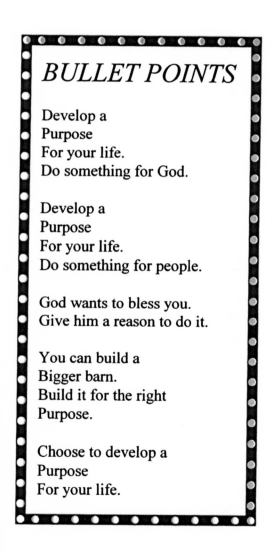

BULLET POINTS

Develop a
Purpose
For your life.
Do something for God.

Develop a
Purpose
For your life.
Do something for people.

God wants to bless you.
Give him a reason to do it.

You can build a
Bigger barn.
Build it for the right
Purpose.

Choose to develop a
Purpose
For your life.

SCRIPTURE ANALYSIS

John 12: 23 - 28

23. And Jesus answered <u>them</u>, saying,

    - And Jesus answered <u>the people [that stood nearby (see verse #29) including certain Greeks, Phillip, and Andrew (see verses #20-22)]</u>, saying,

23. The hour <u>is</u> come,

    - The hour <u>has</u> come,

23. That <u>the</u> Son of man

    - That <u>[I, Jesus,] the</u> Son of man

23. <u>Should</u> be glorified.

    - <u>Shall</u> be glorified.

24. <u>Verily, verily</u>, I say unto you,

    - From the Greek word *amen*, Strong's #281: <u>surely</u>.

    - <u>Surely, surely</u>, I say unto you,

24. <u>Except</u>

    - From the Greek word *ean me*, Strong's #3362: <u>unless</u>.

    - <u>Unless</u>

24. A <u>corn</u> of wheat

    - From the Greek word *kokkos*, Strong's #2848: <u>a kernel of seed</u>.

    - A <u>kernel</u> of wheat

24. <u>Fall</u> into the ground

    - <u>Falls</u> into the ground

24. And <u>die</u>,

    - And <u>[the kernel of wheat] dies</u>,

24. <u>It</u>

    - <u>That kernel of wheat</u>

24. <u>Abideth</u> alone:

    - From the Greek word *meno*, Strong's #3306: <u>remain</u>.

    - <u>Remains [as only one seed]</u> alone:

24. But <u>if it die</u>,

    - But <u>when the kernel of wheat dies</u>,

24. <u>It bringeth</u> forth

    - <u>That kernel of wheat brings</u> forth

24. <u>Much fruit</u>.
- The NIV says: "<u>Many seeds</u>."
25. He <u>that loveth</u>
- He <u>who loves</u>
25. His <u>life</u>
- His [<u>sinful</u>] life [<u>in this world</u>]
25. Shall lose <u>it</u>;
Shall lose <u>his [eternal] life [in the next world]</u>;
25. <u>And</u>
- <u>And [likewise]</u>
25. He <u>that hateth</u>
- He <u>who hates</u>
25. His <u>life</u> in this world
- His [<u>sinful</u>] <u>life</u> in this world
25. Shall keep <u>it</u>
- Shall keep [<u>his eternal] life [in the next world</u>]
25. <u>Unto</u>
- [<u>By converting this life, through death</u>] <u>into</u>
25. <u>Life</u> eternal.
- [<u>A</u>] <u>life [which is</u>] eternal.
26. <u>If</u> any man
- <u>For</u> any man
26. <u>Serve</u> me,
- [<u>Who will</u>] serve me,
26. Let <u>him</u>
- Let <u>the man [who will serve me</u>]
26. Follow <u>me</u>;
- Follow <u>me [by converting his life, through death, into a</u>
<u>life which is eternal</u>];
26. <u>And</u>
- <u>So [that</u>]
26. Where I <u>am</u>,
- Where I <u>am [going</u>],
26. There shall also my servant <u>be</u>:
- There shall also my servant <u>be [going</u>]:
26. <u>If</u> any man
- <u>For</u> any man

26. <u>Serve</u> **me,**
> - [Who will] <u>serve</u> me,

26. <u>Him</u> **will**
> - <u>The man [who serves me]</u> will

26. My <u>Father</u> **honour.**
> - My <u>Father (God)</u> honor.

27. Now is my <u>soul</u> **troubled;**
> - From the Greek word *psuche*, Strong's #5590: <u>heart</u>.

> - Webster's Dictionary defines *heart* as: <u>One's innermost character, feelings, or inclinations</u>.

> - Now is my <u>heart's innermost feelings</u> troubled;

27. And what shall I <u>say</u>**?**
> - And what shall I <u>say [in response to these troubled feelings]</u>?

27. <u>Father</u>**, save me**
> - <u>Father (God) [I want you to]</u> save me

27. <u>From</u> **this hour:**
> - <u>From [having to die at]</u> this hour:

27. <u>But</u>
> - <u>But [it was]</u>

27. For this <u>cause</u>
> - For this <u>cause [to suffer many things, and be rejected of the elders and chief priests and scribes, and be slain, and be raised the third day (see Luke 9: 22) that]</u>

27. <u>Came</u> **I unto this hour.**
> - I <u>came</u> unto this hour.

28. Father, glorify <u>thy</u> **name.**
> - Father, glorify <u>your</u> name.

CHOICE EXAMINATION

1. Why did Galen get excited about the parable in Luke 12: 16-20?

2. Why did Galen know that God would surely deliver him from his affliction?

3. What three words complete the last story in the last chapter of this book, and why did the author cry as he typed them in?

4. In the scripture, why did Jesus compare himself to a kernel of wheat?

5. What was the cause, or purpose, for Jesus having to die at that hour?

6. What choices do you need to make in order to *develop a purpose for your life*?

7. Why do you need to *MAKE RIGHT CHOICES*?

CONCLUSION

Let us hear the conclusion of the whole matter: Fear God, and keep his commandments: For this is the whole duty of man. For God shall bring every work into judgment, with every secret thing, whether it be good or whether it be evil.

Ecclesiastes 12: 13, 14

Printed in the United States
203265BV00002B/76-1023/P

9 781604 779325